FROM HERO TO ZERO

—A True Story—

"Echo Delta Charlie's got a slight problem, we'll just ah......standby one"

CAPT. ROD LOVELL

Rod Lovell Publications
Adelaide, Australia

Author's Disclaimer
Everything in this book happened, but perhaps a few of the dates, times and places may be slightly awry. This story is true to the best of my ability and drawn from memory, facts and numerous government agency statements and documentation, all of which can be verified. Photographs and quotations have been published in good faith and acknowledged where possible. I have endeavoured to find the owners but due to the time-frame elapsed since the occurrence, it has not always been possible. Therefore, I invite any owners to come forward should they have any issues with me using their photographs or quotations in this book for subsequent acknowledgement. Due to the defamation laws in Australia, I have been advised by the legal profession to remove all reference to actual names and position titles of CAA/CASA and BASI staff who were involved in this true story.

Copyright © Rod Lovell 2019
First Published in Australia in 2019
by **Rod Lovell Publications**, Adelaide, Australia
ABN 36 262 815 616
rodlovellpublications@gmail.com

ISBN: 978-1-922565-50-1
Published by Vivid Publishing
A division of Fontaine Publishing Group
P.O. Box 948, Fremantle
Western Australia 6959
www.vividpublishing.com.au

 A catalogue record for this book is available from the National Library of Australia

For those more technically minded readers ...
During the writing of this book, it became apparent that the amount of extremely important technical information and correspondence relating to this event started to over-load the storyline. However, this information is available, for those more technically minded readers, on my website
www.FromHeroToZero.com.au

Cover design by Cherie Fox, cheriefox.com
Typeset in Times New Roman, with chapter headings in Linden Hill,
by Philip Ellison, Encompass Design & Publishing, Adelaide
philip.ellison1961@gmail.com
First printed October 2019
Reprinted November 2019
Reprinted December 2020

The right of Capt. Rod Lovell to be identified as the author of this work has been asserted by him in accordance with the Copyright Amendment (Moral Rights) Act 2000. No part of this publication may be reproduced, stored in a retrieval system or transmitted in any form or by any means, electronic, mechanical, photocopying, recording or otherwise, without the prior written permission of the copyright holder. The information, views, opinions and visuals expressed in this publication are solely those of the author and do not necessarily reflect those of the publisher. The publisher disclaims any liabilities or responsibilities whatsoever for any damages, libel or liabilities arising directly or indirectly from the contents of this publication.

DEDICATION

This book is dedicated to all Pilots involved in an aircraft accident who survived, but particularly those who did not, and who have been wrongly blamed and have had the term *pilot error* permanently associated against their name.

As I was writing this book, I pondered that, if I were the reader, I would conclude that some of these events would have to be fictional. I can assure you, everything in this book happened.

ACKNOWLEDGEMENTS

I would sincerely like to thank the following people for bringing a 25 year aspiration to fruition.

Capt Tony Hannam. Tony and I first met in 1971 whilst we were undergoing training on our respective RAAF Pilot's courses. We became fellow aviators, often being crewed together. He has supported and encouraged me since 1994. In his words 'This is a story which has to be told.' A mate for life.

Jacquelin Melilli, (Jacq of all Trades, Master of Writing). I first contacted Jacqui in late 2017 and she agreed to be my editor. She has given great advice, wonderful support and encouragement. An absolute dream to work with.

Spencer Ferrier, (fellow Pilot and aviation solicitor). I first met Spencer after the accident where he was engaged to assist me in my fight. His legal advice, thoughts and support during the development of this book have been invaluable.

Nickola Ramsey and her son Edward, who created the very descriptive illustrations.

Cherie Fox (cheriefox.com) for designing the incredible front and back covers.

Philip Ellison (Encompass Design & Publishing) who had the massive job of creating a physical book.

Damian Bourne for proof reading.

Jan Thomas (my faithful partner for tolerating my rants and raves) for thousands of hours trying to put my thoughts and memories into a Word document, without a murmur of complaint.

The people above have stood by my side to support me through this and I sincerely, deeply and eternally thank them.

Writing this book has been a roller coaster ride. There have been times where I wasn't going to proceed with it and other times when I was on top of the world with feelings of elation.

Like life, one soldiers on and sees the light at the end of the tunnel.

It is my one chance to tell the world what really happened without the influence of biased and unreliable government departments.

Rod Lovell, September 2019

CONTENTS

Foreword 6
Prologue 12
Flight into Botany Bay 16
The Farm Boy 19
My RAAF Career 25
Gaining My Wings 30
Flying the P-3B Orion 45
Once a Captain, But Not Always a Captain 57
Flying Adventures 71
Civil Flying 80
Back to Flying a DC-3 117
Parkes is Burning 122
The Day That Changed My Life 125
Engine Failure—Left Engine 133
I Take Over 139
A Pilot's Eye View of Failed Engines and a Ditching 151
The Rise to Hero Status 156
The Fall to Zero Status 158
Counselling/Suspension 165
The Paper War 179
Desert Dick 184
The Plane Truth 186
Below Zero 197
Verification and Vindication Finally Obtained 206
Addressing BASI 215
Rod's Final Thoughts and Expectations 223
Appendix 1 – Testimonials 235
Appendix 2 – Rod Lovell's Qualifications 242
Appendix 3 – Glossary of Terms 244
Appendix 4 – Chronology 246

FOREWORD

A momentous event in the history of Australian aviation was possibly the shortest flight that ever took off from Sydney's Kingsford Smith Airport. The 1994 ditching of a Douglas DC-3 in Botany Bay after an engine failed on take-off made headlines because everyone survived with almost no injuries! The Commander of that flight was Captain Rod Lovell, with whom I have worked closely and known very well for nearly 50 years.

Captain Lovell was the architect of Australia's 'Miracle on Botany Bay' long before Captain Chesley Sullenberger followed suit with a remarkably similar occurrence dubbed the 'Miracle on the Hudson' almost 15 years later, when all on board survived his Airbus A320 ditching into the Hudson River in New York. Whilst the parallels between the two events are eerily close, the subsequent investigation and reporting outcomes and their after-effects on the two commanders could not be further apart.

Rod Lovell and I were both highly trained RAAF pilots and flew together in the same Squadron in the same crew, after which our career paths took different directions to pursue our mutual passion to aviate. I went on to spend the next 30 years training and checking pilots in the RAAF, General Aviation and International Airlines' flying propeller driven and jet aircraft up to Boeing 747s on the world's international route network. A lot of aircraft accidents were intensely analysed during ground school courses conducted with those trainees because ultimately a Captain must not only fly skillfully, he must manage every event like a CEO.

It became very evident to me that some pilots were far more conscientious, prepared and capable than others and in fact many were working close to their maximum personal capability when things were going well. Throw in a few 'curve balls' of extreme weather events—fog/thunderstorms/snowstorms/typhoons—or even some partial failures of aircraft systems such as instruments/hydraulic/electrical or the more usual engine surges or fire/failure and combine them with complex ATC instructions and demands and you could now have a pilot who is over-loaded and may no longer function properly. Confusion, disorientation and incapacity to deal with such occurrences inevitably leads to poor judgement/decisions or lack of action altogether. Other crew member intervention may be ignored, or in the worst case, tip the individual over the edge and exacerbate the over-load leading to mental incapacitation.

These are the symptoms that repeatedly show up when reviewing aircraft accident investigations and are often the precursor to a fatal accident and it can all develop very quickly.

However, when the pilot copes with such extreme demands and comes through with flying colours, usually because of a high level of self-discipline, preparedness, knowledge and skill, then the pilot is hailed as a hero, as indeed was the case with the two ditchings—briefly!

As depicted in the subsequent movie 'Sully' the US National Transportation Safety Board (NTSB), like the Civil Aviation Authority (CAA) here, were initially focused in their investigations on 'pilot error' but in both cases the pilots (unusually) survived to defend their actions. Pilots must always assess circumstances and react swiftly—but correctly—without the benefit of investigative hindsight.

'Pilot error' therefore becomes the first easy option in the subsequent lengthy analysis, thus pilots become initially reluctant to say any more than is absolutely necessary to the regulatory authority for fear of reprisal. This does not encourage a good safety ethic and is a root cause of poor pilot/regulatory authority relations and impacts on the aviation industry as a whole. Senator Nick Xenophon's additional comments on the subsequent findings of the Senate Committee Enquiry into Aviation Accident Investigation and Reporting dated 23rd May 2013, were more specific in saying that the general industry attitude towards both the ATSB (formerly BASI) and CASA (formerly CAA) is incredibly concerning; being a mixture of fear, suspicion, disappointment and derision.

In the Hudson River ditching inquiry, the NTSB changed course, sensibly, when they accepted that 'Human Factors' should be addressed and then allowed a time of some 35 seconds for the pilots to confirm, evaluate, act and review their decision before committing to ditch the aircraft which occurred some 173 seconds later (a total of 208 seconds). Why did they back down?

Perhaps the simpler alternative was to accept that the massive ingestion of birds caused the loss of the engines, so no one else could be held responsible? Easy way out!

The pilot quickly recognised that the aircraft was un-flyable! Somehow he had to save his passengers and crew. He did! Accolades followed!

The Botany Bay ditching of the DC-3 'splashdown' occurred just 46 seconds after engine failure and here the authorities went down a very different path! Unbelievably they totally ignored 'Human Factors'—didn't even get a mention, not even when discussing Crew Resource Management (CRM) aspects! If it wasn't deemed largely attributable to pilot error (mis-handling) then somebody else could be held accountable (maintenance/regulatory procedures) and that could reveal a myriad of contributory factors that would have to be explained by relevant parties including the CAA themselves!

'Findings and Significant Factors' of the Bureau of Air Safety Investigation (BASI) report lists a number of such regulatory deficiencies and goes on to expand on them significantly!

By contrast, there are just two short references in the lines of narrative to mis-handling by the Co-pilot (which was never authoritatively defined) and even these contradict each other! So much material appears left out, glossed over or not explored, which is now addressed in this book! 'Pilot error' was the easy way out! This aircraft too was un-flyable, even by one of the best qualified DC-3 pilots around who somehow had to very quickly do something to save his passengers and crew. He did! Career ruination followed!

Captain Rod Lovell is a highly principled and extremely competent aviator. Don't just take my word for it—I strongly urge you to read the testimonials at the end of the book first! There are very few that could have achieved what he did that day and the outcome could have been so tragically different. No pilot can ever physically practice ditching an asymmetrically powered aircraft—when it happens you get only one shot at it and with just 46 seconds notice it is unlikely to be successful. Airlines don't bother practicing it even in their simulators. Perhaps now they should, as there are a lot of very large twin-engined airliners crossing the world's oceans these days a long way from land replacing older three-engined and four-engined aircraft. A ditching could occur at any time with very little warning!

Foreword

Now give consideration to Captain Lovell's situation immediately after take-off with his rapidly unfolding predicament. An old 1944 vintage aircraft, airspeed reducing with the left propeller stopped after engine failure, asymmetric full power set on the remaining right engine, discovering to his dismay that the aircraft won't even fly level in that condition let alone climb! Now he has to plan a new mentally horrifying course of action, commit to that decision to fly the plane onto the water and set it up at the right speed and configuration with flaps and control inputs, to calculate and maintain a required speed to hit the water at the slowest possible safe speed, under control, with the wings level and only engine power available on one side! All that in a 46 second time frame from engine failure to water impact! Again, a remarkable achievement! And that's not the half of it. The unfolding story ahead identifies why it was un-flyable and presents the true cause of the accident—something that the BASI report could only hint at.

Captain Rod Lovell should have spent the intervening years since 1994 speaking at every possible aviation seminar or CASA sponsored training event to pass on the value of his experience as one of a select few who has survived such a difficult exercise. Instead he has been discredited by a report that appears to be as inconsistent as it is incomplete and neglectful, with statements made seemingly to target and discredit the pilot in command.

Hence the regulatory system Captain Lovell respected and complied with meticulously, had absolutely failed him and the very industry it is supposed to protect, for a very long time.

One would hope that in today's more enlightened environment where 'Human Factors' now assume far more importance and relevance than they did when this report was published, that it would be presented in a somewhat different manner, particularly after a desperately overdue Senate Committee Enquiry into Aviation Accident Investigation and Reporting was subsequently convened in 2012.

The revelations and findings of that inquiry are damning in the analysis of the historic relationship between the ATSB/CASA (BASI/CAA replacement bodies) as described on the Australian Government Parliamentary website as being sub-optimal and remain problematic. The Senate Committee considered that CASA's actions had influenced the conduct of an ATSB investigation to the detriment of aviation safety and based on the documentation available to them, the two agencies had placed maintaining the veneer of a productive working relationship ahead of public safety. Alarming revelations indeed on the www.aph.gov.au (aviation accident investigations) website!

It is questionable now to discover where this behaviour began. It would not stretch the imagination too far to believe that 'having got away with it' in the investigation and reporting of Captain Lovell's ditching in Botany Bay in 1994, why not use it as a model in subsequent investigations which ultimately triggered the Senate Committee inquiry? The key elements have the similarity of deflecting criticism away from the wall of bureaucratic invincibility of the regulatory authorities on to the pilots—job done!

All of these points have been challenged by Captain Lovell—their importance cannot be over-stated because they go to the very heart of the problem that the Senate Committee was appointed to investigate. Pilot error is a neat way of sweeping all the problems under the carpet as the last two people to touch the aircraft were the pilots, so it must be their fault.

Regrettably, it's not that simple.

Twenty-five years after his accident Captain Lovell is still trying to clear his name when he hasn't knowingly done anything wrong, the proof being that, like Captain Chesley Sullenberger, he was never charged with any wrong doing by any aviation authority! Yet 'pilot error' was intimated to be the primary factor, conveniently deflecting attention from all the other glossed-over combined causes of the accident—never is it just one thing, it is always a chain of events. The pilots just happen to be the last link in that chain, the last line of defence to save lives—or not.

A 'whitewash' or a 'witch-hunt' will never take anything away from the fact that there was a plane load of young passengers who have more than doubled their age since 24th April 1994 and some no doubt now have children of their own thanks to a brilliant piece of flying from a skilled and conscientious aviator. Thank God for them that Captain Rod Lovell was at the controls that day—a pilot who had endlessly planned and practiced ditching procedures in RAAF Orion aircraft almost down to the point of impact with the water! The DC-3 engine that failed was going to fail sooner rather than later, on the next flight perhaps or one soon after. It doesn't matter where the plane was going, only who was going to handle this extreme situation when it happened. Rod Lovell was my first Co-pilot on RAAF Lockheed Orion P-3B aircraft back in 1974 and I know how good he is. A lesser pilot would have killed all on board. The sad part is that he has since been denied the opportunity to give so much back to and guide the aviation industry in a specific area not visited by many who survive to tell the tale, which has wasted a valuable training resource because of an inadequate process of investigation and a deficient report that destroyed a flying career. That is the tragedy!

Captain Tony Hannam
RAAF
  A2 Qualified Flying Instructor (QFI) and
  Instrument Rating Examiner (IRE)
  Macchi MB326 Jet 2 Seat Trainer
  Lockheed Orion P-3B Long Range Maritime Patrol Aircraft
Air Queensland
  DCA/CAA Authorised Check and Training Captain and
  IRE Swearingen Metroliner 2 Regional Commuter Aircraft
Hong Kong
  Civil Aviation Department (CAD) Authorised Training Captain
  Boeing 747-200/300 (Cathay Pacific Airways) Boeing 747-400
  (Oasis Airlines)

PROLOGUE

A very famous quotation from Captain AG Lamplugh, British Aviation Insurance Group London in the 1930s, which nearly every old aviator has on his wall, states: 'Aviation in itself is not inherently dangerous. But to an even greater degree than the sea, it is terribly unforgiving of any carelessness, incapacity or neglect'.

Life for a young man was always full of action and interest. From an early age, I had a love of motor cars, trucks, tractors and could not take my eyes off the aircraft that flew across my family farm near Middleton in coastal South Australia.

My family were caring but strict. My father was a first-class role model for me. He had been born in 1886, served in World War I and survived without physical injury. My mother was a caring woman who managed six children of whom I was number five. I had the great benefit of a close relationship with both my parents throughout their lives.

After spending my young years as a farm boy on the family farm, I joined the RAAF becoming a qualified aircraft flight Instrument Fitter. I applied for and was selected for advancement and rose to become a Pilot with the RAAF, first learning on a piston-engined propeller-driven training aircraft and ultimately to earn and succeed in gaining the coveted RAAF Wings. This led to flying the Mirage jet fighter and then onto the Orion Anti-Submarine Warfare aircraft which was mostly over-water flight.

My civil aviation career covered flying many jet aircraft to eventually the DC-3. It was in the course of working with my much-loved DC-3 aircraft that the events of 24th April 1994 came to pass.

A Captain, as Pilot in command, is given numerous documents, prior to a flight, which have been compiled and signed off by various authorised/

licensed individuals. The Captain trusts the information provided in these documents, as they are designed to be relied on by him for the safe and efficient operation of the flight. Some of these include engine maintenance, certifying that the engines are in good repair and properly maintained: a load sheet, providing the Captain with details of the load of passengers and freight, a fuel release, certifying the amount of fuel uploaded.

The Captain must make sure that he is licenced and current by the appropriate authority to operate the aircraft and conduct the flight. He must satisfy himself that the weather is suitable for his aircraft and flight, and must prepare the flight track he intends to conduct. It is his task to have this work prepared. He or his Co-pilot are expected to conduct an external inspection of the aircraft to ensure that its critical functions are operating—flaps, ailerons, elevators which is done by conducting a visual inspection.

From these internal and external inspections and checklist completion, the Captain is then able to ensure the aircraft can safely undertake its flight. It has long been the case that the Captain is reliant on the correctness of the information provided to him in this way.

Immediately prior to the ditching flight, all the above documentation and responsibilities were adhered to and complied with.

Unfortunately, however, for this flight I was misinformed by concealment, some deliberate, about the condition of the aircraft's propellers and engines, the weight we were carrying and indeed even the qualifications of my Co-pilot.

On 24th April 1994, I was hailed as a hero when South Pacific Airmotive's 1944 DC-3, VH-EDC (Echo Delta Charlie) under my command suffered an engine failure immediately after take-off and began rapidly descending. With only seconds to analyse the situation, I decided the best option was to conduct a controlled ditching. A ditching is, in the broadest sense, a controlled landing on a body of water. The phrase water-landing is also used as a euphemism for crash-landing into water. That is what I did, although an aeroplane obviously is not designed for this purpose. Forty-six seconds was all the time I had from the engine failure to when we ditched. My decision ultimately saved the lives of all twenty-five souls on board.

I never saw myself as a hero, I was simply doing my job and at that precise moment, my twenty-five years of experience as a Pilot with the Royal Australian Air Force and as a civilian commercial Pilot paid off. I ditched the DC-3 into Botany Bay, Sydney, Australia. Ditching a large aeroplane normally results in fatalities. Therefore, to complete this successfully is an extremely rare occurrence. The price I paid for ensuring the survival of my crew and passengers, was to be made a fall-guy by the then Civil Aviation Authority (CAA—now called Civil Aviation Safety Authority (CASA)), destroying my aviation career and consequently my personal life as well.

This was not my first in-flight emergency. My background in the RAAF, IPEC and several commercial Australian carriers had put me in harm's way more than once. On one occasion, I had taken over the controls of what appeared to be an imminent crash in another DC-3 and brought the aircraft safely to the ground. In DC-3s alone, I had previously experienced no less than three precautionary engine shutdowns, on separate occasions, yet each time still returned to the airfield and landed safely on one engine which was delivering more than adequate power for the aircraft to be controlled and brought safely to land. I had suffered a engine flame-out at high altitude in a Mirage jet and was able to restart the engine and bring myself and the expensive jet fighter to land without incident. This was an event that often, in other cases, resulted in the crew ejecting to safety whilst the aircraft crashed to earth. There were other lesser incidents, but the events of 24th April 1994, at Mascot, Sydney was the most significant event in my flying career.

This story is true and as accurate as I can remember, as recorded by a multitude of notes and official documents that I have in my possession. It is a true story about events where the concealments, failures and inter-department wrangling which slowly became apparent, proved efforts were made to shift all blame. Those who ought to have known better acted wrongly. Those who had done wrong were ignored and critical reactions, which for safety's sake, ought to have been reported to the public, have remained dormant whilst those who nearly caused the calamity have never been held accountable.

Maybe an apparent government cover-up occurred where public servants were protecting their jobs.

This is my story of how I went from hero to zero. My physical body survived the accident, but my spirit, reputation and integrity were well and truly battered to death. The emotional and psychological devastation I suffered at the hands of the Civil Aviation Authority had repercussions that I still live with today. The representatives at the Civil Aviation Authority took most of what I valued in life away from me, apart from my pride. Although my

Prologue

colleagues in the aviation industry supported me from a distance throughout my ordeal, they were reluctant to speak out for fear of reprisal from the regulatory authority. It is widely believed in the aviation industry that the government authorities will conduct reprisals, and often people who rely on government approvals, will be most reluctant to speak about short-comings by government for fear of subsequent discrimination being used against them. I believe that we do not have bad experiences, only bad incidents and if you're wise, you lock them away in the big database called memory, and they all become useful and valuable tools to cope with future challenges.

The irony is that the Australian Government spent well over $1 million to train me as a Pilot in the RAAF and I estimate at least another $1 million (1970s rate) to train me to fly Winjeel, Macchi, Mirage and Orion aeroplanes. Some twenty-two years later, with in excess of 9,000 hours of flying time under my belt accumulated on some thirty plus types of aircraft the Australian government, through the Civil Aviation Authority, spent ludicrous man hours and therefore money to persecute me by questioning my competence, subsequently temporarily revoking my Pilot's licence until I regained it two months later. To add insult, as a taxpayer I was partially funding the Civil Aviation Authority's pursuit of me at the same time as I was draining my own bank account to defend myself over what Australians called an act of heroism, but the Civil Aviation Authority called 'pilot error'. I had the odds stacked against me with no chance to defend myself. To do so I had to do it alone. There was no organisation that would stand and help me with a legal defence. Justice requires money and I was short of that vital commodity because my right to earn an income had been taken away by administrative order. I could not compete with the bottomless pit of cash the government used at their discretion. This book is my chance to present my side of the story to the general public.

I am proud to present a full list of my qualifications in Appendix 2, at the end of this book on pages 242-243.

FLIGHT INTO BOTANY BAY

'Sydney Ground, good morning, Echo Delta Charlie for Lord Howe. Taxi clearance received Golf'[1]

'Echo Delta Charlie clear to taxi for Bravo 3 intersection, the time is on the hour.'

Sydney Airport's Surface Movement Control had granted our taxi clearance and we were on our way. First stop would be Lord Howe Island for refuelling and then on to our destination, Norfolk Island. The time was 09:00 local time on 24th April 1994. Right on schedule.

* * *

As Captain, I occupied the traditional left-hand cockpit seat and, as Co-pilot, Nick Leach the right-hand seat as I had approved for him to manage the first part of the flight in accordance with ordinary procedure. I watched and oversaw his actions and participated in the checks that are done before flight. He then taxied the aircraft for a take-off heading close to south, from the main north/south runway known by its compass bearing as 16 (pronounced one-six), Bravo 3 intersection departure. In normal two-pilot operations, we operate what is known as leg-for-leg. That is the Captain and Co-pilot alternate duties flying the aircraft and operating as Support Pilot. Even (as in this case) when the Co-pilot is flying the aircraft, and the Captain is the Support Pilot, the Captain still retains ultimate control of the aircraft at all times.

The pre-take-off checklist and crew briefing, which included procedures to be used in the event of a malfunction, were conducted whilst taxiing out to the runway. As we were about to take-off on runway 16, we discussed that in the event of an engine failure after take-off, we would anticipate

---

[1] Golf is one of the alphabetical sequences in which recorded aeronautical information (ATIS) is continuously broadcast for Pilots to attain relative information regarding weather and airfield conditions.

returning to the airport for a landing on the east/west cross runway known as runway 25, or as dictated by circumstances. I, as Support Pilot (though still in command of the aeroplane), notified the tower that we were ready for take-off. At 09:07:49 local time, the control tower advised: 'Echo Delta Charlie, contact departures when airborne, clear for take-off.' I acknowledged this take-off clearance. Line-up checklist was completed and the Co-pilot slowly pushed the throttles forward to the full power (or take-off) position. The Pratt & Whitney R-1830s increased their beautiful noise as their power output increased. As Support Pilot, I followed up the throttles with my right-hand, fine tuning the final take-off power setting.

The take-off roll appeared normal. At 81 kt, I reached across in front of Co-Pilot Mr Nick Leach's face to signal V_1 (pronounced Vee One) which is the speed at which the aircraft is committed to flight and after which a landing on the runway runs the risk that the aircraft may overshoot the end. Once the V_1 sign is given, flight becomes the task to manage. This was done by the good old victory sign, as it was almost impossible to hear in the cockpit of a DC-3, even with headsets and intercom. The landing gear was selected up as soon as we were safely airborne. At approximately 200 ft and in excess of 100 kt, the left engine gave a couple of loud bangs. The aircraft yawed slightly to the left—pushed around to the left by the operating right-hand engine which then attempted to turn the aircraft. The left engine had failed and was correctly identified and verbally announced by the Co-pilot. Engine instruments confirmed this and the drills for flying the aircraft and for engine failure were carried out as per the company's Operations Manual. I visually checked that the propeller had stopped and it appeared to be in the feathered position.

All the performance charts indicate that a DC-3 will continue to climb after an engine failure on take-off. All the training we do on aircraft endorsement and recurrency training confirm that the aircraft will fly on one engine. I expected the aircraft to continue the climb and we would continue around to land on runway 25 as briefed. I had trained for these scenarios many, many times. Most of my flying career was in multi-engined aircraft, where the emphasis is on engine-out training. Suddenly, the dramatic shock set in that the aircraft was not climbing and airspeed was beginning to decrease even though the throttles were in full power position and nothing had changed except the left engine had failed. I could not understand why it would not climb with the indications of take-off power on the right engine. It should have climbed with an even lower power setting using the throttles known as METO (Maximum Except Take-Off) power.

The control tower was advised at 09:09:04: 'Echo Delta Charlie's got a slight problem. We'll just, ah ... standby one.' Right at this stage I still intended to climb and return to the airport for a landing. I still could not understand why the aircraft would not accelerate. It did not take long to realise the dire situation we were in. The aircraft was not going to stay in the air. I had the overpowering recollection of the tragic loss at this very point, fourteen years prior, of a Super King Air[2] which crashed and killed all 13 people on board including a one-*week* old *baby*.

At 09:09:18 the tower asked: 'Echo Delta Charlie, confirm operations normal?'

'Ah, negative, we've got ... just shut down the left engine we'll be returning ah ...' I replied.

At 09:09:38 I transmit to Sydney Tower: 'Echo Delta Charlie negative we're going to have to ditch here.'

---

2 Advance Airlines Flight DR4210, Super King Air, registered VH-AAV

THE FARM BOY

In 1900 my father, born in 1886, had enlisted to go to the Boer War. He was only 14 years old, the youngest soldier in South Australia, and was scheduled to sail to South Africa but the night before they were due to depart, orders came through to say all the youngest soldiers were to be left behind. Thank goodness!

At the outbreak of World War I, Dad tried to enlist six times before he was accepted. His false teeth had apparently been his stumbling block. His final attempt on 9th August 1916, was successful, and he was assigned Regimental No. 4737. On 23rd June 1917, he embarked on His Majesty's Australian Transport (HMAT) ship, 'Borda' in Adelaide, disembarking late August at Plymouth, England. Later he was transferred to the 48th Battalion, mainly fighting in France. After the war, he spent six months at Galashiels Technical College, near Edinburgh, Scotland, followed by three months with Paton and Baldwin studying wool classing while awaiting embarkation to return home. It was during this time Dad met Elizabeth Taylor Tait. After returning on the troopship 'Plassy' which embarked in Manchester, England on 5th September 1919, he arrived in Port Adelaide late October. On 30th November 1919 he was discharged from the Army. A short time later, Elizabeth followed on, arriving in Australia and marrying Dad in 1922. Tragically, just over a year later, at the age of 31, during a horrendous childbirth both she and the baby passed away.

Fourteen years later, Dad married Bertha Miriam Sandland who was some 27 years younger, from Broken Hill, New South Wales. Mum bore six children. I was fifth in line. My Dad was 63 years old at the time of my birth.

I was born on 16th September 1949, at the South Coast District Hospital in Victor Harbour, South Australia, later spelt Harbor. I was raised on the family mixed farm which consisted of dairy cows, sheep and cropping. It was just under 400 acres, purchased by my grandfather, John Lovell, in 1896, at Middleton. This was in the days of 32 volt direct current electricity charged by a wind-driven generator mounted on a windmill. I guess back then you could say we were off the grid trendsetters. Near the back verandah of the house was a room with rows and rows of batteries. Looking back, we were luckier than most as a few houses in the neighbourhood only had kerosene-powered lights.

My consistent nightly routine as a child was bedtime at 6.30pm. The ABC News theme Majestic Fanfare was played on the radio. For some reason, I really liked this tune and Mum and Dad always permitted me to listen to it before lights went out. What a good way to transition from a busy day to sleep. How times have changed.

Milking of our twenty or so cows was all done by hand and Betsy became my cow. I can still see the old girl walking with a limp from an unfortunate accident. This was the era of sitting on a three-legged wooden stool and milking into a 2 gallon (9 litre) stainless steel bucket. At the tender age of around four or five, I believe I probably managed approximately two minutes of milking before Dad would discretely take over from me so we could finish before the day ended. I can still remember the warmth of the cow on a cold winter's morning, pressing against my cheek to keep me warm. The buckets of milk were then transferred into 10 gallon (45 litre) cans and transported by tractor and trailer to our back farm gate for collection by the local milk truck.

Whenever we went for a Sunday drive, we would have to be back home by late afternoon as the cows would be lined up, waiting to be milked. I remember Dad saying; 'got to get home to milk the cows'. I still use this phrase today, even though I have no cows, to excuse myself from friends.

On 19th September 1954, after I had just turned five years of age, my Dad took some of our family to the Mallala RAAF Station to view the Air Pageant to commemorate Air Force Week. I remember high speed (for that time) jets flying past. This ignited my fascination for flying.

Whilst growing up on our farm in Middleton I remember watching aeroplanes as they flew over on the odd occasion, again further ingraining my love for these amazing machines. Robby's Aerial Services would do top dressing of superphosphate over the nearby hills after reloading the hoppers from makeshift airstrips. These aircraft were based at Parafield which was the only civil airport until Adelaide Airport was opened in 1955. They flew de Havilland Tiger Moths and the occasional de Havilland Canada DHC-2 Beaver. Watching the wheels of the Tiger Moths rotating, whilst it was flying, absolutely intrigued me.

I remember being allowed to drive Dad's 1948 Massey Harris 44K tractor on my own, around the farm, when I was just six years of age. I was so thrilled, I raced up and told mum about my achievement and she promptly reprimanded my Dad. I still have that same tractor after restoring it many years later. Dad would be pleased.

* * *

On 6th May 1956, my mum wrote the following note in my Baby Diary: 'Top of first finger on left hand chopped off when Dad chopping up meat. Dr Collins gave anaesthetic and stitched it back on.' Let me explain how this happened. Dad was chopping up the meat from the recent sheep kill when one piece started to fall off the table. I made a grab for it at the same time as Dad swung the tomahawk down to stop the meat from falling. Obviously, I was quicker than Dad as my hand was under the down swinging tomahawk. Four stitches later, and contrary to all medical expectations, I regained full use of my finger and fingertip. The joke around town was that Dad must have been running short of meat on the farm.

When I was about five or six years old, I received a Wyn-Toy semi-trailer car carrier as a present. I thought that, in real life, if this car carrier could go at a certain speed along a road, a plane would just lift off it and fly and could return to land on the same moving semi-trailer. In the early 1950s families did not have a lot of access to media, so this scenario was something I had created in my mind. These aerial exploits have now become quite common at air shows in the United States and elsewhere for some years. As most boys did, growing up in this era, I constructed plastic model aeroplanes. I can still remember receiving a model of a Beaufighter, or similar, as a gift from a godparent, which was made from melted down gramophone records. I wish I still had this toy as I've never seen anything like it since.

My first two years of schooling was by correspondence due to the travelling distance to school. Economically, those were hard times, hence the car was not used by Mum to deliver us to school. Lessons were delivered via post which Mum would administer. At the time this was the only form of education available for younger children. As we lived quite a few miles from the local primary

Getting ready for Sunday School (Author's Collection)

school in Middleton, it wasn't until we were in third grade that we were allowed to bike to school on a limestone road, which was uphill on the way home.

* * *

One of my fond memories, as a young teenager, was when Dad and I used to park on the side of Tapleys Hill Road, on the western side of Adelaide Airport, and watch the planes take-off and land. It certainly spurred my desire to fly, but as none of my relatives had anything to do with aviation, there was no one to guide me into making my dreams a reality. I wrote to various flying schools at Parafield, and also the Royal Australian Air Force

(RAAF), for information on how to become a Pilot. I carried around their brochures in my pocket until they were all tattered and falling apart.

* * *

I completed the highest education level to be studied at Victor Harbour High School[1] which was the Leaving Certificate but without the necessary standard in English and therefore did not have the educational qualifications needed for direct entry into the RAAF as a Pilot. At that time I lacked a certain amount of drive and ambition to attend a school within the Adelaide region to obtain Leaving Honours. Even though I was keen to fly, I had no personal guidance or mentoring to give me the incitement needed to push me to follow my flying dream. I left Port Elliot and boarded with my sister, Lorraine, finding employment with a linen laundering company as a Trainee Manager, just south of Adelaide. My first set of wheels was a 125cc Lambretta Scooter which I used to visit home every Friday night for the weekend. Looking back, I now realise how dangerous it was riding an underpowered scooter on country roads, especially at night, with only one dim (three watt) tail light to warn drivers of my presence on the road. Some nights were cold and raining and I would wear an ex-army tank suit under a grey plastic raincoat to keep the wind and rain out. A few months later, I decided to update to a 1964 Holden EH ute.

I did a couple of other labouring jobs, one of which was as a Sanitation Engineer. The job paid very well and in those days all I did was run between the truck and the garbage bins. Over the course of a day, I probably ran between 30 and 50 km. I became quite physically fit as a result.

* * *

In the late 1960s, my mate, John Barton and I were driving his 1939 four-door Renault down to Waitpinga Beach, just west of Encounter Bay in South Australia. The car had cable operated wheel brakes so that when you pushed on the brake pedal, through a system of levers and cables (one to each wheel), a cable applied tension and thence torque to each wheel brake shoes.

Before we drove down Dennis Road towards the beach, we stopped at the top of the steep hill to conduct a risk assessment as to whether the questionable brakes on the old girl would cope with the sharp right-hand bend at the bottom of the hill. We knew if we missed the right-hand bend, we would slam head-on into a cliff face at high speed. In true-blue Aussie style we decided to give it a go. John slowly eased his foot off the brake and the car

---

1   Victor Harbour was spelt as Harbour in my youth. It wasn't until the 1980s that it changed to Harbor

proceeded down the slope in first gear. At his first application of the foot brake, we both heard a twang, signifying a brake cable had snapped. The significance of this was that in those early cable brakes if you lost one, you lost all braking including the park brake.

Not having been presented with this type of scenario in the past, John nervously asked 'What should I do?' As speed was probably at a fast walking pace, I immediately said 'Steer into the bank'. He did, and the car came to a halt. As cars in those days had bumper bars, no damage was done to the vehicle. We were both relieved that disaster had been averted and we probably had a slightly nervous chuckle. We got out to survey the situation. I have no doubt that had we continued down the hill, we would have slammed into the embankment at the bottom with disastrous, possibly tragic, results for both of us.

We decided that John would reverse back up the hill with me following closely with a rock to place in front of a wheel in case the engine stalled. All went well, and the car was reversed back up to level ground and securely parked. I got a pair of side-cutters out of the car boot and went over to the closest fence and cut about twelve inches of plain fencing wire, climbed under the car and repaired the broken cable. We hopped back in the now 'serviceable' Renault and drove back to Port Elliot without any problems. Isn't youth grand!

MY RAAF CAREER

In late 1967, I applied to the RAAF for entry as a motor mechanic and in early 1968, whilst driving home after completing the interview in Adelaide, I was stopped for exceeding the speed limit on Main South Road, Bedford Park by a solo motorcycle policeman whom I had observed a few miles earlier booking another car. I was so elated at the outcome of the interview that the only thing on my mind was to get home and share the good news with my parents. I didn't notice the policeman following me through my rear vision mirror until it was too late. A few weeks later, I received the speeding fine in the mail. The notice stated that I had to produce the document to a Justice of the Peace (JP). As my father was a JP, I handed it to him. Regrettably, due to my misdemeanour, it was the first and only time I ever saw him cry! Obviously, I had brought shame upon him, the justice system and his family. I then realised his immense sense of pride and have never forgotten his reaction. It has haunted me my entire life. The court case was heard after I had joined the Air Force, and my father, forever supporting me, appeared on my behalf at the Darlington District Court. Fortunately, I received a fine but no conviction. Thanks, Dad!

* * *

On 8th April 1968, I enlisted in the RAAF to undertake No. 925 Recruit Course. I was allocated Service No. A46271. This was a ten-week basic recruitment training course at No. 1 Recruit Training Unit, Edinburgh, South Australia. Three months later, I was posted to RAAF School of Technical Training (RSTT) in Wagga Wagga, New South Wales for No. 139 Trainee Mechanic course. When I joined the RAAF, I had indicated that I wanted to be a motor mechanic, which seemed a normal vocation for a farm boy, as I did not possess the educational qualifications to qualify for Pilot entry.

From Hero to Zero

Joining the RAAF 1968 (Author's Collection)

Whilst in the early stages of training, the RAAF conducted assessments to ascertain each trainee's progress and aptitude. After one such assessment, I was called into the office and advised that in their opinion, I was capable of a more technical career than that of a motor mechanic. The options they suggested were radio, electrical or instrument trades. I decided to enlist in the instrument mechanics course.

The RSTT just outside of Wagga Wagga, New South Wales, provided apprentice and adult trade training for technical and other ground personnel. At this time, only males were permitted to undertake such technical training. Adult trade training was normally provided in two stages. The first stage was basic mechanics training to bring the trainee to a level of proficiency in his particular trade, to enable him to be employed as a qualified tradesman. He was then normally posted to an operational squadron for a period of approximately twelve months to gain valuable hands-on experience under supervision. After the twelve months, he was posted back to the RAAF School of Technical Training to undertake advanced fitters training on higher level training courses.

This was a terribly daunting and also exciting time in my life. It was the first time living away from home. This meant having to do my own laundry, using an old copper wash tub, and my own ironing, mending and darning socks. Oh, for the good old days! Mum was not close by to do these small jobs and in those days one very rarely phoned home as the cost of a phone call was exorbitant. Christmas and Easter were the only times I was granted leave to drive back to South Australia for a home visit. I remember before driving home, we all had to go to the Base Cinema to watch a film produced in 1961 by the Highway Safety Foundation and Safety Enterprises Incorporation called *Mechanised Death*. It was a legendary driver education scare tactic film that underscored the danger of speeding and reckless driving. The film was produced in an era when automobiles lacked the kind of modern safety features and crash-resistant designs that we take for granted today. It featured bloody, real accident footage of carnage and destruction supplied by the Ohio Highway Patrol.

Whilst attending No. 76 Instrument Mechanics Course during the day, I studied the Services General Certificate of Education (SGCE) course in English at night. As English comprehension was not my strong point, I thought, when doing the examination, if I quoted a lot of Shakespeare it would show that I had put a lot of hours into studying. I remember my roommates jokingly saying they would pay the examination markers to pass me, just so they would not have to watch me standing on my bed and then listening to me quote Shakespeare any longer. I successfully completed the SGCE course, thereby fulfilling the educational requirements to apply for the RAAF Pilot's course. It was during this time, whilst undergoing the mechanic's course, that I was finally able to touch an aeroplane up close. The

RAAF were using Commonwealth Aircraft Corporation (CAC) de Havilland Vampires. The smell and feel of those mighty machines gave me just the incentive and determination I needed to drive me towards Pilot training.

I successfully completed No. 76 Instrument Mechanic Course with a credit and was posted to No. 11 Squadron RAAF Edinburgh as an Instrument Mechanic in May of 1969, preceded by a temporary attachment to Unit No. 1 FTS (Flying Training School), Point Cook, Victoria for the first two weeks. A mechanic normally works in the workshop under supervision, until fitter status is attained, and very rarely gets to work on an aircraft. This gave me the encouragement and ambition to take the next step of becoming a Pilot. The sight of Winjeels constantly buzzed overhead gave me the inspiration I needed.

My first ever flight was at Edinburgh, South Australia. As an Instrument Mechanic, I was allowed to sit in the cockpit of a P-3B Orion for a local flight. I remember that flight vividly. Although I had seen cockpits and take-offs in the movies, my first time ever airborne was awesome and will never be forgotten. This again, just enforced my dream to become a Pilot. It was while I was an Instrument Mechanic that I applied for Pilot training but heard nothing for months.

* * *

During my time at RAAF Edinburgh, I was able to travel home to Port Elliot in South Australia every weekend. In the summer of 1969, I joined the Port Elliot Surf Life Saving Club and after suitable training was awarded my Bronze Medallion. This is the core award before becoming a surf lifesaver in Australia. In order to be able to participate in lifesaving operations, the Bronze Medallion course is offered which provides participants with the skills and knowledge of patrolling and surf awareness. A surf lifesaver is a trained volunteer that patrols our beaches on the weekends. Becoming a surf lifesaver is satisfying, fun and rewarding. It instils great qualities in that person, such as respect, trust, leadership, teamwork, decision making, responsibility and safety. However, as a young buck, I can clearly remember one sunny day whilst on patrol at Horseshoe Bay, South Australia. I was standing in a canvas beach shelter looking out to sea with the binoculars when I allowed my field of vision to drift around to the left to check out the beach. A lovely, dear old lady came down to me, pointing her finger at the ocean. 'Don't you worry about those young fillies sunbaking up on the beach. You just concentrate out to sea' she said. Caught in the act! This was the start of my desire to give back to the community. Later in my life, I would become a regular blood donor, a puppy raiser for the Guide Dog Association New South Wales, much later a Justice of the Peace and very recently a Legacy Legatee.

* * *

In May of 1970, I was posted back to the RSTT in Wagga Wagga to complete No. 55 Instrument Fitters Course. During this time, I was called to the Education Office.

'Is this yours?' questioned the Education Officer, holding up my Pilot application form.

'Yes Sir!' I answered. It was a complete shock to me as I had almost forgotten about it.

'I can't understand why this hasn't been actioned and processed' he replied. He assured me he would hasten the application process.

I was sent by train to Sydney to undergo a Farnsworth Lantern Test. This test consists of showing a pair of vertically oriented lights consisting of combinations of either red, green or yellow-white. The test subject is asked to identify the two colours, some of which are identical. Nine colour pairs are administered during the test, beginning with a red/green combination, to allow the patient to see these two colours prior to seeing a white light, which decreases testing errors. The examinee is shown the target for only two seconds, as colour-deficient patients can sometimes correctly identify the colours with prolonged exposure. Shortly after, I embarked on a train trip to Melbourne for an eye check with Dr John Colvin, at The Royal Victorian Eye and Ear Hospital, who was also a qualified Pilot and became a consultant ophthalmologist to the RAAF.

Sometime in 2008, I wrote to Dr Colvin thanking him for passing me and therefore opening the gates to a wonderful, exciting and extremely rewarding career. I also told him about my DC-3 ditching, which had received vast national media coverage, and mentioned that due to his support at the beginning of my career, I was able to captain the plane through a successful ditching, saving all lives on board. His wife wrote back, informing me that Dr Colvin was in a nursing home and had very poor vision, so she read my letter to him. She advised that on reading my letter to her husband, he had tears in his eyes. Apparently, when I did my aircrew medical in 1970, my eyesight must have been borderline resulting me in requiring more intense testing by a specialist. This was the reason the RAAF arranged for me to see Dr Colvin.

GAINING MY WINGS

I passed my Instrument Fitters Course early in January 1971. On that very same day, my dream came true as I was posted to No. 1 Flying Training School at Point Cook, Victoria again, however, this time I was assigned to No. 80 Pilots' Course, with the rank of Cadet Aircrew, flying CAC CA-25 Winjeel basic training aeroplanes.

My first training flight was on 29th January 1971, in a Winjeel A85-422 under Instructor, Flight Lieutenant Graeme Szczecinski. The elation I felt walking out to the flight line is seared in my memory.

My Pilot training started in earnest on 22nd February 1971. This was followed by my first solo flight in a Winjeel A85-403 on 17th March 1971.

Every walk across the tarmac to your aeroplane is so exciting. It's an ever-changing environment—the weather, the wind, the sounds and smells of aviation. The magnitude of the task, the self-confidence tempered with the reality of the consequences of inadequacy that will put you to the test grows, as does the size of the aircraft you approach—it can equally be a thrilling and a daunting walk.

Even though your flight is planned to the nth degree you are always aware that sometimes things won't always go according to plan. Matt Hall, ex RAAF Fighter Pilot Top Gun Instructor, and 2019 Red Bull Air Race World Champion once said:

> 'The difference between confidence and arrogance, in my definition, is that a confident person has the utmost belief that they can do a very good job and win a fight, but they'll always listen to advice. Whereas an arrogant person has the same amount of confidence, but they don't actually listen to anything'.

I would often discuss aircraft accidents and what-if scenarios with my very good friend and aviator mate, Dave Foulkes, who has since passed away. Pilots don't consider this a morbid subject, but one where your knowledge and experience increases. You never know when you might have to draw on this invaluable knowledge during your career. For me, this happened on 24th April 1994, when I ditched my aeroplane at Botany Bay, Sydney.

* * *

Whilst undergoing Pilot training at Point Cook, I did one of my best landings to date. As most take-off and landing areas were on grass (just like a huge paddock), plastic cones marking the active runways were moved as required to ensure you always took off into the wind. So proud was I about my landing, that even my instructor's comment didn't faze me.

'Cadet, that is one of the smoothest landings I have ever experienced. It's a pity the runway is fifty yards over there' he said pointing to the right. I was obviously concentrating so hard on my approach and landing that for a few minutes 'situational awareness' escaped me.

Another landing that comes to mind was years later in a RAAF Lockheed P-3B Orion at Learmonth, Western Australia. Thankfully there was a long runway and from memory, our flight had been fairly bumpy due to the mechanical turbulence in the air on a hot day. When an aeroplane takes off or lands into the summer sky, it flies through these areas of upward and downward moving air, and it reacts accordingly, sometimes violently. This is why flights in the summer are often uncomfortable near the ground, on landings. I can vividly remember approaching at our normal speed and flaring the aeroplane. In the flare, the nose of the aeroplane is raised, slowing the descent rate. In the case of conventional landing gear equipped aeroplanes, the attitude (this is the aircraft's orientation with respect to the horizon) is set to ensure the aeroplane touches down on the main landing gear first. Runway length is very critical for landings and take-offs and all aeroplane performance is predicated on that runway length.

Getting back to Learmonth, the runway length was far more than that required. Therefore, I knew I could attempt a smooth landing by flaring at the appropriate height and speed and waiting for the normal touchdown vibration of machine contacting the ground. This did not happen and as speed bled off, I thought to myself, when it hits, it is really going to hit hard. However, there was no jarring, no screeching of tyres or vibrating. Nothing. Therefore, at about 100 kt, I slowly lowered the nose of the aeroplane expecting any time for the abrupt jolt. Still, nothing. Wow! We had landed and no-one on the plane felt a thing. There was still plenty of available runway to slowly pull up and exit via the taxiway.

Point Cook basic flight training was normally only about fifteen one-hour

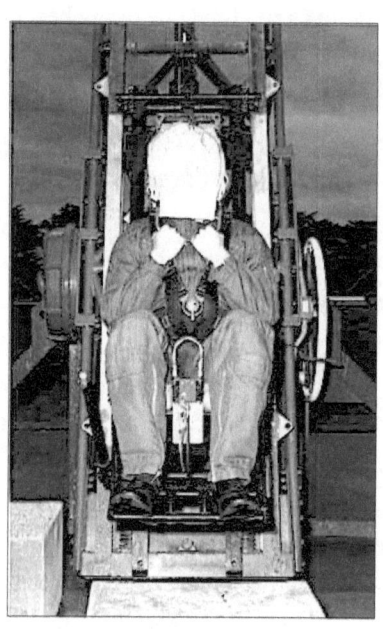

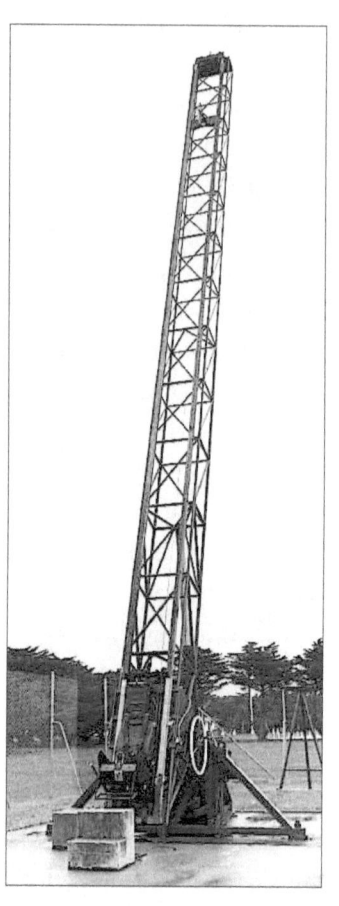

(above) Ejection Seat Trainer at Point Cook (Mike Medhurst)
(right) Ejection Seat Trainer at Point Cook (Mike Medhurst)

dual flights, with an instructor. In that time some cadets flew solo and some didn't, although this was not in any way an indication of the cadet's ability. I was lucky enough to go solo.

Whilst at Point Cook, we undertook ejection seat training in a rig which gave aircrew practical experience in ejection from aeroplanes as our next training aircraft would have these seats fitted. This rig was an ejection seat on rails which ran approximately 30 ft (9 m) vertically. We were told by the Aviation Medical Section that the rig used only one explosive cartridge as opposed to the real aeroplane which had two. These cartridges are used to propel the Pilot and seat clear of the aeroplane in an emergency. I remember pulling the protective face blind down over my helmet. A face blind is a canvas blind attached to the top of the ejection seat. Once this handle is pulled the blind covers the face of the occupant of the seat and the ejection sequence commences, to protect the face from the effects of wind experienced on a real ejection. After feeling no jolt or acceleration whatsoever, I presumed the seat had not fired. I removed the face blind to be surprised it had and I was way up the top of the rails.

* * *

In early April 1971, I was subsequently posted to No. 2 Flying Training School at RAAF Pearce, Western Australia. When travelling from Point Cook before crossing the Nullarbor, we stopped at Kevin Rasmus', a fellow course member, mother's house at Port Augusta for a fantastic lunch. We had five cars in convoy. Our next stop was on the South Australian/Western Australian border where we lined all our vehicles up across the road for a Le Mans start. This entailed all the drivers lining up about 100 m on the Perth side of the border. One of us shouted GO, to which we ran across to our cars, climbed in, started our engines and drove away at breakneck speed! Naturally, Rod in his hot EH Holden Ute was first away.

Pearce is where I finally flew jets. The MB-326H (Macchi) was an Italian designed light military jet trainer. It had been developed and ordered dur-

Nullarbor 'Le Mans' start (Rod Trower)

From Hero to Zero

Yours truly seated in a Macchi Jet Trainer (Author's Collection)

ing a period in which the 'all-through' jet trainer was considered to be a fashionable concept within many air forces. An all-through jet trainer negates the requirement of a piston-engined, propeller-driven basic trainer, as historically used. It was intended to provide a single type of aeroplane that could be used to perform both elementary and advanced training right through to a near combat-ready standard. However, the RAAF soon found that 'all-through' jet training wasn't effective and switched back to operating the Macchi in conjunction with a cheaper piston-engined type (Winjeel) for basic training, having had a brief flirtation with all-through jet training between 1969 and 1971.

This was a great time in my life. The excitement of the ground school and the flight training was beyond my wildest dreams. Flying down the Avon Valley, to the east of Pearce was unreal, but it had to be flown dual with an instructor. Cadets were not allowed to do it solo as flying down a valley at high speed allows no room for errors of judgement. On navigation exercises, a favourite trick for an instructor was to ask you to pass your navigation map back to him in the rear seat so that he could compare them. My answer was: 'Sir, I prepared both, so they are both the same'. The reply was: 'Now, cadet!' Obediently I passed it back. After a few seconds, I asked for it back. 'No' was the answer. This meant I had to navigate back to base without a map. The map also contained a lot of other pertinent information, such as fuel, heading, true airspeed (TAS), time and other essential information to navigate back to base. Due to 'situational awareness', you try to remember your next turning or waypoint to continue the flight. If you were wrong, the instructor would certainly berate your actions. Fortunately, I was not berated. This experience taught me a valuable lesson and from then on, I carried a smaller cheat sheet in a flight suit pocket just in case. Many old Pilots have lost their navigational maps when sliding open the cockpit window of a DC-3 to allow cool air to circulate. The draft created would quickly suck out all loose paperwork. The countryside was probably littered with numerous navigation maps and charts.

* * *

My whole life revolved around flying and the Air Force. I was extremely shy and not confident around women. I always found it hard to understand why they would want to talk to me as I thought that my looks on a score between one to ten was probably a two or three. I met Leone, a nurse, when I attended a party put on by a friend. Leone's good friend, Cecily Smith, had two brothers, Frank and Robert who were also cadets on my Pilot's course. Prior to meeting Leone, I had only been in a couple of short-term relationships.

Robert was a great friend to me during the Pilot's course. Whenever I would visit Perth, from Pearce, Robert was very kind and would make up my navigation maps for my next sortie. Cadets quite often were given a change of instructor and I was assigned to Squadron Leader Craig Couzens who was the Chief Ground Instructor at No. 2 Flying Training School. He was fantastic and similar to Lieutenant Commander Chris Konczey, who I was to meet later when he was on exchange duties at RAAF Edinburgh from the United States Navy. Both of them saw specific qualities in me and encouraged and helped me enormously in my career. At that time, there were about four Pilot courses at any one time at Pearce and only the senior course participants were allowed off base during the week. As I was an ex-groundie (ground crew), I knew most of the airmen on the guard gate at Pearce and so I would boldly drive down to Perth most evenings without being questioned.

Leone and Cecily were renting a unit in South Perth so I would visit them often. One night after having a few beers at the Cadet's Mess I drove down for a visit. Knowing I liked a beer, the girls offered me one from their fridge that had already been poured into a beer mug. I thought that was very nice of them until I took a mouthful.

'Yuk! What the hell is this?' I spluttered as the girls laughed wholeheart-

edly. They had concocted a tea brew and used dishwashing liquid to make the froth. I learnt a valuable lesson that night—open the bottle yourself!

Unfortunately, both Frank and Robert failed to graduate. As one RAAF flying instructor told me, they can basically train anyone to be a Pilot, but they only have a limited time to accomplish this. If progress is not up with the timeline, then that cadet must go. This was at the time when the Vietnam war was winding down. This resulted in a limited number of places being available.

After leaving the Air Force, Robert John Smith was only twenty-one when the Macair Cessna 206 VH-MKK he was flying as Pilot in Command crashed in Papua New Guinea on 4th December 1973, at approximately 2.30pm. Also on board was twenty-six-year-old Robert Bruce Smith who sadly lost his life in the accident. As odd as it seemed for them to have similar names, they were not related to each other. Robert John had been flying with Macair for three months. Upon hearing the news from Cecily about Robert John, Leone and I drove to Adelaide to support her during this horrendous time of her life.

On 14th December the search to find the wreckage was called off. Two days later, after the authorities received a report from some villagers, the wreckage was spotted from the air. A ground party found the body of Robert Bruce Smith beside the aircraft and medical opinion was that he had lived for at least 48 hours. There was no sign of Robert John Smith until 21st December when his body was found face down under a tree fern covered in tufts of grass. It was deduced he had lived for approximately 12 days after the crash. It was estimated he had walked a total of approximately 30 km at altitudes between 2,590 m and 2,743 m but ended up only 6 km from the crash site. Very sad.

* * *

One aspect of the flying training I thoroughly enjoyed was formation flying. This type of flying is incredibly mentally and physically exhausting. Most times we would hold close formation for only about twenty minutes and then move out to a loose formation which is nowhere near as demanding, allowing us to recoup before re-joining in close formation. The larger the aeroplane, the harder it is to conduct formation flying due to the weight and inertia involved. The largest plane I have flown in formation is the P-3B Orion.

I thoroughly relished everything about the Pilot's course apart from the physical training. A couple of times we were required to board a bus which would take us way out the back of Pearce—approximately 10 km. We would then have to run back to the main gate of the base. As a strong believer in the conservation of energy, I would lag to the back of the pack and put out my hitchhiking thumb. Sooner or later a car would stop and pick me up. I would duck down in the back seat so my course mates could not see me, and when the driver asked where I would like to be dropped off, I would give him a drop-off point that was about 1 km before the main gate to the base. When the car pulled over to drop me off, I would give my heartfelt thanks and find a spot to sit, under a tree, until my course mates came along and then I'd re-join the back of the pack.

* * *

On 6th November 1971, I was asked to call the Orderly Officer who advised me of the sad news that my brother, Malcolm, a South Australian Police Officer (and ex-Army) had passed away at the age of thirty-two. He was ten years older than me. He apparently had been feeling unwell at his home and, as was done when we were children, went and sat outside in the car in the sun. He had then suffered a heart attack. On the Monday arrangements were made for me to fly back to Adelaide for his funeral. I was very impressed at his funeral to see a cavalcade of around fifty motorcycle policemen escorting the hearse to the cemetery.

When talking with my parents later, they related a strange and concerning event. Apparently, on the day my brother passed away, two policemen came to their home in Port Elliot and said that they had some bad news about their son. For some twenty minutes or so, the words 'your son' were the only words used without naming him. Eventually, they said 'Malcolm' and my parents were shocked as the whole time they had assumed it was me that had passed away due to my fledgling flying career.

My siblings and I were not very close due to the significant age differences between us. At my earliest memory, my eldest sister Margaret was undergoing nursing training at McLaren Vale Hospital and Malcolm was in the Army. I was reasonably close to my other sisters Jennifer and Lorraine. My little brother, Colin, followed many years later.

* * *

One of my course mates was Phillip Sbizzirri and I remember fondly how we used to have a 'pipe-in' session in one of our rooms quite often. As

From Hero to Zero

we were young cadet Pilots, it was super cool, at that stage, to be smoking a pipe. Around three or four of us would light a pipe and within minutes it was hard to even see a mate across the room. Looking back, although senseless and not at all healthy, we had a great time. Oh, the joys of youth! Phillip was also an ex-groundie (Instrument Fitter), but he came through the RAAF Apprentice Scheme, not as an adult trainee as I did. Phillip came up with the phrase *'M'ol China'* which translates to best mate. Unfortunately, Phillip did not complete the course due to health reasons. Just recently he sent me a birthday greeting and this phrase is still used.

On 3rd March 1972, I passed my RAAF Wings test and was awarded the National Mutual Trophy for the Student who has Shown the Most Improvement on No. 80 Pilots' Course. I was very proud of this achievement. I started No. 80 Pilots' Course with forty trainees and only sixteen graduated. On graduation, I was promoted to the rank of Pilot Officer and presented with my coveted wings. My service number changed from airman rank A46271 to officer rank O46271.

Our Graduation Ceremony was held on Thursday, 23rd March 1972. The reviewing officer was Air Marshal Sir Valston Hancock, KBE, CB, DFC

The Officer Commanding, Officers and Cadets
of the
Royal Australian Air Force, Pearce
request the pleasure of the company of

LT COL & MRS A S M. LOVELL

at the
Graduation Parade of No. 80 Pilots' Course
at 6.00 p.m. on THURSDAY, 23rd MARCH, 1972
to be reviewed by
Air Marshal Sir Valston HANCOCK, KBE, CB, DFC (Ret'd)

to be followed by a
RECEPTION in the OFFICERS' MESS (between 7.00 and 9.00 p.m.)

R.S.V.P.: By 9th March, 1972
to O.C'. Secretary
RAAF Pearce 6085
Phone 095-711200 Ext 256.

Lounge Suit
Summer Uniform
PTO

No. 80 Pilot's Course Graduation Invitation (Author's Collection)

(Retired). It was an impressive ceremony and I was very proud to have graduated. My father, Lieutenant-Colonel Lovell and my mother Bertha (known as Biddy), flew across to RAAF Base Pearce, in Western Australia, for my graduation. Fellow graduate Cadet Aircrew Steve Knudsen and his father, Group Captain Fred Knudsen, were also in attendance and all four of us were interviewed and photographed for a story in the Daily News that appeared on 23rd March 1972. I'm sure that both high-ranking military fathers were proud of their sons.

I recall AVM Hancock's speech, printed in our Graduate Ceremony booklet[1] as if it was yesterday. He had this to say:

'Your graduation day is an important stage of your Air Force and Navy careers. By hard work you have overcome the difficulties of a rigorous training course; now you face the challenge of converting to operational aircraft in your new squadrons.

'For your efforts so far, I offer my congratulations. However, the hard work, dedication and personal application does not stop here. From this point onwards, your careers as Service Officers will be largely in your own hands—you will be required to show sound judgement, discretion, integrity and self-discipline in all your activities. Later, you will accept a solemn responsibility for the defence of our country.

'Finally, the aircrew of the Royal Australian Navy and the Royal Australian Air Force have high reputations which you have a duty to maintain. I am sure that this responsibility is well placed and I wish you continued success for the future.'

* * *

Towards the end of my Pilot's course, we were allowed to submit posting preferences. To be honest, I cannot remember what my preference was. Just prior to graduating, we were advised of our postings to take effect after graduation. Initially, I was told I was going to fly McDonnell Douglas F-4E Phantom II if another already qualified Pilot rejected that posting. There was something big and powerful about the Phantom. It was nicknamed the Rhino by United States Service personnel. The McDonnell Douglas F-4E Phantom II is a tandem two-seat twin-engined, all-weather, long-range supersonic jet interceptor and fighter-bomber with a top speed of over Mach 2.2 and was used extensively during the Vietnam War. It served as the principal air superiority

---

1 RAAF publication for No 2 Flying Training School

No. 80 Pilots' Course just prior to graduation (Author's Collection)

fighter for both the United States Navy and Air Force and became important in the ground-attack and aerial reconnaissance roles late in the war. Whilst on Pilot's Course, the RAAF significantly wound down their air support from the Vietnam War.

Unfortunately for me, he accepted and I was posted to No. 2 Operational Conversion Unit (OCU) at Williamtown, New South Wales to fly Macchi and Dassault Mirage III fighter aeroplanes which to me was just as exciting. The Dassault Mirage 111O was known as the French Lady. This was a very apt description. She was certainly good looking with all the right curves in the right places and moved with a certain dignity and poise. The French Lady was very popular with her Pilots. The aeroplane, in a clean configuration, had a sparkling supersonic performance despite a relatively modest thrust/weight ratio, with exhilarating acceleration and rate of climb in full afterburner. Very few aircraft could match its amazing roll rate. All this, coupled with the best feeling flight controls of any contemporary aeroplane, made it a sheer delight to fly.

* * *

Whilst on Pilot's course we were not permitted to be or get married, but once my graduation had taken place, Leone and I tied the knot as Leone was

First solo in Mirage A3-06 on 14th August 1972 (Author's Collection)

pregnant with our first child. On my posting to Williamtown, after graduating, we passed through Rosanna near Melbourne, Victoria for our planned wedding as her family lived in that area, and my parents flew across to attend. We had decided this was the best option for the majority of guests. It was a rushed trip as the RAAF had only granted me seven days leave to travel from Pearce to Williamtown. Although I was not Catholic, our ceremony was held in a Catholic Church followed by our reception. As her parents had made all of the arrangements for the wedding, we did in fact go and see the priest the following day. I do remember him commenting that the usual protocol was to meet the couple prior to the wedding for his little chat, not after as we had done. This certainly caused a good laugh between us. I was twenty-two and Leone was twenty-one when we married. On reflection, I feel I was way too young and immature to have been married at the age of twenty-two.

* * *

Part of the conversion course at No. 2 OCU was to conduct a Mach 2 run in the Mirage. On 5th September 1972, after completing the Mach 2 run (twice the speed of sound, or approximately 2,500 kph), the aeroplane suffered an engine flame-out. In aviation terms, a flame-out refers to the rundown of a jet engine caused by the extinction of the flame in the combustion chamber. It can be caused by a number of factors, including fuel starvation, compressor stall, insufficient oxygen (at high altitudes), foreign object damage such as caused by birds, hail or volcanic ash as in the case of British Airways Boeing 747 G-BDXH on 24th June 1982. That aeroplane, radio call sign Speedbird 9, flew into a cloud of volcanic ash thrown up by the eruption of Mount Galunggung, West Java Indonesia, resulting in the failure of all four engines. Capt Eric Moody glided this huge 747 out of the ash cloud, and all engines were restarted.

From Hero to Zero

Although one engine failed again soon after, the aeroplane managed to land safely. An outstanding display of airmanship by the entire crew.

My flame-out at Mach 2 happened off the coast, north east of Williamtown, New South Wales at a height of 40,000 ft. The timing of the relight procedure, which could only be carried out under 25,000 ft, had to be delayed. This was due to the fact that above this altitude, the atmosphere was less dense than required. In that time I gave a Mayday (distress) call on guard at frequency 243 Mhz, which was received by Richmond RAAF base, near Sydney, and not Williamtown. Richmond then alerted Williamtown to activate the appropriate response.

They say that the Mirage has the gliding properties of a brick! However, it is a requirement to be at the 300 kt optimum glide speed without delay. It only took seconds to descend to the required 25,000 ft with the aeroplane's attitude seeming to be around 60 degrees nose down. I remember seeing a lot of ocean! Because of the enormous rate of descent, there were now only two options—if the engine would not relight immediately, then the only choice left was to raise the nose to reduce the rate of descent and airspeed and eject from the aeroplane. There is an old aviation saying: 'nothing on the clock but the maker's name'. This was a jovial phrase referring to an engine not producing power.

This was an intense moment for a brand-new Pilot with only 300 hours total flying time and 26 hours 'time on type', even having trained for such an event. Only seconds later, and below 25,000 ft, my attempt to relight was successful as was the subsequent landing. Interestingly, I later spoke to a Williamtown Air Traffic Controller who told me they had assumed my Mayday radio call was merely a position report. An investigation was carried out, in house, after my incident with inconclusive results as to the cause of the flame-out. The outcome of this incident came down to seconds, not unlike the ditching of the DC-3—some 22 years later.

Shortly after my incident, a colleague on my course also suffered an engine failure in the Mirage. He attempted to land the aeroplane on a country road. He was not so fortunate and subsequently met his end. There is still conjecture as to why he didn't eject.

* * *

Whilst at No. 2 OCU I seemed to be having personality problems with some instructional staff, although most instructional staff were fantastic. Unfortunately, some of these staff saw themselves as the 'gods' of the aviation world. At no time did I ever aspire to be an arrogant Top Gun. However, I did aspire to be one of the best Pilots. Through the unit adjutant, I made an appointment to see the Unit Commanding Officer (CO). At the agreed time I was ushered into his office, and I naturally assumed that I would be able to present my side of the problems. Wrong! As soon as the door was closed, I received the greatest dressing down of my life. I was not allowed to utter a word. He was a largeish, balding guy who was standing in an extremely dominant position. His body language spoke volumes! He protected his instructors to the hilt and did not want to even listen to the reason I requested an audience with him. I was made to stand the whole time during his four or five-minute tirade and was not allowed to utter a word. He finally concluded with: 'Do I make myself clear? Now get out!' Nobody could ever accuse the military of being caring and understanding.

I readily admit to some personality conflicts during my Mirage training at No. 2 OCU. The last example of how vindictive some of these people could be was when I had to sit for a written exam on a Monday morning at 9.00am. Naturally, I studied all weekend to prepare. Immediately after completing the exam, I was called into the Chief Flying Instructor's (CFI) office to be told that I was off-course, meaning my training had been terminated, hence the end of my high-performance fighter Pilot career. I felt it was vindictive of them to let me study all weekend for a difficult exam, sit the exam and immediately it was finished, to be advised of my course termination due to certain people deeming me to be unsuitable for high-performance fighter/strike aircraft. I believe the CFI was genuine when he told me that he had nothing to do with this decision. My Mirage instructor also advised me he was unaware of the decision. I know deep down that this had nothing to do with my flying ability of the Mirage but due to not having the Knucklehead (Fighter Pilot) persona. This is by no means a derogative title; it is used merely within the military as an endearing slang word just as transport Pilots are known as Trash Haulers. The Fighter Pilot is well depicted by Tom Cruise, who starred in the film Top Gun portraying the 'I am the greatest Pilot' role.

After I had been off-coursed, whilst still at Williamtown, I was allowed to go back and fly Macchis whilst the RAAF decided on my new posting.

* * *

During this period, I experienced another hair-raising moment at Williamtown Airport. Flying a Macchi, I was number five in the landing sequence behind four Mirage aeroplanes. It is common practice to have a mixture of aircraft types in the landing circuit area. Most aeroplanes create wingtip vortices, but with Mirage aeroplanes having delta wings they are more pronounced. These are circular patterns of rotating air left behind a wing as it generates lift. One wingtip vortex trails from each tip. If the atmospheric conditions are suitable, you can sometimes see them on airliners coming in to land. At low speeds, a delta wing requires a nose up attitude (high angle of attack) to maintain lift. If you can imagine the turbulent air created by four Mirages all within a lineal distance of about 4 km, then you would understand the impact this had on my relatively small and light Macchi. Well, on final approach to land at about 500 ft above the ground, all of a sudden I flew into those unseen vortices and in a split second my aeroplane rolled sharply, about 120 degrees to the left. I considered ejecting, but thought to myself, all I'm going to do is bury my head in the dirt, as the aeroplane was still rolling into the inverted position. I immediately applied maximum thrust, a lot of right rudder and some aileron to slowly roll back to a normal flying attitude. Fortunately, it worked, but this manoeuvre now had my Macchi pointing in the direction of downwind, with the potential to meet aircraft flying in the opposite direction head-on. Fortunately, no other aircraft were in the circuit, so all was ok. I extended out a bit further before re-joining for a normal landing. I must admit, this shook me up a little.

* * *

Given the opportunity to apply for a posting of my choice, I chose Transport Support Flight RAAF Butterworth flying Dakota (DC-3) aeroplanes. Again, I missed out, which I assume was due to no vacancies at that time thus I was subsequently posted to No. 11 Squadron, Edinburgh South Australia, to fly Lockheed P-3B Orion aeroplanes. This posting turned out to be a blessing in disguise. I thoroughly enjoyed the aeroplane and the team crew environment.

FLYING THE P-3B ORION

I commenced flying the Lockheed P-3B Orion in 1974. The following article was written some 45 years later and sums up the crews' appreciation of a fantastic and very capable aircraft.

Wing Commander Marija (Maz) Jovanovich (awarded the Conspicuous Service Medal in 2019), Executive Officer of the RAAF's 92 Wing wrote (in part) a great article in the Australian Aviation January/February 2019 magazine.

'Australia is a maritime nation. Our national character and concerns are heavily influenced by the fact that we are surrounded by the sea, and our dependence on it as a defence barrier as well as a treasure trove of resources and a primary mode of trade. It follows that this maritime nation has always turned towards its maritime patrol assets to protect the things that matter. The P-3 has answered this call with distinction.

The majestic P-3 Orion (Author's Collection)

'As a weaponised warfighting platform, capable of delivering torpedoes, mines and anti-ship missiles if required, the P-3 has a deterrence presence that contributes to rules-based order and stability in our region. On the flip side, the P-3 and her crews also excel at providing humanitarian assistance in disaster situations.

'There are few things as fun as flying such a large aircraft to the edges of its envelope. [So true]

'The Orion is a real 'Pilot's aircraft', the last one in the RAAF inventory.

'In the hands of a swept-up crew, the P-3 is a deadly hunter, capable of locating and tracking multiple submarines and attacking them with torpedoes.

'A good ASW [Anti-Submarine Warfare] mission is pure euphoria, and ASW is highly addictive.

'Proficient in its main roles, the Orion is the queen of re-tasking. It was not uncommon to head out on one kind of mission only to be redirected while airborne to something completely different.

'The remarkable aircraft notwithstanding, the most special thing about flying the P-3 is the maritime crew. This motley collection of disparate individuals, all technical experts ... have always made life both challenging and fun. Nowhere else have I encountered the camaraderie and close teamwork environment that characterises life on a maritime crew.

'There would be no great flying, no successful missions without the men and women who maintain the aircraft and keep them serviceable.'

* * *

Around Christmas of 1972, to take up my new posting with the No 11 Squadron in South Australia, Leone and I, along with our two-month-old son, Gary, were driving across the Hay Plain in our Holden EH Ute. It was the middle of summer and I can still recall the brutality of the forty-degree heat. There was no air-conditioning in those days and the wide-open windows and speed of the car gave little relief to our overheated bodies. Under the circumstances, Gary coped well. We used damp towels to keep him as cool as we could. In those days you just did what you had to do. This was the only way we were going to get our family over to South Australia. Oh, how times have changed.

* * *

Flying the P-3B Orion

Dad and I photographed at my parent's home in Port Elliot (Author's Collection)

No. 11 Squadron acquired Lockheed P-3B Orions in 1968. I vividly remember, whilst on recruit course, watching them flying into Edinburgh. At the time, I never contemplated that I would eventually become a Pilot of these magnificent aeroplanes. The Orion (endearingly referred to as son of 'Neptune', which it replaced) is a four-engined turboprop anti-submarine and long-range maritime patrol (LRMP) aeroplane developed for the United States Navy from the civil Lockheed Electra and introduced in the 1960s. Crew complement is normally twelve, however, for non-operational sorties (e.g. air displays or Pilot, flight engineer training) it can be as little as four. Once on station, one engine is normally shut down (usually the No. 1 engine—the left outer engine which had no electrical generator) to conserve fuel and extend the time aloft and/or range when at low level. Above 1,000 ft we could extend this capability by shutting down No. 4 engine as well.

* * *

In the RAAF, when you convert onto an aeroplane type and successfully complete the conversion course, you do a quick flight on that aeroplane as 'Pilot in command'. After completing conversion onto the P-3B, my Co-pilot for my first command flight, on 24th March 1973, was none other than Flying Officer Tony Hannam, who wrote my foreword. This was the beginning of a lifelong friendship. One story regarding Tony that comes to mind is when we both flew into Nadi, Fiji on a temporary assignment. At that time, Tony was a Captain, and I was a Co-pilot. One evening we were at one of the hotels having a few ales when we got chatting to a young couple who were think-

Orion Co-Pilot (Author's Collection)

ing about getting married. Well, as we had all had a few beers, some bright spark (not mentioning any names) stated that if a ship's Captain could marry a couple, then there was no reason that an aeroplane Captain could not. No sooner said than done. As no ring was available, Tony offered to lend them his, but fumbled and dropped it under the table. After a frantic search and recovery, the 'marriage' was formalised and the process was completed. To this day, we often wonder if there is a couple out there who still believe they were legally married in Fiji by an aeroplane Captain. They may be in for a very rude shock the day they find out the truth.

* * *

As part of aircrew training, one is required to go on a survival course. This was normally about a week long and entailed living off minimum food and general survival techniques—not my favourite pastime. This was to be conducted down the Rapid Bay area, South of Adelaide, close to where I was raised. I did a bit of reconnaissance prior to the event and went and bought a whole lot of non-perishable supplies, stashing them near where I thought we would be camping. Sure enough, we were dropped off by bus, reasonably close to where I had hidden my cache. My fellow crew members and I thought it not prudent to recover the rations immediately, and so we waited until late in the afternoon before striking out for the recovery operation. It probably took us around half an hour to find the site. Apparently, the other guys at the campsite could hear us coming from quite away off. Allegedly we were calling out at the top of our voices: 'Hey, Bushy'. Bushy was the nickname given to the organiser of the survival course, Flight Lieutenant Brian Kavanagh. Obviously one of the good guys, he apparently ignored us.

A year or so later, I had to undertake another survival course at Canungra, in South East Queensland. We were briefed to never go on local roads as the instructors were patrolling them. Being the energy conservationist that I was, when the opportunity arose I would make my way onto the road and walk along it in my green flight suit. At some point, I would come across elderly couples at picnic tables having a cuppa and afternoon tea. Naturally, one would embellish the situation when asked what I was doing.

'I'm on a survival course in the bush and haven't eaten in a while'. I would tell them trying to look forlorn. It worked like a charm.

'Oh, you poor boy. Sit down and share our food and drinks'. To have a nice hot cuppa and some homemade fruit cake and biscuits was pure heaven. I loved it even though I didn't fare as well as one of the other guys. I heard that every evening his girlfriend would meet him at a pre-arranged location and he would spend the night with her then get dropped off early the next morning. What a trooper!

* * *

The RAAF followed the UK Royal Air Force (RAF) traditions in many areas. One was that Pilots and other commissioned aircrew in the RAAF are classed in the General Duties Branch, whereas other officers that held positions such as medical, dental, chaplains and legals were deemed to be in the Specialist Branch.

As a Pilot, you are expected to be an officer and manager first, and whilst the flying part is important, you need to understand that the General Duties Branch usually gets all the top rating jobs. These include Squadron Commanders, Wing Commanders, Base Commanders and other senior ranking positions which involves more desk work and less flying time. It's important that one has the ability to perform secondary duties just as well which could also include Sports/Entertainment Officer.

One of my secondary duties at No. 11 Squadron was as Officer in Charge (OIC) of the squadron crew room. This was when I was in Edinburgh in 1973, when I was a lowly Pilot Officer, commonly referred to as a bog-rat. The crew room was very old with absolutely no appeal, so I decided it needed modernising and sprucing up. At one of the morning briefings, I announced my plans. The squadron members were asked to contribute a small amount of their wage every payday and when that member was posted out of the squadron, he could either donate his contribution or receive a percentage of it back. From memory, I think everyone donated their contributions.

My crew room modernisation plan was received enthusiastically and started to gain momentum. This entailed mainly constructing a false ceiling and faux-brick bar and generally making the whole room homelier and more modern. However, within a few months, Squadron Leader Les Fisher called me into his office to advise that the project was becoming too big for me to handle and he would take over the project, effectively jumping on the band wagon and taking all the credit. I obviously assisted him on his career path as last I heard, he was Air Marshall LB Fisher AO. He never did thank me for his career boost!

* * *

In 1973, I bought a beautiful 1968, 4.2 litre Mark X Jaguar with a sunroof. It was a magnificent car. We had a growing family by then and my old EH Holden ute was no longer suitable. I paid cash for the Jaguar and over the next twelve months, I spent money sprucing it up.

A devastating tragedy occurred that same year. We had borrowed a caravan from my sister Jennifer and were holidaying at Moonta, in South Australia.

Leone was heavily pregnant with our second child. In the very early hours of the morning on 11th July 1973, she told me that she thought things were not right with the baby. I hooked up the caravan to our Mark X Jaguar and left the caravan park for home at Smithfield Plains. The 140 km trip was done in a very short time. On arrival at Smithfield Plains, at around 6.00 am, I uncoupled the caravan and took my wife straight to the Hutchinson Hospital in Gawler. Our second child was born very premature and I remember touching her in the humidicrib as she was placed in an ambulance to be transferred to the Queen Victoria Hospital. She only survived a few hours. A nurse from the hospital rang me at home to inform me of her death. I drove back to Hutchinson Hospital to inform my wife. As soon as she saw me walk into her room, she knew what had happened. I can still remember, to this day, the hospital staff saying to us 'You'll get over it.' You never get over things like this in your life. You simply learn to deal with it in different ways. Our daughter, Suzanne, is buried in West Terrace Cemetery in Adelaide and there is a plaque with her name on it at the Baby Memorial.

A disturbing report surfaced in 2001 about a government cover-up regarding stolen baby parts. This scandal reported the South Australian Government's involvement in the removal of babies' organs, hearts and brains, without consent, during autopsies performed at the Adelaide Women's and Children's Hospital, the Queen Victoria Hospital and the Queen Elizabeth Hospital. This practice was carried out between the 1960s and the late 1990s mostly for medical research. On hearing that, I made an enquiry to the Department of Human Services' Tissue Retention Hotline. Christine Charles, Chief Executive of DHS wrote back to me enclosing a counsellor's letter stating that their investigation team found no evidence that an autopsy had been conducted following Suzanne's death.

Later that same year, two suited gentlemen came to my home.

'Is that your car in the carport?' one of them asked.

'Yes, it is,' I proudly replied.

'Well, I'm sorry to inform you that it's not. It's ours,' stated the other.

'We are from the Beneficial Finance Corporation. The person you bought this car from has not paid off his loan. You are required by law to return the car or pay off the amount owing if you would like to retain the car,' he informed me.

As you can imagine, I was devastated. The amount still owing was more than I had paid for it. I drove it down to the Beneficial Finance Corporation in Adelaide. When I went to hand over the keys, I asked to be reimbursed for the fuel.

'Surely, you don't want to be reimbursed for such a small amount', sneered the Office Manager. When I insisted, he begrudgingly took $20 out of his wallet and handed it to me.

After that incident, I purchased an old 1954 Morris Oxford Series MO for a few dollars. I then convinced Tony, shortly afterwards, to buy a black one advertised for $20. I towed it home at night with Tony steering his new acquisition after we taped a Dolphin lantern torch covered in red cellophane as a tail light. Having adjusted the timing, it ran very well and he would regularly pass me on the uphill Oxford Outings (OOs) but not for long, as his would overheat. I would then pass him and wave as he waited for it to cool down. This quite often repeated on various trips and created much merriment. When Tony left the squadron, I took over his Oxford which then became part of my entrepreneurial fleet. Overseas exchange officers would normally sell their vehicle in preparation for returning to their own country. As they would need an interim vehicle, I would sell them the much cheaper Morris Oxford, on the condition that I was guaranteed to be able to buy it back, immediately prior to them departing Australia. This would entail purchasing it back for a much lower price—hence my profit-making abilities. This was a small venture which kept everybody happy. They had a vehicle to travel around in without the stress of finding a buyer in the last couple of days prior to their departure.

* * *

My first trip as Co-pilot with Flying Officer Tony Hannam and his crew occurred on 3rd February 1974. It must have been around this time that as Flying Officers in the RAAF, we had to sit for what were known as B exams, which were a necessary requirement for promotion to the rank of Flight Lieutenant. There were five non-technical exams, only involving administrative subjects, taken over two and a half days that had to be passed prior to promotion. After one examination sitting, Tony and I were driving home for lunch when we decided that we should pick up our respective wives and go to the local pub for a counter lunch, basically abstaining from the afternoon exams. We found the afternoon in the pub far more interesting than sitting a boring exam. On reflection, I was never a 'career officer'. I just wanted to fly aeroplanes.

As Tony and I were close friends and lived very near to each other, we used to travel in either his car or mine to work each day to Edinburgh. One day, Tony tried to kill me. He arrived at my house in his late 1940s MG TC (the car of choice for most Air Force Pilots), with the roof up, as usual. I always told him that if you had a sports car, you had to have the roof down, so each time he arrived at my house, we would put the roof down. On this particular day, Tony turned right at a roundabout, at breakneck speed, as only a young Air Force Officer in a sports car would. About halfway through the turn, the passenger door, which was hinged at the rear, (commonly referred to as suicide doors), flew wide open and I was almost ejected from the vehicle. I saved myself by grabbing hold of the steering wheel. That, in itself, was not a smart idea to do on a roundabout.

I think it was at the same roundabout that Warrant Officer Col Asimus, who was a Flight Engineer on the Orions, was detained by the police. Apparently, he was driving home from a dining-in night at the Sergeants Mess, when he entered the roundabout. According to Col, it took him five circuits of the roundabout before he found an exit. When he did, the boys in blue were waiting for him. Col, like most flight engineers, was a great guy, very professional and a pleasure to fly with.

* * *

The Mess Dining-In, or dining-in nights, as they are more customarily known in the RAAF, are a regular feature of mess life, both in the Sergeants Mess and the Officer's Mess. The essentially simple procedures, which are traditional, heighten the enjoyment of the meal and impart a graciousness to the occasion often not found elsewhere. A Mess Dining-In differs from a normal dinner, insofar as both non-resident and resident members are required to attend. Attendance at a dining-in night is obligatory

I only attended minimum dining-in nights, but one thing I do remember was the tradition of 'Passing the Port' in preparation for the Loyal Toast. During the first passing of the port, several decanters are placed, without stoppers, in front of nominated members, who fill their glass and pass the decanter to the person on their left without allowing the decanter to rest on the table. This action symbolises a toast and the chain of unbroken loyalty to the Sovereign, hence signifying that nothing should come between a member and the Sovereign.

Although these nights were very formal, they normally ended with most

From Hero to Zero

1974 Fincastle Crew : (L-R) Graham McCloy, Dave Reynolds, Ray Ruming, Darryl Redding, Rod Lovell, Neil Clifford, Col Asimus, Jim Farquar, Ken Buch, Rick Jones, Des Dorsman (Author's Collection)

members having a good and merry time.

* * *

In June 1974, three junior Pilots, myself included, were chosen and trained as relief and restricted Flight Engineers due to No. 11 Squadron being undermanned in the flight engineer section. This qualified us to occupy and carry out the duties of a flight engineer (in flight) except for take-off and landing phases. It is always enlightening to experience other crew member roles. It certainly gives you a new perspective and appreciation for what they do.

In August 1974, I was very proud to be selected to fly the P-3B Orion as Co-pilot representing Australia in the Fincastle Competition—an amazing feeling. We then commenced practising for fly-off. The competition is a contest of skills between the Commonwealth air forces of the United Kingdom, Australia, Canada and New Zealand. During the competition, crews compete in anti-submarine warfare, anti-surface warfare, and intelligence and surveillance gathering. Maritime crews from the RNZAF (New Zealand), RAAF (Australia), RAF (Britain) and RCAF (Canada) compete each year for the Fincastle Trophy. The trophy was originally donated by Mr and Mrs Aird Whyte in 1960, to commemorate their late son, Sergeant Nairn Fincastle Aird Whyte. He was an Air Gunner in RAF Coastal Command who was

Flying the P-3B Orion

killed in action in 1943. The first competition was held in 1961 and was a simple bombing competition between antisubmarine crews. It was held early in November 1974, in New Zealand, at the Royal New Zealand Air Force Base, Whenuapai.

During this time in Whenuapai, it was obvious that the aeroplane Captain (not Tony in this instance) could not relate to his crew. Early one morning, whilst we were in New Zealand, we were all in the crew bus waiting for our fearless leader. Eventually, he turned up at the bus.

'I thought I'd walk to help me wake up,' he stated.

'We can't wait that long' replied the normally quiet and sometimes grumpy, Air Electronics Officer (AEO) Neil Clifford. His reply brought the bus down, giving us all a good belly laugh.

* * *

That year the Fincastle Competition was won by the Royal Air Force who flew a Hawker Siddeley Nimrod, which was a maritime patrol aeroplane developed and operated by the United Kingdom. It was an extensive modification of the de Havilland Comet, the world's first operational jet airliner.

On one occasion I was privileged to be part of one of the yearly squadron's Christmas flights, in the Orion, to Cocos Islands. On landing at Cocos Islands, and taxiing to the terminal, we shut down the inboard engines to keep Father Christmas safe as he stood on the Flight Engineer's seat with his upper torso emerged from the cockpit's overhead escape hatch. It was spectacular to see Father Christmas waving to the children. On shutdown, Father Christmas distributed gifts that had been donated by various Adelaide department stores to the delight of the island children.

* * *

My RAAF training also qualified me to be granted a commercial Pilot's licence, which was issued in 1973 by the Department of Civil Aviation, (DCA)—the forerunner to the Civil Aviation Authority. In the mid-1970s I undertook studies for my Senior Commercial Pilot's Licence (SCPL). At this point in time, a Pilot had to be employed by an airline before being able to gain an Airline Transport Pilot's Licence. The study for the SCPL theory examinations was one of the most challenging and demanding courses I have undertaken. Thankfully I successfully passed all and was awarded my SCPL in July 1976. Further study allowed me to be granted an Airline Transport Pilot's Licence in December 1979 when I was employed by IPEC (Interstate

Parcel Express Company).

In early 1975, I volunteered to fly civilian aeroplanes on bushfire patrols, as a reserve Pilot, above the Adelaide Hills in a two-seater Cessna 150. These patrols were called Smokey South or Smokey North obviously depending on which direction one was despatched. Taking off from Parafield Airport to the south or north over the ranges and hills, we spotted and reported any smoke or fires. These were usually bumpy flights as we were flying over high terrain on hot days.

ONCE A CAPTAIN BUT NOT ALWAYS A CAPTAIN

On 27th May 1975, I attained P-3B Non-Maritime Captain status. This allowed me to operate as Pilot in Command of Orion aeroplanes in non-operation roles such as ferrying of aircraft from one place to another, post maintenance flights, other required flights over the Australian mainland. I was previously bypassed for this coveted position by three junior (time in the squadron) Pilots. As much as I loved flying, there were times of frustration when I was at the mercy of certain military personnel who revelled in their power and used it at their whim to punish people like me who called a spade a spade.

In June 1975, I took four weeks of recreational leave for the birth of our daughter, Kylie. This birth was especially important to us due to the loss of Suzanne only two years prior. Fortunately, everything went according to plan and Kylie was a welcome addition to our growing family.

After not flying for 30 days, and hence not being current on aircraft type, I was asked to take an Instrument Rating Renewal test on my first flight back, although this flight check of mine was not required for another four weeks. I was not signed off on this test as a pass and the Commanding Officer of the Squadron revoked my Non-Maritime Orion captaincy. I was back to being a Co-pilot again. Although there is no laid down currency pre-flight test, common sense dictates that when a Pilot has been on leave for an extensive period of time, involving a major life change, they would normally be given refresher flights prior to a flight test.

I mentioned this to another Pilot who said that the same thing had happened to him when he was required to take a test with a Qualified Flying Instructor (QFI). His outcome was entirely different from mine. When it was ascertained that the test was not going well, the QFI changed the test to a training flight. End of story. I should have been offered the same courtesy. Five weeks later, after about six more flights and relevant study, I was given the Instrument Rating Test again, and this time I passed. I would not give him the satisfaction of failing me twice. I can't remember if my flight was any different, but he had previously had his glory in humiliating me.

Butting heads with military personnel was causing me grief until I met Lieutenant Commander Chris Konczey. He was on an exchange posting from the United States Navy (USN) and we hit it off right away. He saw a lot of potential in me and I became his Co-pilot for a while. He reiterated to me on how the military system worked, and basically told me to keep my thoughts to myself, and my mouth shut. For his confidence in me and good advice, I am eternally grateful. I actually caught up with him when he visited Australia around 2013 and presented him with a book called *Catalina, Neptune and Orion* by Stewart Wilson, as a token of my admiration and respect for him.

* * *

On 19th August 1975, our crew was tasked to fly Edinburgh to Townsville with an overnight stay. On arrival, as was customary, we were met on the tarmac by a crew welcoming committee. We were relaxing after the flight when the Orderly Officer came rushing up and told us to prepare for an imminent medevac flight. We had to fly a scuba diver suffering from 'the bends' down to Sydney on a medical evacuation (medevac). This flight was carried out at a relatively low level, for an Orion, as the medical staff wanted a sea-level cabin pressure so the patient with the bends would not be in further pain. The Orion would normally cruise at around 28,000 ft (this would give a cabin pressure of around 8,000 ft), however, in these cases, we fly at a lower altitude to around 18 to 20,000 ft which gives a sea-level cabin pressure.

Medical evacuations (medevacs), along with Search and Rescue (SAR) flights were a common occurrence with our Squadron. Medevacs could involve accident victims, neonatal retrieval and other medical emergencies which sometimes entailed international flights as the Orion had long-range capabilities and a comfortable cabin environment.

Search and Rescue missions, more often than not, involved searching for disabled, stranded or lost boats and yachts. A search that I was involved in was the motor vessel Blythe Star. This vessel was a coastal freighter which

Once a Captain But Not Always a Captain

'F Troop' (back row L-R) Bob Hudson, Dave McDonald (RAF), Rod Lovell, Ian Filsell, Holger Hildebrandt, Spike Jones, Al Chiesa, Tony Morgan (front row L-R) Steve Byrnes, Russ Vance, Steve Gray, Danny Williams, Ross Bishop (Author's Collection)

foundered off south-western Tasmania in October 1973, leading to the largest maritime search operation conducted in Australia at that time. Our aeroplane was tasked to search the eastern side of Tasmania, to no avail. The freighter's crew had managed to board a lifeboat but the ship itself was never located.

* * *

After serving my time in the sin bin as a Co-pilot, I regained my Non-Maritime Captain status in February 1976 and on 25th May 1976, I was awarded full Maritime Captain status. This position gained me command of F Crew, affectionately known to all as 'F Troop'. The Squadron had six operational crews, and to differentiate between the crews, they were allocated letters of the alphabet from 'A' through to 'F'. However, this did not refer to a level of competency of the crews. Under my tutoring this crew became the crew to be envied. I was extremely proud of them all. We would work hard together, but we also enjoyed a good social life. I think I may have been hard on the crew, but they responded, and 'F Troop' became a very respected operational crew. It came to the point where aircrew were asking the Squadron CO if they could be transferred into the (in)famous 'F Troop'. On at least one occasion Operational Command specifically requested 'F Troop' to carry out a particular operational flight. It was an honour to be held in such high regard.

I remember one time, we were tasked to transport our Base Officer

Commanding (OC) to somewhere over east, probably Richmond if I recall correctly. As the time to close the doors approached, there was no sign of our Tactical Coordinator (TACCO). I went to the flight hut and rang his home. He was still at home and I advised him that he'd better hurry as the OC was on board, waiting. From memory, I made some lame technical excuse as to our delay. I secretly advised one of the crew members at the back of the aeroplane, that when I saw our TACCO drive past on the service road, between the administration side and airfield side of the base, I would use the intercom to give him the heads up. He was then to ask the OC to visit us in the cockpit for the engine start. This was a normal and common invitation for dignitaries onboard. Sure enough, our TACCO raced down the service road enabling the allotted crew member to ask the OC to the cockpit. Immediately the crew member raced to the cockpit advising that the OC did not want to come. I sternly told that member that no matter what, he had to come to the cockpit. This allowed our wayward crew member to approach the rear of the aeroplane and climb aboard up the aeroplane ladder without being observed by the OC. I don't know what was said to the OC, but he did come up to the cockpit for engine start. Phew! I'm not too sure if he was ever the wiser.

Other day-to-day operations would include coastal surveillance, now referred to as border control, where we would check and report on shipping, yachts, fishing trawlers and any other suspect vessels. Normally these were detachments away from home consisting of anything from a week to a month. One thing I didn't realise at the time was the effect on our private life and how nothing ground to a halt if I was away for a month. My wife Leone, along with all the other crew members' partners, continued to carry out all the everyday duties to keep our homes running smoothly ready for our return. I remember on returning from such a month away, I would always immediately step into the role of head of the house again without giving any thought, or thanks, to what Leone had accomplished. Interstate and international phone call costs were exorbitant at the time, hence were usually made in an emergency situation only. Mail was not an option as we were constantly on the move without a base camp. None of us gave enough thought and credit to our partners. I am sure, upon reflection, we were all remiss in this regard.

We had an extremely understanding neighbour called Mary. As soon as I would drive in the driveway, after returning from a lengthy detachment away from home, she would come over and immediately take our children back to her place, barely uttering a word. After the appropriate timeline, Leone and I would go to her place to have a cuppa, a chat and retrieve our crew.

* * *

In late October 1976, we were on detachment to Amberley for exercise Kangaroo II, a joint warfare exercise held by the Australian Defence Force in Queensland. HMAS Melbourne also participated in this exercise. At this time this was the largest peacetime military exercise to be held in Australia. It took place in the Tasman and Coral Seas and along the eastern Australian coast and included troops, ships and aircraft from Australia, New Zealand and the United States.

I knew one of the RAAF Air Traffic Control (ATC) Officers, who I believed was working at the Brisbane ATC centre at this time. I asked him whether we would be permitted to do a low-level reconnaissance flight along the beach around Surfers Paradise to Coolangatta upon our return from our exercise. This was not a normal flight pattern for such a large aeroplane. He advised me to give him notice at around the time we were ready to proceed. As agreed, on our next return from a long exercise, we contacted ATC and requested a low-level reconnaissance flight. We were given the clearance with instructions to follow the coast, not above 500 ft, to which we gladly complied. Now that's what I call a clearance. Flying below 500 ft was normal operations for us over open water, but to have this clearance to fly down to 100 ft, so close to shore, was an exhilarating experience, particularly for the people on the beach. It was quite a buzz for us to look up at the apartment blocks and hotels along the coast. In fact, we did this on a few different days. I can remember other crews enquiring how to get this clearance and I said 'just ask.' Well, they did, and most of them received a clearance coastal at 5,000 ft. It pays to have contacts.

That week, back at the Amberley Officers Mess, whilst reading the Brisbane Courier Mail newspaper, there on the front page was a fantastic picture of an Orion flying low up the surf line, whilst in the foreground was a couple, laying on their backs, resting on their elbows, appreciating their defence force at work. Knowing that our crew was the only one doing these passes, and in consideration for my fellow crew members, I rang the newspaper and requested a dozen or so copies be forwarded to me back at Edinburgh.

Ensuring our shores are safe (Author's Collection)

Some days later, after arriving back at home base, at the morning squadron briefing, the Commanding Officer held up one of these newspapers and requested that the Captain of the aeroplane see him immediately after the briefing. Sprung! Before the CO had a chance to tear strips off me, I quick as a flash, told him of the invaluable publicity the RAAF would get and I bet him that applications for RAAF recruits would increase. Reluctantly, he could not disagree.

On 24th November 1976, we participated in a search and rescue public relations activity called Operation Blue Hull, for an Adelaide-based 'Water Sport' magazine. Peter McDermott (our crew Tactical Coordinator) drafted much of the verbiage which was used in the magazine. A key theme of the activity was small craft safety at sea. It covered information boat owners needed to know to assist rescue crews to help find them if and when they were in trouble out at sea. Most boat owners have no idea how hard it is to spot boats

Front cover of 'Water Sport' magazine (Author's Collection)

with blue hulls and white tops in choppy seas. This is the preferred colour scheme for a lot of small watercraft. Bushy Kavanagh was the Survival Officer of our squadron at the time, so he was appointed to go floating in a dinghy and grace the cover of the January 1977, Vol 9, No 1 issue.

In mid January 1977, we were crewed to undergo a training exercise south of Adelaide. I thought my Dad, who was ex-military and over 90 years of age at the time, would appreciate a flypast. I arranged for Mum and Dad to be parked near the Obelisk at Freeman's Knob, Port Elliot. At the prearranged time we flew back to Port Elliot in the Orion. I spotted our family's two-tone brown Holden HQ, so proceeded to fly a mini air display for my highly respected father.

What I was not aware of was the fact that at the next beach towards Victor Harbour, Boomer Beach, there was a surf lifesaving carnival underway. Apparently, the television cameras were delighted with my performance and a still photograph appeared in the next edition of the Victor Harbour Times. I was invited into the Commanding Officer's office once again to explain. As much as I have pointed out my shenanigans during my career in the RAAF, at no time was anyone or any aircraft put at risk. These deviations were simply innocent fun for my crew which was necessary, in my view, to keep up crew morale. It must be remembered that at the time the Cold War (1947-1991) was very real and simmering. This was a period of tense relationships between the USA and its allies and the USSR and its allies. Included in this period was the Suez crisis of 1956, the 1960 CIA U-2 spy plane (Francis Gary Powers) shot down in the USSR and the Cuban missile crisis 1962. We could have been called into combat at any given time.

Flight Lieutenant Mike Bray, a Royal Air Force exchange officer, was in my crew and was very upfront. Like myself, he called a spade a spade. He made me very proud, when, during his farewell speech before returning to the United Kingdom, he told the audience I was the best Captain he had flown with anywhere in the world. What an accolade.

On 22nd February 1977, our crew undertook another one of the medevac missions. This was a flight from Darwin to Adelaide to transport a newborn baby in a humidicrib. A photo of our Orion, and St John Ambulance crew and the humidicrib appeared in the Advertiser newspaper. Some forty years later I still wonder the outcome of this patient. I remember the impact of this situation as I was immediately taken back to the loss of our daughter Suzanne in 1973. It never

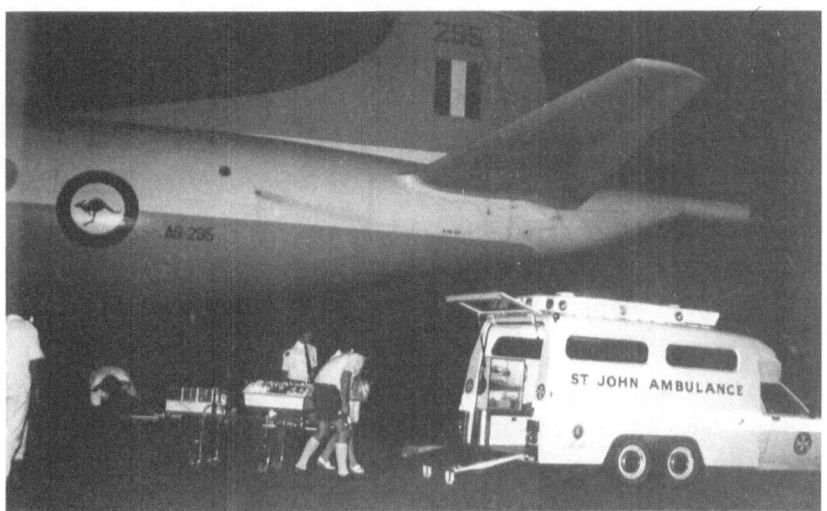

(above) Arrival at Adelaide Airport with humidicrib (Author's Collection)
(below) Letter of thanks (Author's Collection)

THE UNIVERSITY OF ADELAIDE
DEPARTMENT OF PAEDIATRICS

019301

PROFESSOR G.M. MAXWELL
TELEPHONE: 332 4888

The Queen Victoria Hospital Inc,
160 Fullarton Road,
Rose Park, S.A. 5067.

February 24, 1977

The Honorable D.J. Killen,
Minister for Defence,
Parliament House,
CANBERRA. A.C.T. 2600

Dear Mr. Killen,

    I am writing on behalf of the Neonatal (Newborn Infant) Retrieval Unit attached to the Queen Victoria Hospital.

    I wish to express my gratitude to the R.A.A.F. for supplying an Orion aircraft from Edinburgh Airfield to fly a three man Retrieval Unit from our hospital to Darwin on Tuesday, February 22nd.

    A critically ill newborn infant who required constant ventilatory support was transferred from the Darwin Hospital to the Queen Victoria Hospital. It is possible that surgery will be required because of an unusual respiratory condition.

    I would like to thank, through you, the Commander of the Base, Air Commodore Connaughton and the members of the crew of the Orion Aircraft, led by Flight Lieutenant R.D.M. Lovell, who could not have been more helpful to us throughout the whole operation (flight not medical) which took some eleven hours.

    I do realise that there is an enormous cost involved in long distance retrieval, but where intact survival will occur, as in this circumstance, then surely there is justification.

Yours sincerely,

G.W. DAHLENBURG
Reader in Neonatal Paediatrics

From Hero to Zero

fails to amaze me what situation can trigger these memories and flashbacks.

* * *

In March 1977, I flew the P-3B Orion in the RAAF air displays at air shows at Laverton, Canberra, Edinburgh and Pearce. This was a great honour and morale boost to be selected to demonstrate the capabilities and manoeuvrability of this great aeroplane before huge crowds and television audiences. It normally culminated in a mock attack on a plywood submarine silhouette being blown up in a lot of smoke and flame. It was very impressive for the audience.

On 22nd June 1977, the RAAF awarded me with a Category B Maritime Captain status on the P-3B Orion. I previously held a Category C Maritime Captain status. According to my logbook statement, this meant above average ability. For the RAAF to consider me to have above average ability as a maritime Captain was significant. I'm always amused that I was awarded this above average ability and selected to fly the Orion air display, when, only a few years prior, my flying ability was doubted by persons in authority who thought otherwise. It demonstrates how fickle your career can be when it hangs in the balance of the powers-that-be. It became evident to me over the years that non-combat flying ability could take a backseat to kowtowing. I doubt that this would be the same situation in wartime when they are calling for their best Pilots to get the job done.

On 29th August 1977, I was awarded the Right-Hand Seat Check Captain status. This entitled me to command and fly the aeroplane from either Pilot seat, otherwise a Captain is restricted to only sitting in the left-hand seat.

Around this time there was to be a crew selected to fly in the upcoming Fincastle Competition. The senior squadron aircrew assessed crews via simulator exercises. At No. 11 Squadron we had a simulator for the cockpit and a simulator for the tactical section, which could be electronically coupled together. For this fly-off, the cockpit crew were assessed by a senior squadron Pilot. One of the rules of the competition was that you flew over the submerged submarine with just its periscope visible and breaking the surface and then had to fly outbound for a period of time. From memory, it was two and a half minutes before the aeroplane could turn back. In this time, the submarine had submerged completely, and we had to then locate it and drop a small sound signal to simulate an attack. The normal procedure was to fly outbound level at approximately 200 kt. Our now infamous,

F Troop, had devised a method where we flew outbound for the required time, but not level and not at 200 kt. We would add power, lower manoeuvre flap, which lowered the stall speed of the aeroplane and then climbed at approximately 145 kt. What this effectively did was decrease our horizontal distance out from the submarine before we turned inbound. Most times, we could still see the submarine wake, hit them with a mock attack and bingo, we got a hit. Well, this did not impress the Squadron Leader Pilot assessor, probably because he didn't think of it. He told the Squadron Commanding Officer that I was dangerous and should not be in command of an aeroplane and should have my wings taken off me. After I had left the Air Force, an Orion crew member told me that they had adopted my tactics at a later stage.

During my service in the RAAF, I had numerous great times with my crew and we did a very professional job. Part of our work included medical evacuations (medevacs) and search and rescues (SAR). These were sometimes either extremely rewarding or extremely frustrating and saddening. The frustration came from the Orions being the last to be called for a search and rescue event, because of authority protocol. Had we been the first, particularly for marine searches, the success rate would have been higher. One such case of bureaucratic intervention was the ditching of Rockwell International 685, VH-WJC, on 17th July 1983 near Bass Strait. The ABC television network's Four Corners program produced a documentary on the case calling it, *Search Without Rescue*. A survivor was sighted clinging to the wreckage of the ditched aircraft some fifty minutes after the accident but after approximately another two hours, contact was lost. Helicopters were not launched, but an Orion would have had the capability to drop life rafts at the scene within two hours of the event.

One such out-of-the-ordinary trip I captained was a mail drop on Macquarie Island, located around 1,500 km south-east of Hobart. On 7th September 1977, our crew dropped three storepedoes onto a little narrow neck in the island. A storepedo is a cylindrical storage container about the length of a three-seater couch and up to about a metre in diameter with an attached parachute. They were used to airdrop supplies to troops and civilians. There is no airfield on the island and members of the Australian National Antarctic Research Expedition (ANARE) were very grateful and excited upon our arrival. The round trip from RAAF East Sale recovering to

From Hero to Zero

Macquarie Island mail drop aircraft heading from west to east looking south (Danny Williams)

RAAF Edinburgh lasted a little under eight-and-a-half hours.

A crewman on the flight, Danny Williams, wrote the following:

'Macquarie Island Mail Men

'In 1977, 11 Squadron's F Crew (affectionately known as F Troop) conducted what we believe was the RAAF's first mail drop to those hardy souls occupying Australia's scientific Research Station at Macquarie Island in the Southern Ocean. The Hercules guys have done Macquarie Island mail drops since and claim theirs was the first, but I believe we beat them by some years.

'Flying out of East Sale for fuel planning purposes, we were all kitted out with very hot and uncomfortable immersion suits which we borrowed from Navy and spent some hours 'past the point of no-return' during our flight down south. We had media and other passengers on board for the occasion. The airdrop was arranged after a visit to the Island by Tasmanian Senator, Michael Townley, earlier that year. One of the passengers was Officer Commanding RAAF

(left & below) Public relations exercise with HMAS Otway 6th October 1977 (Author's Collection)

Base Edinburgh, Air Commodore BJ Connaughton. The female journalist onboard was closely guarded by her Army Defence PR Liaison Officer who stuck to her like a second coat of paint. Our trip got lots of coverage in RAAF News and the local Adelaide Press.

'Challenges in the air were of course weather and fuel planning as we were heading beyond the point of no return for engine failure, and the risk of mid-air collision with very large albatross, of which we sighted a few enormous ones. With landing lights on, they dived out of our way. The target was a very thin piece of beach which the locals had to chase clear of elephant seals for the drop which was conducted in some very challenging wind conditions. Two of the three storepedoes landed on the beach but the third landed in the

From Hero to Zero

very rough ocean. Fortunately, that container only held non-critical food items and reading materials; the more important mail from their loved ones arrived safely on the beach (though had we told the guys on the ground that crew had snuck in a few Playboy and Penthouse magazines, I'm sure some hardy souls would have braved the surf). One of my most memorable missions on the P-3B.'

Site through periscope of a P-3B running in for attack (Patrol Sqn 6 VP-6)

FLYING ADVENTURES

My association with flying was not only a passion and career, but my hobby as well. On 31st March 1977, I test flew ex RAAF ab-initio trainer A17-168 Tiger Moth VH-DDA at Northam, Western Australia and later purchased it. A Tiger Moth has no wheel brakes, no tailwheel (just a tail skid) and no electrical system and you need to understand aviation to fly this aeroplane well. It was a perfect training platform. However, I did install a VHF radio to communicate with Air Traffic Control. This was powered by a small 12-volt battery which I would take home to recharge at the end of a flight. The Tiger Moth is a fantastic aeroplane for real aviators and I had to learn how to fly this little beauty all over again. The RAAF very kindly allowed me to operate and hangar this aeroplane at the Edinburgh Base. I enjoyed flying it enormously.

My beautiful Tiger Moth (Author's Collection)

Yours truly preparing for take-off in my Tiger Moth (Author's Collection)

I fondly remember flying my Tiger Moth up the coast abeam Adelaide Airport on nice calm summer evenings. The airport radar could only pick me up when I was approximately within three nautical miles (5 km) from their antenna due to the Tiger Moth having very little metal and mainly constructed of wood and canvas both of which are non-radar reflective. This was long before the days of mandatory transponders which are electronic devices that produce a response when they receive a radio-frequency interrogation. All aeroplanes now have transponders to assist in identifying them in a busy air traffic control environment.

One of the qualities of a true aviator is finesse. Sometimes, you will overhear Pilots saying, 'I gave it a good boot full of rudder.' This means the Pilot suddenly used a great deal of foot pressure on one of the rudder pedals. This is totally unnecessary. In fact, when I was flying my Tiger Moth, I used to rest my feet on the rudder pedals and instead of pushing, for example, the right rudder, I would *ease* the pressure on the *left* rudder pedal and the aeroplane would turn slowly and smoothly to the right just from the weight of my right foot. The same technique can be used for pitch control. You will often see video clips of Pilots carrying out what I call pumping the control column which is vigorous and forceful forward and aft movements. This is totally unnecessary. Manipulating flight controls should always be done with smoothness and finesse. Flying up the coast on a calm summer night, I would trim the elevator so that I could fly hands off. I would fold my arms and control the pitch just by leaning forward or sitting upright. The feeling one has when bonding and feeling a machine is awe inspiring. My dear old dad, who grew up farming with a horse team, told me once. 'You can't talk to machinery.' Sorry, Dad, but I totally disagree. I believe you can, and you can definitely feel when the machine, whether it is a plane, tractor or truck is trying to tell you something.

My four children all went flying in the front seat of my Tiger Moth when they were four years of age, with the exception of my youngest son, Kris, who pestered and pestered me to take him. He was two weeks shy of his fourth birthday when I relented. I had fitted an automotive mirror to one of the vertical struts so I could view the front passenger. I had a foam booster seat for the kids to sit on. They were under strict instructions to place their hands on the side cockpit doors and never take them down. That way I could view them, wave to them to give assurance and they could see me. Because they were hanging on so tightly to the side doors, they would raise just their forefinger in acknowledgement of my wave. I would give them a smile and another wave. It made me so proud that they would listen to my instructions with such enthusiasm. It was imperative that I could see where their hands were at all times as I didn't want them near the seatbelt buckle.

On 24th and 25th September 1977, Leone and I participated in The World's

From Hero to Zero

First Tiger Moth Air Race at Rutherford (West Maitland), in New South Wales. This great air race attracted competitors from all over Australia. The entrants came from all manner of aviation backgrounds such as airline Pilots, flight and aerobatics instructors and air force Pilots.

Prior to this event, I developed a plan that listed available refuelling stops and/or accommodation. Around a week in advance, contact was made with the refueller to ensure aviation fuel was available. Leone was a good passenger but was not a trained navigator; therefore, I took responsibility for that as well. Navigating from the air is entirely different to navigating in a vehicle. You look for different features which stand out and are not readily evident from a ground level vehicle. Examples are railway lines, lakes, rivers, high hills and coastlines. Radio towers are very obvious from the ground but much harder to see from the air. It is a trained and acquired skill. Navigating then was all about map reading, but it is easy to fool yourself into believing that what you see on the map is what you are looking at on the ground. It's important that you identify specific features. There was no GPS for intrepid aviators back then. After around one hour of flying in an open, noisy, windy cockpit with all its challenges the crew are starting to look for somewhere to land and rest.

A few days before the air race, Leone and I flew our recently purchased Tiger Moth from Edinburgh to West Maitland, via Parafield, Renmark, Mildura staying overnight at Hay. Leone was a trained nurse and was a good passenger, but not the best at navigating. This was back in the good old days where there were no fees for parking your aircraft. We tied the plane down by rope, to pegs hammered into the ground to prevent it from moving in the unlikely chance of winds arising that were not forecast. A canvas cover was placed over the two cockpits. Once the aeroplane is tied down and 'put to bed', you can usually take up the offer of a lift into town from a friendly airport worker or a taxi to a local motel.

The next day we completed our trip to West Maitland via Griffith, Parkes and Mudgee, the starting line of the race, where we were interviewed by the local radio station, as I think we had travelled the furthest distance to participate. The usual questions were asked along the lines of my flying experience, where we had come from, how the flight had gone etc.

The race began with the first flight from Rutherford Airport, West Maitland to Port Macquarie via Knobby's Head in Port Stephens. We stayed overnight

Two equally beautiful aeroplanes—though vastly different in their performance (Author's Collection)

before heading back to West Maitland via Taree the following day. On that weekend we met legendary aviators, Bill Hitchcock, Bruce McGarvie and Don McBain. Bruce was Pilot in command and Don navigated a Tiger Moth VH-ASB. Our flight went exceptionally well but paled into insignificance when compared to Bruce and Don's story. Bruce was a crafty old aviator and thought he'd bend the rules and shorten the route by cutting the corner at Knobby's Head despite Don strongly advising against it. The noise of the engine did not make communication easy and finally having cut out the turning point to save considerable time, at some point north of Knobby's Head, Bruce asked Don why they shouldn't have done that. Don was finally able to get through to Bruce that there was a Cessna 172 full of scrutineers circling overhead near that turning point. With that information, Bruce turned the Tiger Moth around to head back to the turning point. What he hadn't anticipated was running headlong into a flock of Tiger Moths flying north along the proper route. Apparently, there were Tiger Moths flitting in all directions in an attempt to avoid a head-on collision with Bruce and Don's Tiger Moth. It all sounded hilarious when we met in the bar at Port Macquarie that night. We were all doubled over in laughter when Don related this story to us. Bruce merely stood there sucking on his pipe saying he couldn't understand

An intrepid aviator and his trusty Tiger Moth (Author's Collection)

what the problem was. He was such a character. If there's one thing I remember about Bruce is that I don't think I ever saw him without a tobacco pipe hanging out of his mouth. Perhaps it's pertinent to say that we didn't win this race with this kind of skulduggery going on.

We decided to take three days to return to South Australia travelling via Scone and Dubbo with an overnight stay at Condobolin. These comfort stops were purely for a quick bite to eat, fuel up and any other personal requirements. The following day we travelled via Griffith and Hay with an overnight stay at Mildura. Then it was on to Renmark arriving at Edinburgh on the 29th September. An absolutely fantastic adventure. Where else can you fly magnificent old biplanes, meet and chat with equally old aviators and tell yarns and many exaggerated truths. When I went back to flying Orions, it increased my appreciation of basic aviation, the way our forefathers flew.

I later approached the RAAF with the idea of conducting a formation flight with my Tiger Moth and a P-3B Orion for public relations purposes. This might sound impossible because of the vast variation in the flying speeds of the two aircraft, but the idea was taken up and took place on 12th October 1977. Formation flying is a disciplined flight of two or more aircraft under the command of a flight leader. There were lots of photos taken on the tarmac of the Tiger Moth alongside the much larger Orion. The flight was a huge success as the Tiger Moth was safely capable of 130 kt in a dive whereas the Orion was getting close to minimum safe approach speed as it overtook me in my aircraft with multiple passes. The story made the Adelaide Advertiser the next day and the Australasian Post a bit later and also appeared in The Tiger Club (UK) magazine 'Tiger Tales'. It is always a good public relations exercise when you or the RAAF make the media. It highlights our defence force and puts a little human side to the military.

* * *

It is always a pleasant surprise when you meet high ranking officials who are actually nice people. Two who particularly impressed me were General Sir Arthur Leslie MacDonald, KBE, CB and Jack Anderton, General Manager of Steel Planning at BHP. I once flew General MacDonald, who

An intrepid aviator and his trusty Tiger Moth (Author's Collection)

was at the time the Chief of the Defence Force Staff, to RAAF Pearce in an Orion. He sat behind me on the radar cabinet, in the cockpit and even offered to serve me a coffee. Jack Anderton offered me a Pilot position with Associated Airlines flying Gulfstream corporate jet aeroplanes out of Essendon Airport. Silly me, declining at that time, thinking that it was more professional to apply through the normal channels, obtaining success by my own merit, without the help of people high up within organisation. Wrong!

On another occasion, I was interviewed for a Pilot's position with Trans Australia Airlines (TAA). One of the questions the panel asked me was whether I was related to Captain Arthur Lovell. I replied that I was not. Again, silly me. I should have said something like: 'Good old Uncle Arthur. I haven't seen him for a while. How is he?' Later I was to find out that Arthur Lovell was a highly respected B727 Captain who on 16th October 1964, delivered Australia's first domestic jet airliner and Ansett's first Boeing 727, VH-RME, to Essendon Airport from Seattle.

* * *

In late 1977 I made the decision to resign from the RAAF. Prior to this I had been considering what my options would be if I were to leave the RAAF for a civil aviation career. The following incident cemented my contemplation.

After my crew had arrived back at Edinburgh early evening from an all-day flight, and as was the custom, a few of us went for a beer. Being in our green flying suits, we were only allowed to drink in a small sidebar of the Officers Mess. When it came time to close the bar, I, during a little bit of horseplay, objected to the bar being closed and took the key from the female bar attendant who was a member of the Women's Royal Australian Air Force. Eventually, I returned the key, the bar was locked and we all went home.

The next morning I was called into the President of the Mess Committee's (PMC) office, to be informed that because of my horseplay I had been banned from the bar for a month. This I accepted without question, left his office and went about my duties. Later that morning, I was approached on numerous occasions by various members of my crew telling me that they had also been banned from the bar.

'No, that's not true. Only I was' I replied to each of them. After the fourth member came to me, I decided to investigate and went back to the PMC's office. When I told him what was occurring and that I had accepted my punishment without complaint, I questioned why the other crew members, who had not even gone to the bar, were banned. 'To teach you a lesson' he replied. Well, it certainly did and at 8 am the next morning my resignation was on the Commanding Officer's desk. This incident was the final straw that broke the camel's back after numerous degrading incidents that curtailed my flying career. When I handed in my resignation, I was aware of numerous civil aviation positions available at that time. Although not taken lightly, it was not a hard decision to make. I took leave over the upcoming Christmas period. This allowed me to gain the training I needed to take up a civilian Pilot position I was interested in. I purposely delayed my actual resignation date from the RAAF Services until 10th April 1978, thereby accrediting me with just over 10 years' service.

At the time of my decision to resign, I didn't have another position to walk into as the RAAF required three months' notice which did not suit any potential employer. However, civil aviation was expanding and I believed I would have no trouble swapping straight over to becoming a civilian Pilot. After all, years prior I had obtained my Senior Commercial Pilot's Licence. With Leone working as a qualified nurse, the thought of not bringing in an extra income was not an issue as we were not in a vulnerable financial position.

From Hero to Zero

CIVIL FLYING

I fulfilled a dream to fly into Langley Park located on the banks of the Swan River, Perth, Western Australia on 27th February 1999. It is grassed, rectangular in shape and was the site of Perth's first airstrip. Major (later Sir) Norman Brearley used the area as a landing strip when he pioneered civil aviation in Western Australia in the 1920s, a time when aviation was routinely perilous.

It literally was an aviator's dream to fly into and out of such an historic place that had not been used as a landing strip in decades. My choice of plane then was VH-PKL, a Cessna 150 Aerobat and I flew with a group of enthusiasts who gained a permit for its use on this day. It is doubtful if the strip will ever be used again due to the encroaching high-rise buildings and environmental consideration. It was a very memorable flight and one that

Langley Park (Mir Zafriz)

Langley Park as seen from the Pilot's seat (Daryl and Jane Grove)

will never be forgotten due to its historical significance.

* * *

In 2003, I crewed a brand-new Cessna Citation Bravo from the factory in Wichita, Kansas, back to Australia, along with the owner and an American Pilot who had thousands of hours experience on these particular aeroplanes. This was a very interesting trip in many ways. At one stage we spent a couple of days at Anchorage, Alaska where the sun didn't set at that time of year, awaiting clearance via Russia. The route chosen was necessary due to the fact that the Cessna did not have the fuel range to fly more directly to Australia over the Pacific Ocean via Hawaii. Whilst in Anchorage we stayed at a hotel that was right on the edge of Lake Hood which is the world's busiest sea plane base. Lake Hood has an average of nearly 200 movements per day and there are around 800, mostly single-engined, sea planes based there. I could walk around this huge lake to my heart's content. Here I participated in a two-hour joy flight to view the wildlife, which incorporated numerous landings on the water. From Anchorage, we flew west to Nome. Nome is also the place where the yearly Iditarod Trail Sled Dog Race ends. It's a very interesting place as I don't think anything has changed in the last 100 years. Access is either by air or sea which is frozen over for part of the year. We were taken on tours of the local area and made aware of the bears that could suddenly appear from behind a bush. I always wanted to return to Alaska and take more time to appreciate its beauty. We then flew from Nome to Magadan, Russia for a short refuelling stop. The mosquitoes there were huge, but we were assured, that because of the cold, no viruses could live in their bodies. From Russia, the route we chose was via Japan and other islands which included Guam. Whilst taxiing out at Guam, we had an electrical malfunction indication in the cockpit. As this was my leg to fly as Captain, I ascertained by deduction, fault finding and confirmation, that it was a comparator failure and not a failure of critical components. Whilst going through this process, it was quite clear that the other qualified Pilot could not completely understand what I was trying to explain and the owner, also a Captain on type, did not contribute to the discussion at all. I said to them both that I was 100% sure in my analysis of the situation and I proved that both critical components were working satisfactorily and that it was just the comparator that had failed, which was later found to be the case. I also stated that safety was always paramount to me and that if I wasn't 100 per cent sure, I would abort the flight. As safety was not compromised, the take-off and flight continued. My assessment was confirmed later by aviation technicians.

* * *

Another dream of mine, though not flying related, was to drive steam engines. In 2009 the Australian Prime Minister Kevin Rudd offered a Stimulus Package to more than thirteen million Australians. It was designed to stave off a recession and limit job losses. This consisted of up to $950 per person. Most people I knew decided to put that money toward things like a payment off their mortgage or buying a flat screen TV etc. I chose to put my money back into the volunteer community whilst achieving another lifelong dream, to undertake the 'Train Driver for a Day' experience with the Bellarine Railway in Victoria. This entailed a morning of instruction and orientation and in the afternoon, I drove under instruction from Queenscliff to Drysdale and return. The train I drove was a 0-6-0ST 1916 Steam Locomotive—named Arthur T Middleton—built by the Vulcan Iron Works, Wilkes-Barre, Pennsylvania, USA. How appropriate, considering I was raised at Middleton. What a thrilling and exciting time to stand on the footplate and operate the controls of such a magnificent piece of machinery. I would do it again in a heartbeat. I cannot recommend this experience highly

Train Driver for a day (Author's Collection)

enough should you ever get the chance. At the end of the day the driver instructor complemented me on my smooth manipulation of the controls.

* * *

My first civilian flying job was with IPEC Aviation, a freight airline based at Essendon Airport, Victoria, mainly flying to Launceston in Tasmania and return. Terry Blyth, IPEC's Chief Pilot, came to Adelaide in late 1977 to interview me whilst I was still serving in the RAAF. They were in the very early stage of their business and at that time IPEC did not have any aircraft flying. It was very exciting being involved with a new airline that had not even got off the ground. When Terry interviewed me, we talked about my Tiger Moth as Terry had a lot of flying experience in Tasmania on classic aeroplanes. He subscribed to the old school interview style where you sit down and have a chat about your flying career, what you have done, your achievements etc. When I got home that afternoon, Leone asked me if I got the job.

'I don't know. Terry didn't tell me' I replied. In those days, calling people interstate was expensive. It was a couple of weeks before Terry rang me.

'Are you bringing your Tiger Moth over?' he asked. What superb news. I took this to mean that I had been successful in my application and would soon be relocating to Victoria. As this now fell into my leave taken at Christmas of 1977, Leone and I drove from Adelaide to allow us to attend her family Christmas function and also for me to undergo the ground school training required for the Argosy aeroplane at Essendon Airport.

Once my resignation from the RAAF became official, we uprooted the family and moved in with Leone's parents in the suburb of Rosanna, just outside Melbourne, Victoria, for a short time. It was around six months before we moved to an old wooden rental property in Woodend as it was more convenient for the commute to Tullamarine and Essendon Airports than from the eastern suburbs. We learnt that Woodend got extremely cold in the winter, so much so that the night before you would always fill up the kettle for your morning cuppa as the water in the pipes would freeze. Sometimes it would be between 10 and 11 am before they would thaw out.

* * *

Our four children were very special to me as each of the children were individual in their own right. No favouritism was ever shown.

Whilst holidaying at Ulladulla, New South Wales in the early 80s, we took along a popular electronic handheld game called Donkey Kong. Being a mere male, I needed peace and quiet to concentrate on this new acquisition. This was far from achievable in the caravan we were staying in. Early one morning, I decided to go to the toilet block to sit and play my game in peace and quiet. Halfway through a game, I heard the block door open.

'Dad, are you in here?' called out Gary. There were muffled chuckles from other guests as they knew full well what I was doing. Sprung!

On 12th September 1981, our firstborn Gary, then eight years old, accompanied me on a freight flight, along with First Officer Tim Davies, in a DC-3 from Essendon to Canberra to Sydney and then back to Essendon. It was a total flight time of nearly seven hours to deliver Melbourne newspapers to Canberra and Sydney. Children often accompany Pilot parents from a very young age and are taught the basics.

I can remember Kylie coming home from junior primary school one day and said the 'F' word in the presence of her mother. Shock, horror!

'What did you say?' asked Leone. So, Kylie repeated it. 'You go and tell your father what you just said.' Kylie came to me and repeated the 'F' word. Again, shock, horror! Naturally I responded with;

'What did you say?' So, Kylie repeated it. It's funny how we respond to such things. Kylie got to say the 'F' word four times that day in front of us—and got away with it!

Even though Mark joined in the usual 'boy' things, he was always a very quiet child and didn't need people around him. He was happy in his own world. I remember one time when he climbed up a tree and was bitten by bull-ants. He came inside crying and Leone put some Stingose on his bites. To my amazement, he immediately went back outside and climbed that same tree again.

I used to call Kris 'Twok' as he appeared to look like Mr Spock and at the same time was small, like Twiki, from the TV series Buck Rogers in the 25th Century. At social gatherings in cold Victoria, I would place him inside my jumper to keep him warm whilst we were conversing in the outdoors. Kris was similar to Radar, from MASH, in his intuition of his surroundings. He could spot the golden arches of Macca's long before I could.

When in Woodend, our children were taught life strategies such as Stranger Danger. These were drilled into them and we had a household fire-drill in place, due to the risk of bush fires and possible in-house fires. They were also taught to cook basic items to ensure, that if we did not get home on time for some reason (there were no mobile phones at the time), they were able to take care of themselves for a short period of time. When we visited large areas, like a national park or showgrounds, etc, the children were briefed that if we became separated, then as soon as they realised it, they were to sit down immediately. They were not to go looking for us, but to stay in one spot. This would make it much easier for us to find them if the situation ever arose. We always believed that kids should be allowed to be kids and enjoy the outdoors and get dirty! We had purchased two mini-bikes which they were permitted to ride and race under very strict conditions, on the few acres we lived on.

Some very close friends, Tony and Jenny Redmond, built a mud brick house only a couple of kilometres away. They had three young boys of their own. If we knew ahead that we were going to be home late, we would arrange for the Redmonds to pick our children up from school and look after them until we got home. I took it as a huge compliment when they used to say that they would look after our four children at any time. Wow! These days hardly anyone would mind one child, let alone four.

In the early days, we owned a Morris Minor Panel Van and the children would sit in the back on upturned wooden fruit boxes. There were no seatbelt rules back then. If they got tired, they would lay down on the carpeted floor. The panel van had one major flaw. There was a rubber seal between the cabin roof and the rear van section which was not waterproof. In winter we would sometimes drive with an umbrella up inside the car to keep the rain off the driver and passengers. One day this leak actually proved to be an asset. Kris had contracted whooping cough in his younger years. I remember standing in the shower, holding him, hoping that the steam would relieve his cough, but it didn't. We then opted for a one-hour drive to the Royal Children's Hospital in Melbourne. Funnily enough, this drive on a Victorian wet winter's day fixed him. By the time we arrived at the hospital, he had stopped coughing.

I believe that country living allowed our four children to enjoy an idyllic, healthy childhood. We would go water-skiing in our old wooden clinker inboard ski boat named Turkey Shoot, enjoyed many holidays and they went on numerous flights in my aeroplanes.

* * *

When I joined IPEC, I was slightly disappointed about being assigned the position of First Officer (Co-pilot) on the Argosy aeroplane. My position in the RAAF was a right-hand seat check Captain on Orions. This disappointment lasted only a couple of weeks. I was crewed with some of the older and far more experienced Pilots, such as Captain Terry Blyth, Captain Jack McDonald and Captain Keith Beattie, DFC (Distinguished Flying Cross), who was a quiet and unassuming man. I only recently learnt more of his career after reading his book The Wind Beneath My Wings. Captain Beattie was born in Wellington, New Zealand in 1922 but grew up in Christchurch and Auckland. He was a Pilot for forty-four years, including serving in Bomber Command during World War II as a Pathfinder where he earned the Distinguished Flying Cross for bravery. This included being the only survivor of a head-on crash with a German Junkers-88 night-fighter plane. Beattie's right wing was shorn off in the collision during a night mission over Germany in March of 1945. Not only was his survival miraculous, but his escape from the wreckage through a small pilot's window was incredible. He spent six weeks as a prisoner of war. When he got back to his squadron, they questioned how he could possibly have gotten out of such a small window. He affirmed that he had, but when his squadron asked him to try it again, he couldn't fit through. It was said that Captain Beattie was not easily rattled. That is an understatement. He was the original *Captain Cool*. I learnt so much from these older, experienced, wise Pilots and

IPEC Armstrong Whitworth Argosy VH-BBA (aussieairliners)

will be forever grateful. What I first saw as a disappointment at being assigned a Co-pilot, became a valuable opportunity to learn new skills. These aviators had so much to give. I soaked up their knowledge like a giant sponge.

When I gained my command on Argosy aeroplanes, it was with very mixed feelings. I was extremely pleased to once again attain the rank of Captain, but at the same time saddened by the fact that I would quite possibly never fly with these incredible aviators again. As Captain of an IPEC Argosy freighter bound for Tasmania, I recall a particular flight departing Tullamarine Airport in the early hours of the morning. We were in complete darkness when the Co-pilot announced to the Air Traffic Controller that we were ready for take-off on runway 27.

'There's a racehorse loose on the airport, but if you want to take-off, you can. There's nothing in the rule book to guide me in a situation like this', was the response we received from the Air Traffic Controller.

After quickly assessing the situation of the possibility that a dark racehorse could gallop from one end of the airport to the other in the time it took us to take-off, and knowing full well that an aircraft colliding with a large animal, does not end nicely for either party, I declined to take-off until the racehorse had been secured. As we were first in line, we taxied back to the hanger advising the tower to phone us when they had caught the racehorse. Two other aeroplanes, one of which was the Ansett Electra VH-RMX, followed our actions. The Tower Controller then closed the airport. When the horse was found by the northern boundary, we were advised by the tower, but again did not venture forth until the capture of the racehorse had been confirmed. I guess I can lay claim to the fact that I was instrumental in closing Melbourne's Tullamarine International Airport. This was not to be the only Australian International Airport I would be involved in closing.

* * *

In May 1979, I commenced command training with IPEC on DC-3 aeroplanes. I was trained by Captain Terry Blyth, whom I and others refer to as 'The Master'. He was an exceptional aviator and became a great personal friend. As IPEC expanded its road business, it naturally also wanted to move into air freight. However, IPEC faced difficulties with the Two Airlines Policy implemented by the Australian Federal Government between the 1940s and the 1990s. Only two airlines were permitted to operate flights between state capital city airports. At the time, these were Trans Australia Airlines (TAA), which was government-owned, and privately-owned Ansett Airlines. The Menzies government fought tooth and nail to prevent Gordon Barton, Founder of IPEC, from being allowed to get import licences for aircraft with which he intended to operate air freight services. In 1979, after a fifteen-year battle, IPEC finally received permission to operate a national cargo service. However, it was far from fair and open competition. IPEC were not allowed to fly their Argosy aeroplanes to Sydney due to conditions placed on their Airline Licence, so Gordon Barton persisted with a DC-3, VH-EWE. The Fraser government still reserved 80 per cent of the business for Ansett and TAA and imposed restrictions on what sort of aircraft IPEC could use, precluding the most efficient option.

In December 1979, IPEC was offering voluntary retrenchments as the general economy suffered a downtown. A friend of mine Paul Murphy (ex RAAF P-3B Captain) was flying Learjet 35 aeroplanes for Stillwell Aviation at Essendon Airport. He advised me that vacancies were available with Stillwell, so I took the opportunity to accept a redundancy package with IPEC and then joined Stillwell's as a direct entry Learjet Captain.

* * *

I used the Morris Minor Panel Van to commute between my home at Woodend and Essendon and Tullamarine airports. It had a fuel tank capacity of approximately 43 litres, so I decided to fit it with an auxiliary fuel tank with a hand operated changeover tap in the engine bay. One winter's night, around midnight, I was driving to work when one tank ran out of fuel at a most inopportune time, right opposite The Black Lagoon which is in the Black Forrest just south of Woodend. I couldn't believe it! I had to unlatch the bonnet, get out of the car, lift the bonnet, change the position of the tap and close the bonnet and get back in the car. The whole time, I was aware of the eeriness of a gentle wind causing a rustling of the gum trees. A fine mist caused by low cloud surrounded me and I was imagining seeing the figure from the 1954 black and white horror movie, *The Creature from the Black Lagoon.* I've never done a fuel tank change so fast in all my life! The hairs on the back of my neck still rise at the memory.

* * *

On 16th June 1980, Wards Air Cargo took over the Learjets from Stillwell Aviation. I was now employed by Wards Express flying as Captain on night freight operations to bases that included Melbourne, Perth, Darwin and Brisbane. These were testing times for our family. I was an owner/builder of our home which entailed subcontracting and organising tradesmen and completing some of the building requirements myself. After completion, Leone and I and our four young children moved into our new house on four acres just outside Woodend, in Victoria. When I would arrive home in the morning following night flights with Leone working days as a nurse, Kris, who was two at the time, would have his nap whilst I dozed in a Jason rocker recliner chair. This was to prevent me from falling into a deep sleep as I was in charge of minding our youngest son. This allowed him to easily arouse me when he awoke and called out.

On one occasion we were tasked to fly from Sydney to Canberra to pick up $2 million in new gold coins. When we landed in the middle of the night, numerous armed guards surrounded the plane in preparation to load the coins. Once the coins were loaded, I was asked to sign the paperwork.

'What? You want me to take responsibility?' I said with tongue in cheek. I summoned the Co-pilot over and persuaded him to sign for the $2 million cargo. Easy! On our way to Essendon, I asked the Co-pilot what he would do if we received a radio call stating that because of a security breach we had to divert to Shepparton. The scenario passing through my mind was that it could have been a robbery. Nothing of significance came out of his mouth but I told him if we did receive such a call, I would divert to an unspecified aerodrome and not tell anyone on the radio. Once on the ground I would phone the company and tell them where their plane and coins were and await further instruction.

* * *

My employment at Wards Express had been challenging. Fellow Pilots had also clashed with the Manager of Wards Express Air Freight Division over various aeroplane operations. As practically all our work was at night, we would arrive at our port mostly around daybreak and obviously go to sleep. It was not uncommon for management to ring up after I had been asleep for only a couple of hours and question why I had done certain things, like landing at Kalgoorlie to refuel. I had to explain that the weather forecast showed a probability of Perth being covered in fog. Shortly after falling back to sleep, another phone call with unnecessary questions. Their approach was straight-out bullying and harassment. Though I would get the required legal rest period, the regulations never mention the word sleep. Whenever I would ask to see the company's operations manual or the aeroplane manufacturer's checklists, I was told it was none of my business. The manager and I never did see eye-to-eye.

On 26th March 1981, I received a phone call just after midnight from the manager asking me why I wasn't at Tullamarine Airport. I advised him that I was not rostered for the flight, but he advised me that I most certainly was and to get to the airport immediately. My house at Woodend was a fifty-minute drive to Tullamarine Airport. In the previous few days, he had called me on numerous occasions to advise roster changes. Like many general aviation companies, we were given a written roster, but as soon as ours was printed, it was out of date. Hence, it had become normal practice to receive a phone call advising of roster changes. One particular week, the phone calls had been numerous. I drove to Tullamarine, where my Co-pilot, was waiting for me. I remember thinking it extremely strange that the Co-pilot had not called me, so I suspected something fishy was going on. Normally, there is camaraderie between crews. We look after each other and only consult with management if the situation is way out of the ordinary. We conducted the pre-flight and flew to Perth where we arrived prior to our scheduled time. In the evening of that same day, we flew back from Perth to Tullamarine, arriving around midnight. As soon as I landed, I was handed a sealed envelope by one of the aeroplane loaders. On opening this letter, I found a letter from management stating that my employment was terminated.

31st May 1981 three Setair DC-3s flying over Melbourne for PR exercise (Ben Dannecker)

I drove home, got what little sleep I could, and early the next morning called Buck Brooksbank, who at the time was president of the Australian Federation of Air Pilots (AFAP). He offered to try and get my job back, but after my discussion with Buck, I felt this would be futile.

I'm sure the manager relished the opportunity to be done with me once and for all. Little did we both realise that we would meet again in the mid-1980s when he was appointed Aviation Manager with IPEC.

* * *

In April of 1981, I was employed by another great gentleman and aviator, Joe Salfass who was the Operations Manager of Setair. I was appointed to the position as a DC-3 Captain again mainly flying night freight from Essendon to Launceston and Sydney and the occasional passenger trips. These DC-3s, VH-MIN, 'UPQ and 'MWQ aeroplanes were all very well maintained. During the time I was employed by Setair, I did not hear of one engine failure or precautionary engine shutdown. This was significant due to the number of aeroplanes and the number of hours these aeroplanes were flown per year.

Probably a little-known fact about the old DC-3s is that they are not watertight, as is proven later in this story. When flying in the rain, it was common for the Pilots to wear a plastic raincoat worn back to front so that the buttons were on your back. The old rubber seals around the windscreen leaked profusely and this was the only way for the Pilot to try and keep dry. If there was no

My first DC-3 VH-EWE (Geoff Goodall)

raincoat available, then large plastic garbage bags would suffice. The old girl handled icing in cloud very well. If you were remiss in applying carburettor heat to prevent ice building up in the carburettor throat, then naturally the ice would build up in the throat to such an extent that the engine would backfire with a hell of a bang and consequently clear itself and settle down to running smoothly again. Some propellers were fitted with alcohol de-ice. This is where alcohol was metered to run down the propeller blades under centrifugal force preventing ice from building up. However, if this was not a feature of the plane, or not turned on, ice would build up on the propeller blades and at the appropriate time centrifugal force would fling it off, normally hitting the side of the cockpit just behind the Pilots. This was another way we would be jolted back into reality. It was all in a day's work. That is why some DC-3s have an extra layer of aluminium skin, that is often dented, in that area of the fuselage.

A funny story was related to me about Joe Salfass. Quite often our cargo out of Tasmania for the mainland was crayfish. Some DC-3 Pilots carried a bag needle in their navigation bag. This was considered an essential tool by them and often on those long dreary flights, they would go down the back and avail themselves of the self-service that had been provided in the cargo—an expected quality control check by the distributors. On one particular flight, Joe was the ultimate diner. After acquiring his meal, he laid newspaper across his lap and with a pen knife attached to his keyring, he went about dissecting, devouring and checking the quality of the cargo. Once quality control had been confirmed, he wrapped all the newspaper up, slid back the pilot's window and recycled the evidence into Bass Strait! After landing at Essendon, when walking to his car, he searched his pockets for his keys. Oops; nowhere to be found. Sadly, he then realised he had thrown them out of the window with the cray remnants. Poor old Joe!

One time taxiing out of Launceston, Tasmania, for a flight back to Essendon, we had just left the freight apron and were slowly taxiing north. At this time a Pilot is basically concentrating on where the aircraft is going and conducting cockpit checks, which involves a significant amount of concentration inside the cockpit. Out of the corner of my eye, I noticed a movement behind the wire fence and looked around to see that we had just passed a mother holding a very young boy. His waving little arm dropped in a very dejected manner as he had not received a response. On seeing this I slid open the cockpit window and gave him the biggest wave I could muster. Well, he almost leapt out of his mum's arms in jubilation!

* * *

In June 1982, I returned to IPEC. Our retrenchment agreement had stated that once there was an upturn in the company, we were to be offered our previous seniority position. I took this up flying Argosy aeroplanes. When IPEC acquired its first DC-9-33F (registered VH-IPF) in 1982, TAA (Trans Australia Airlines) were responsible for training and checking Pilots. In

Yours truly in the Captain's seat of IPEC's DC-9-33F taking off on Runway 26 at Essendon (Author's Collection)

From Hero to Zero

January 1983, I commenced DC-9 training under TAA's training and checking organisation. Eventually, IPEC had suitable Pilots who could undertake the role. Therefore, TAA relinquished its training responsibilities to IPEC. However, as we had been trained to TAA standards, IPEC retained their training procedures. My line training was conducted by Captain Phil Westh, and I was checked to the line as a DC-9 Captain by Captain Rod McCullam. Two years later, I was appointed Line Training Captain on DC-9 aeroplanes.

Whilst a Captain on the DC-9, I was elected President of the IPEC Pilot's Technical Committee (IPTC) which I formed along with Check and Training Captain Dave Foulkes. The committee allowed Pilots a forum to discuss operational views to be passed onto management in a non-union like environment. From memory, management embraced and endorsed all our proposals.

* * *

In October 1983, I purchased a 1952 Beechcraft D18S VH-FIE Serial Number A-808, a fantastic eight-seater aeroplane with twin-radial engines. This was imported into Australia as VH-CRT in 1956 by the heavy construction and mining company Thiess Brothers Pty Ltd and used for executive transport. Originally N721D, owned by Birdwell Oil Company in the USA. This Beech 18 had many modifications to enhance its flying range, performance and was beautiful to fly.

I flew my Beech 18 in the final leg of the re-enactment of The MacRobertson Trophy Air Race, also known as the London to Melbourne Air Race. It was held on the 23rd October 1984, marking the race's 50th anniversary. It was such an honour to be asked to participate. The invitation was due to my Beech being a red twin-engined aeroplane, similar in appearance to the de Havilland DH88 Comet which won the race in 1934. A crowd of 40,000 people gathered at Flemington Racecourse to watch the race leader de Havilland DH88 Comet, *Grosvenor House*, piloted by CWA Scott and T Campbell Black, pass overhead before landing at Laverton. They had completed the 11,300 mile (18,000 km) flight in just 71 hr 1 min, which included refuelling landings.

On another occasion on the 23rd February 1985, I was invited to display both my Tiger Moth and Beech 18 at Tullamarine, Melbourne Airport Open Weekend. This event was staged to celebrate the Australian state of Victoria's 150th anniversary. I flew my Tiger Moth in first, landing on the grass just to the east of runway 16. I was then taken by car back to Ballarat to pick up the Beech 18. On this trip, I was accompanied by a neighbour, Bill O'Halloran from Woodend.

December 1983 at Goolwa Airport: L-R Leone, brother Colin, sister Margaret, nephew Richard, sister Jen and myself—front row my children L-R Kylie, Gary, Mark and Kris (Author's Collection)

'What are all the people looking at?' asked Bill as we taxied in.

'They are looking at a rare classic aeroplane' I replied. My Beech 18 was one of only three of its type in Australia at that time. It was a wonderful era for aviation in Australia at the time. Country airshows were numerous and aircraft owners were paid to participate.

The Australian film industry was also in full swing. In 1985, my Beech 18 and Tiger Moth planes were used in the film productions of *A Thousand Skies;* an Australian mini-series about the life of the famous early Australian aviator Sir Charles Kingsford-Smith. *The Lancaster Miller Affair* was another Australian mini-series about the relationship between Bill Lancaster and Jessie Miller. The story is of their record-breaking flight from London to Brisbane in 1928, the sex scandal that followed and consequently an unsolved murder mystery. Again, it was an honour to have my aeroplanes involved in the re-enactment of this era of Australia's aviation history.

On 2nd June 1986, Leone, the children and I were returning from a few days in Sydney in our Beech 18. The kids always thoroughly enjoyed flying in any aeroplane, but they particularly loved the Beech 18 as it was

From Hero to Zero

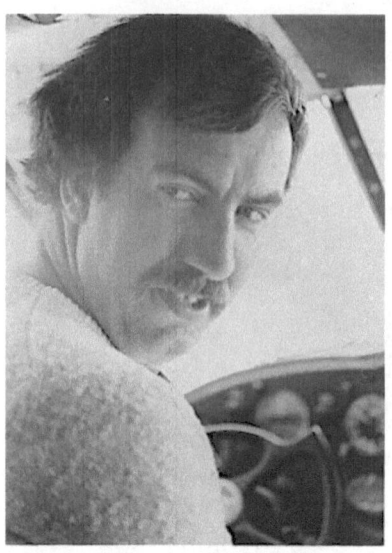

In my Beech 18 at Goolwa Airport (Author's Collection)

very spacious and they could move around freely inside. Our little getaway was a business trip to appraise the Aero Professional Flying School at Bankstown Airport, which subsequently led to its purchase. On reflection, this was probably the worst financial move I had ever made. It was dark when we returned home via Ballarat, where the aeroplane was hangered, and our car was parked. We entered cloud prior to our descent. I flew a non-precision (Non-Directional Beacon) instrument approach, with a missed approach as I was unable to gain visual reference with the runway due to the low cloud. I flew another approach and again missed for the same reason. I decided to divert to Essendon Airport, Victoria, where we had an uneventful landing. This meant we had to catch a taxi back to Ballarat Airport. A week later I made the trip to retrieve the aeroplane and return it to the hangar.

The Beech 18 is the most ergonomically difficult plane I have ever flown. It is certified to fly in Instrument Meteorological Conditions (IMC) single-pilot which is a huge challenge. There are buttons, knobs, levers, handles and switches everywhere, even under the seats. Just to confuse things further, both the layout of the primary flying instruments and the power control levers are completely non-standard. A centre console is configured with the prop levers nearest to the Pilot, mixtures nearest the Co-pilot and throttles in the middle, along with levers that control each engine's manifold heaters, oil shutters and flap and undercarriage selectors. A flat sub-panel below the console carries the fuel valves; T-handles for the tailwheel lock and park brake; plungers for oil bypass and oil shut-off; engine primer and fire suppression selectors. Two handles next to the Pilot's right knee, which resemble handbrakes from a vintage car, operate the cowl flaps, while a large red lever by the Co-pilot's left hip works the fuel pressure plunger pump. These are just some of the very complicated features of the cockpit. To carry out an instrument approach in IMC, overshoot and keep flying, whilst constantly

Beech 18 Cockpit (Author's Collection)

manipulating levers and handles is an incredible workload for a single Pilot. To do the same manoeuvre in, say a Cessna Citation (certified for two-pilot operation), is a walk in the park. But what the hell, it's such fun!

* * *

In September 1986, I resigned from IPEC after purchasing the Aero Professional flying school at Bankstown Airport. I believed, wrongly, that I could contribute and give something back to aviation by passing on my flying skills to new students. It wasn't until after I purchased the business that the CAA informed me that as I did not have an instructor's rating, therefore I was not permitted to instruct. This I found incomprehensible as I was a Check and Training Captain for numerous companies on far bigger aeroplanes up to and including Douglas DC-9 but was prohibited from instructing in a basic two-seater Cessna. I remember stating to the authority that practically every instructor at Bankstown was there to accumulate their flying hours and gain qualifications to be eligible for the airlines. No young Pilot takes up instructing as a chosen career. I decided to fall back to an administrative and advisory role and left instructing to the far less experienced Pilots.

To try and economise I decided to reduce the half a dozen casual instructors down to two full-time instructors. That was another bad business move.

As soon as they were employed on a full-time contract, their hunger for acquiring students and their job enthusiasm waned. I recollect witnessing a prospective customer enter the premises and approach one of my instructors who was two bites into his hamburger. The instructor looked at the customer, turned back to look at his hamburger, then looked back at the customer and was about to take another bite of his hamburger when I slammed my hand down on the front desk and shouted for him to serve the customer, immediately. Gee! I might sound like I was a really cruel boss but watching him compare his $2.50 hamburger with a customer who was potentially worth $30,000 to the business, made me livid.

As a matter of interest, I was extremely proud that most of my instructors, after working under my tuition and gaining the required hours, were successful in gaining employment with QANTAS Airways. This gave me a huge sense of achievement. How ironic that for decades I had applied to fly for QANTAS, but due to the timing in the industry, my attempts were unsuccessful.

* * *

Around this time, I also gained employment with Norfolk Island Airlines as a Beech 200 Super King Air Pilot, based in Sydney. The flights were mainly to Lord Howe as well as Norfolk Island. On one occasion, my first flight for the day was scheduled from Sydney to Lord Howe Island and on board was the new customs officer, who was to take up his new posting. On my second trip for the day, I was to fly his wife out to join him. The terminal staff at Sydney Airport advised me that she was a little apprehensive about flying. When it came time for her to walk out to the aeroplane from the terminal, she became extremely distressed. When she appeared, walking towards me, she was supported, and I mean literally supported, by a guy on each arm holding her up. She was crying and shaking.

'Should we sit her down the back?' asked one of the staff. I told them to put her up in the front right-hand seat alongside me. The poor woman was beyond petrified. Once she was seated in the Co-pilot's seat (these aeroplanes only required one Pilot), I began to explain to her exactly what I was going to do and the associated noises and aeroplane responses she would see, hear and feel, prior to and after my actions, to prepare her for the flight. I did this prior to every movement on the pre-flight checks: engine starts; taxiing; take-off; landing gear retraction; flap retraction, etc. By the end of the flight to Lord Howe Island, she was very relaxed, and I believe enjoying herself.

I felt a great sense of pride and achievement after seeing her transformation from a nervous wreck to a calm, happy passenger.

Prior to every flight a passenger briefing must be conducted, so on each trip back from Lord Howe Island or Norfolk Island, after I loaded the passengers and closed the rear door, I would position myself at the back of the aeroplane amongst the passengers. Some Pilots would take their seat up the front and brief the passengers by the public address system. My approach was a little different.

'So, did you all fly out here with Norfolk Island Airlines?' I would ask.

'Yes,' they would answer.

'Then you should remember your passenger brief from a few days ago.' I would then ask some questions regarding the positioning of life rafts, life jackets and other emergency equipment. More often than not, like most typical airline passengers, they had not paid any attention to any previous emergency briefings and had no knowledge of safety equipment whereabouts. This interaction with passengers, rather than a rote explanation, is far more effective. I could confidently say that to this day, after my briefing, those passengers would know how many life rafts, life jackets and emergency exits there are on a Super King Air.

As much as I enjoyed flying the Beechcraft Super King Air 200, I found the strain of running my new business in Sydney and the fact that my family were still living in Woodend, Victoria too much to handle. I was at the time living in my new business premises.

* * *

On 22nd March 1987, I was conducting a scenic coastal flight around Sydney in a twin-engined Piaggio P166. These were a beautiful plane for scenic flights as they had huge windows for the passengers to look out and a high overhead wing which did not obstruct the scenic views. All was going fine until I returned to the circuit area at Bankstown for landing. I selected the landing gear down and could not achieve three green lights to signify the landing gear was down and locked. I advised my seven passengers that we had a slight problem with the landing gear. I recall several passengers aged in their twenties who thought it was a real hoot. They were looking forward to the emergency vehicles and the possibility of appearing on the evening television news. An older couple, seated in the first row behind me, looked like they were going to faint when they heard our predicament. Fortunately, I was able to manually

Left main gear extended, right main gear retracted, nose gear half-way down (Author's Collection)

Captain Terry Blythe in the Piaggio P166 Cockpit (Author's Collection)

pump the gear down via a handle between the Pilot's seat and the side of the aeroplane. Unfortunately for me, when the owners restored the aeroplane, they carpeted the side wall, so every time I pumped the handle another layer of skin came off my knuckles.

* * *

Eventually, I was appointed Chief Pilot of my own business on 15th April 1987 and later gained approval to conduct endorsement training and testing on my Tiger Moth and Beech 18 aeroplanes. As part of Aero Professional's flight training, it owned an ATC-810 twin-engined CPT/IFR Flight Simulator. At one stage, I was training a commercial Pilot to fly on instruments. In this simulator exercise, the Pilot was required to carry out a Non-Directional Beacon (NDB) at Wollongong Airport. This entailed flying east over the airport and out to sea at 4,200 ft (1,300 m) flying down to 2,200 ft (670 m) whilst conducting a left-hand turn heading back to the airport. In a not uncommon scenario, this Pilot actually flew west over the top of the airport and descended heading west carrying out a mirror image to the published procedure. The only problem with this is there is an escarpment west of Wollongong airport rising to above 3,000 ft (915 m). When I deemed it appropriate to intervene, I simultaneously turned off all power to the simulator, leaving us in near complete darkness and clipped the Pilot over the back of the head.

'You're f…… dead!' He was in complete shock as I told him he had just killed himself and everybody on board the aeroplane. I very rarely swear and when I do it is only to emphasise a critical situation. Because of my shock approach method of instruction, I can guarantee that Pilot has never carried out a mirror image instrument approach since.

* * *

We took some wonderful family holidays during the 1980s. These included flying from Bankstown to Noosa in the Beech 18 to see my good friend and mentor, Terry Blyth and another time, we flew from Ballarat to Coffs Harbour for a two-week holiday. They were the days when everything was a lot simpler and cheaper.

To support my family, I would look for additional flying jobs, one such was as Chief Pilot of Airtex Aviation. I was entrusted to look after numerous aeroplanes and Pilots as well as captaining their Learjet. The corporate jet scene was a highly responsible role as well as being very rewarding and enjoyable. However, you had to be flexible enough to change your route at a moment's notice to cater for the passenger's adjusted plans. Our passengers included various dignitaries, company CEOs and television personalities. What surprised me the most, was that once they were on board, all they generally wanted was peace and quiet. We undertook numerous heart runs and organ transplant flights. In the early days, we had top priority of the airways and once cleared for take-off, we flew directly to the destination airport. We considered ourselves an aerial ambulance, without the lights and sirens. It gave us immense personal satisfaction to think that we may have been helping save someone's life.

* * *

Approval to conduct renewal of command instrument ratings, as an Approved Testing Officer (ATO), on PA31 (Piper Navajo) and PA60 (Piper Aerostar) followed soon after. A Pilot must have his Instrument Rating renewed every twelve months either by a departmental Flying Operations Inspector (FOI), or by a designated Pilot (ATO). This permits him to fly without outside visual reference. Because there is a lengthy wait, and also a preference to avoid department people at all costs, another way to get the permit is to get an ATO to conduct the test. At this particular point in time, as I was Chief Pilot for Airtex Aviation at Bankstown Airport responsible for about a dozen pilots, it was logical that I become an ATO.

Whilst Chief Pilot of Airtex Aviation, I was invited out to dinner one night by the General Manager of a rival air charter company. He offered me the role of Chief Pilot of his company, on a larger corporate jet and a much higher salary package, which included a BMW car. All I had to do was provide Airtex's charter client details. I don't think so! I politely declined the offer.

On 20th November 1987, I was flown to Brisbane by Rob Poynton who owned the DC-3 (VH-SBL), used to carry out scenic charter flights and para-

Beech 18 formatting on the TAA DC-3 (Author's Collection)

chute jump operations at Oakey Airfield. My Co-pilot, Glenn Atkinson, was a great aviator and friend. About a week later, Glenn and I were at the bar with a group of people, in Brisbane Airport, waiting to catch my flight back to Sydney when I met Helen. She was a Co-pilot for Flight West Airlines, flying Beechcraft Super King Air aeroplanes. As a fairly new Pilot, she was impressed with the fact that I was an ex-RAAF Pilot who had flown at twice the speed of sound and was a DC-9 and Learjet Captain. She was seventeen years younger than me, yet we hit it off straight away. I couldn't wait until the next time I saw her. Fortunately, as I was flying Learjets on charter flights, there were frequent trips to Queensland.

* * *

My marriage to Leone was good and stable for the most part, but I had nothing to compare it to. We really just took each day as it came. Meeting Helen changed everything. She inspired me like no one else. My marriage to Leone didn't deteriorate like most do, it was just an unexpected happening. I would never consider putting any blame on Leone. At the end of July 1988, I separated from Leone to pursue a relationship with Helen. I moved into a unit after seeing an advertisement for shared accommodation close to Bankstown Airport. At this stage, Helen was still living in Brisbane.

* * *

In October 1988, I successfully completed the Bicentennial Around Australia Air Race in my Beech 18. My crew consisted of Tony Hannam, Paul

Salmon and Steve Shaw. Once word got around that my Beech 18 would be competing, strangers offered to pay me substantial amounts of money to be part of my crew. I declined their very generous offers. My selection of crew was dictated by their abilities and qualities to perform as a united team in an old classic aeroplane and, even more importantly, we would be facing a fortnight in close company with each other. The race was sponsored by General Electric (USA). It covered more than 6,100 nautical miles (11,300 km) and virtually circled Australia, anti-clockwise. The race started in Narromine, New South Wales and landed at Toowoomba, Rockhampton, Longreach, Mount Isa, Alice Springs, Tennant Creek, Katherine, Darwin, Kununurra, Broome, Port Hedland, Carnarvon, Geraldton, Perth, Kalgoorlie, Forest, Ceduna, Adelaide, Hamilton, Melbourne, ending in Canberra. It was more than an air race, it was a bicentennial event which brought the celebrations to remote places and people in the vast outback of Australia, as well as to its capital cities. The line-up of 105 competitors was quite a spectacle. Military, and civilian single and multi-engined aeroplanes taxied into line to await their flag-off.

Conventional tricycle geared aeroplanes are much less susceptible to ground looping than tail wheel aircraft such as the Beech 18. A ground loop occurs when directional control is lost on the ground and the tail of the aeroplane swings past the nose, swapping ends, in some cases completing a full circle. A nose wheel, or conventional, aeroplane is steered from ahead of

Peeling away from the formation (Author's Collection)

From Hero to Zero

The crew at rest under the wing
L-R Paul Salmon, Steve Shaw, Tony Hannam and myself (Author's Collection)

the centre of gravity, whereas a taildragger is steered from behind, much like driving a car backwards at high speed. This means that on the ground a taildragger is inherently unstable, whereas a nose wheel aeroplane will self-centre if it swerves on landing. In addition, some tailwheel aeroplanes must transition from using the rudder to steer to using the tailwheel while reducing through a speed range when neither is wholly effective due to the nose high angle of the aeroplane and lack of airflow over the rudder. This event can result in damage to the aeroplane's undercarriage, tyres, wingtips, propeller and engine. Avoiding ground loops requires further Pilot training and skill.

On 16th September 1988, my 39th birthday, we positioned the aeroplane from Bankstown to Narromine to start the race. On approach to runway 11 the main wheels touched down. In a taildragger, the Pilot keeps the tail up and hence the rudders in clear air for directional control for as long as he can. If conditions aren't right, as in speed and attitude for the flare and touchdown, the aeroplane can start to porpoise. This is where the nose of the aeroplane rises and falls with ever-increasing deviation as the main wheels bounce off the runway. The only real solution is to apply take-off power to the engines and carry out a go-around, which I did making a lot of radial engine noise not often heard. I continued on for another circuit and an uneventful landing. On taxiing to the club rooms and shutting down, a few guys came out to say that they liked my beat-up or low-level pass prior to landing. They obviously did not observe the porpoising but enjoyed the show, so why should I deflate their illusion?

We had a fantastic time in this race. I think there were only two places where we had to pay for motel rooms. Everywhere else someone on the crew knew someone, who could put us up or we made our own arrangements. At our overnight stop in Alice Springs, the boys chose to sleep under the wing of the aeroplane, on army camp stretchers, as the old aviators used to do. As I was aware that these inland places can get very cold at night (4°C), I opted to sleep on the bench passenger seat in the plane. Sure enough, at about 4 am, I was awoken by loud knocking on the cabin door.

'Let us in, it's freezing!' Funnily enough, word got around and at Broome, the local TV crews came over to us after we landed to ask if we could recreate the scene so they could televise it on the news. So we did, at 7.00 pm, as soon as it was dark! Once the film crew were satisfied with the footage, the boys got out of bed and we all headed to the bar for a beer. On other occasions, I caught up with a RAAF Pilot's course colleague, the Captain of the RAAF Dakota, who handed me the keys each night as they left the aeroplane—allowing us warm and dry sleeping quarters and clearly to guard their plane! Again, the camaraderie of the Air Force was very evident. The RAAF entrants had a great time showing the flag but were not competitors.

Because the Beech 18 had two Pratt &Whitney R-985 radial engines, our biggest logistical problem was engine oil consumption. The flight time was close to seventy hours, so therefore the old girl would use about 360 litres of oil on the trip. That equates to eighteen, 20 litre drums. I had six drums pre-positioned in Darwin and another six at Jandakot, and we left Bankstown with six drums.

Our only big hiccup during the race were spark plug problems which occurred when we tried to leave Forrest, on the Nullarbor, in Western Australia. This called for engine cowls to be removed; 'cold pot'[1] the cylinders; remove the cold plug(s) and clean and reassemble. We did all this in the hot sun, whilst the rest of the contingent continued on to Adelaide (Parafield). We were probably an hour or so late landing there, after the last plane, but when we taxied in, we were greeted with a standing ovation from the other contestants. What a lovely gesture!

---

1 Cold potting is where you start a cold engine and let it run for approximately 30 seconds and then shut it down. You then immediately feel all the cylinders, one at a time, with your hand. The cold cylinder(s) indicate that this cylinder has not been firing and the spark plug should be inspected for fouling.

At the presentation dinner in Canberra at the end of the race, the Trans Australia Airlines (TAA) DC-3 VH-AES got a special mention for completing the race in a classic old aeroplane which had undergone a complete rebuild and restoration. Tony remarked to me that it was a shame that we didn't also get a mention for completing the race in our classic aeroplane without any major problems or maintenance issues, considering, unlike TAA, we had no support staff throughout the race. After all, both of these aeroplanes were basically the same engineering complexity and age, but we differed enormously in our support crews. I don't mention this due to having sour grapes over the situation. I just feel that a simple acknowledgement would have been appreciated for an outstanding effort by my crew. As a privateer in an event such as this, I have the utmost admiration for fellow privateers who want to do this, or follow any other passion of theirs, but just don't have the money or resources compared to the big company sponsored entrants.

Tony Hannam, one of my crew members, penned a poem called 'Four Men in a Beech 18' in relation to our experiences during the race. It's available to read on my website www.FromHeroToZero.com.au

* * *

Leone and I continued to run our business for a few months even after our separation. In December 1988, my precious Tiger Moth was reluctantly sold, with the proceeds going to try and prop up our business, Aero Professional, which was struggling to keep afloat financially. The business was placed on the market, and an offer soon appeared, which I accepted. However, this was overturned by Leone who believed she could still make a go of it even though, at the time, our working relationship had deteriorated enormously. She and her new boyfriend admitted to letting down the tyres on my Beech 18, to stop me from moving it to Hoxton Park where the parking fees were a lot cheaper.

I learnt a lot of valuable lessons in that flying school business. Why would you operate a business when your competition was only a few metres away? You would see prospective customers window shopping all the flying schools when they knew nothing about the industry. It did not matter who had the best planes or the most qualified staff, it was all about who had the most tinsel and the cheapest rates. A lot of flying schools treated their activity as a hobby, not a viable business. We were the first business to have the company name on the side of all our aeroplanes. This soon caught on and the other businesses at the airport followed suit.

* * *

On 22nd May 1989, Airtex Aviation flew their General Manager and me to Florida in the United States to gain experience and qualifications on corporate jets. We were trained by FlightSafety International. The Learjet 35 Recurrent Training Course entailed approximately one week of attendance encompassing a mixture of ground school and simulator exercises. The Learjet training in the simulator was invaluable. By its very nature, simulator training is safer than aircraft training. Abnormal and emergency procedures may be learned and practised without risk to students, staff or aircraft. Severe weather, terrain or obstruction conflicts can be demonstrated in the simulator without the risk of exposure to the actual condition. In-flight failures of systems and instruments can be created exactly as the failure would occur in the aeroplane. Whilst in Florida, I took it upon myself to gain the internationally recognised Federal Aviation Administration (FAA) Commercial Pilot Certificate. This was issued on the strength of my Australian Pilot Licence and experience.

Whilst on a month-long detachment in Wewak, Papua New Guinea (PNG), carrying out photographic work for PNG mapping in a Learjet 35, VH-FOX. Helen, now a QANTAS Pilot, took leave to join me for a week before the end of the detachment. I was asked if I'd like to test fly a 'lighty' (light aeroplane). On 13th July 1989, Helen and I agreed to test fly a Wren

A unique photograph of a Learjet and Mirage flying together—I have been extremely fortunate to have flown both types of aircraft (Greg Meggs)

From Hero to Zero

Learjet XA-WIN completing a low pass as the opening number for 'Aeroexpo Xalapa 2007 Airshow' (Rafael Cordero Torres)

460 registered P2-UIH, which is a highly modified Cessna 182. It had been sitting in the hangar for years so on take-off, all was fine until I rotated the aeroplane. It was then that with obviously a change of airflow inside the aeroplane, all the dust, swarf and whatever else was on the floor defied gravity to fly up into my eyes. Struggling to wipe these foreign objects quickly away was a big priority in this critical phase of flight. Once the dust settled, we went on to do a low-level scenic flight of the area. This was vastly different from most of my Learjet flying which was around 45,000 ft.

We all have embarrassing moments in life. At the completion of the detachment I was to return to Sydney via Brisbane. Helen flew as a passenger on Air New Guinea to Port Moresby to crew her next QANTAS flight. She asked me to take her laundry back home. When I went to clear customs at Brisbane Airport, the Customers Officer who inspected my bags came across Helen's clothing and underwear whilst rifling through my bag. Standing over him at six feet, two inches and weighing 110 kg, the gobsmacked look he gave me made me realise he thought they were mine. If it was possible to shrink from embarrassment, I certainly did as I walked away feeling two feet tall and glowing red from head to toe. It was the quickest I ever recall exiting a building.

* * *

Unfortunately, in October 1989, due to a very bitter separation with Leone and no options left to explore, I was forced to sell my Beech 18 aeroplane. It was a very sad farewell to a truly beautiful aeroplane. Shortly after, I replied to an advertisement from QANTAS Airways for the position of Pilot Instructor Simulator (Under Training) Boeing 747. The interview was conducted by Captains Ray Saunders and Geoff Tyler. At this interview, I was required to give an instructional brief on an aviation subject of my choice. No way was I going to brief on jet aeroplane theory or aerodynamics, as with the extensive knowledge these guys have in this area, they would have eaten me alive. I mean to say, I had flown jets, but for these pilots, it was their way of life and as Check Captains there was very little they did not know about those subjects. So, I chose to talk about an aviation subject that they may not have been conversant with—the ground operation of tail-wheeled aeroplanes as this was more my area of expertise. My enthusiasm on the subject included whiteboard diagrams and I remember Captain Geoff Tyler, who apparently had no tail-wheel experience, asking Captain Ray Saunders if what I was saying was correct. Ray said he couldn't remember as it had been so long ago. We all had a few laughs. A few days later, much to my delight, I received a letter which notified me that I had been successful in my application and I resigned as a Director of Aero Professional. The training I received from QANTAS complimented my RAAF training. The ground school training was conducted in Sydney, whilst the simulator training was conducted by QANTAS instructors in Taipei, using China Airlines' simulators, as the QANTAS simulators were fully booked.

I met and started a strong friendship with Senior Check Captain Geoff Jones who was my simulator instructor for this period. His wife Laurel accompanied him to Taipei whilst on this assignment. It was quite the norm that after a simulator session, Geoff would come back to my room for a quick drink and debrief the simulator session and talk about DC-3s. More than once, we got caught up in shop talk and Laurel would ring my room in the early hours of the morning to ask if her beloved Geoffrey was still with me.

In Taipei, I worked and studied extremely hard. There were only two afternoons in that fortnight when I went for a relaxing stroll. The rest of the time, I was either in the books, sleeping or in the simulator. As part of my learning, I would walk around my hotel room imagining flying a circuit in the B747. This would always help me to firmly memorise checklists and procedures. It is something I have done for my entire career. In one simulator session, Geoff decided, at a moment's notice, to give me instant fog, resulting in zero forward vision as soon as the main wheels touched down. This was completely unbriefed. Immediately, I focussed my concentration completely on my instruments and brought the simulator to a halt on what I hoped was the runway.

'Now we'll see how good you are,' said Geoff, as he returned to unlimited visibility. I looked out the front cockpit window to see where I had pulled up. Wow, I couldn't believe it. The nose wheel was probably some 2-3 m (6-10 ft) left of the centreline. Considering I had no visible reference for this landing, and it takes a B747 about 1,830 m (6,000 ft) to pull up, I was exceptionally thrilled with this outcome.

After each simulator session, the Check Captain writes a critique of that particular exercise. On 15th December 1989, Geoff wrote the following:

'Considering the appalling state of this simulator (not QANTAS'), the exercise was flown to a high standard with very good management & awareness. Procedures very good, 3 engine instrument approach (ILS) very accurately flown.'

For this simulator exercise, I was awarded a rating of 4 (High Standard) by Senior Check Captain Geoff Jones. A rating of 4 is the highest rating QANTAS ever awards to any exercise. When I told Helen, she said it was unbelievable as 'no-one is ever awarded a 4 rating'.

* * *

My employment at QANTAS was a bittersweet experience due to a Pilot's dispute that commenced on the 18th August 1989, when the Australian Federation of Air Pilots (AFAP) embarked on an industrial campaign ostensibly in support of a 29.47% pay rise and a limitation on the hours pilots were prepared to work. This action precipitated one of the worst and most expensive (financially and emotionally) industrial disputes in Australia's history. The airlines caught in the dispute were Ansett, East West, IPEC and Australian Airlines.

Although I had not been employed by IPEC since resigning in 1986, some people in the industry had been misinformed and linked me as a participant in this strike action. The dispute caused a major downturn of international passengers, made apparent when QANTAS flights, returning from Japan to Australia, carried few passengers. In February 1990, I became one of the many casualties of the dispute when QANTAS terminated my contract, along with my colleagues on the simulator instructor's course.

* * *

After my termination from QANTAS, I consistently faxed applications to IPEC for a Pilot position and was perplexed when the end of the year was approaching and I had never heard back. Then someone advised me that someone at IPEC had been destroying my faxes as soon as they arrived. That prompted me to phone management directly and I was then granted an interview. In November 1990, I re-joined IPEC Aviation as a DC-9 First Officer. When I was with IPEC previously, I had been a Line Training Captain on DC-9 aeroplanes. The airline was a highly disciplined, and a thoroughly professional outfit. Captain Frank McIntyre, (ex TAA DC-9 simulator instructor) had written reports in regard to my training that stated:

3rd December 1990—'Intensive period covering Base Check Ex, abnormal circuits, emergency descent, wind shear, and locator approach were all completed to an above average standard.'

5th December 1990—'All of First Officer Lovell's periods have been of an above average standard and this was no exception. A good demonstration of how the simulator should be flown.'

* * *

After the pilots' dispute, the standard of most pilots dropped significantly. Now, after leaving IPEC only four years earlier, I was shocked by the lower standards. The standards were satisfactory, but not to the level of my expectations. As a First Officer, there was very little I could do to influence improvement. One example I was informed about was when an IPEC DC-9-33 taxied out for take-off from the Ansett freight apron at Tullamarine one night with the main cargo door wide open. Obviously, the external pilot pre-flight inspection, the checklist, the amber caution lights and the increased noise level from the jet's engines did not stop this intrepid crew. Fortunately, the aeroplane was stopped prior to take-off, or the attempted flight would have been a disaster. It is critical for the huge main cargo door to be closed and locked as this ensures the structural integrity of the aeroplane. Aeroplanes weren't even allowed to be towed empty with the main cargo door unlocked, and here we had a fully loaded aeroplane taxi with it wide open.

On another night when I was Co-pilot, the loadmaster brought the load sheet to the aeroplane which the Captain duly signed. When it was handed to me to ascertain the take-off performance figures, I noted the load sheet indicated that we were 70 kg above the maximum take-off weight. I advised the Captain and loadmaster as I've always regarded maximum weights as absolute and refused to fly otherwise. The Captain stated it was insignificant, and we would burn that in fuel taxiing out, even though this had already been allowed for in the load sheet. I stood my ground and said I would not be on that flight until a new legal load sheet was produced. Having made my intentions clear, I started packing my flight charts back into my navigation bag in preparation for walking off the aeroplane. When the Captain and the loadmaster saw that I was serious, they acquiesced to comply with my demand. To some, 70 kg in a 51 tonne aeroplane may seem insignificant, but that is not the point. Rules and limitations are put there for a valid reason and if one dares to disregard these, then they may incur penalties or at worse cause serious injury or loss of life.

On 12th April 1991 an ex TAA Captain, suspended me from flying duties with IPEC as I dared to question a Captain regarding his actions whilst conducting a simulator exercise. One of the main roles of a First Officer is to monitor, advise, and if necessary, question a Captain's actions and logic. A First Officer is a very necessary component of a safe flight crew. Any Captain who cannot be questioned is extremely arrogant and dangerous. I was reinstated shortly thereafter.

On 31st May 1992, due to the economic climate and the downturn in air freight, I was retrenched, along with others, by IPEC Aviation. No staff had any inkling of the situation developing within the company. It certainly came as a shock to all of us. Even though Helen and I had purchased a seven-acre hobby farm at Riddells Creek the year before, there was nothing else holding us to Victoria. Due to the fact that I was now unemployed, this allowed us to consider our future which resulted in our move to Camden in NSW.

* * *

On 5th September 1992, Helen and I were married at her mother's rural property just outside of Rockhampton, Queensland, with Tony Hannam acting as my best man. It was by far the best wedding I have ever attended. As we were both pilots, what better way for the bride to arrive than in a helicopter. The family were sworn to secrecy. Helen and I discussed the cost, as a helicopter would have to come from Gladstone to carry out our wishes. I remember saying to her; 'Let's just do it'. We went to Lloyds Helicopters at Gladstone Airport and explained that we wanted Helen, and her bridal party,

Wedding photo at Rockhampton Airport (Author's Collection)

to be picked up by helicopter at Rockhampton Airport and then flown to her mother's property which was about a five-minute flight. We requested that the helicopter do a couple of circuits around the property before landing around 100 m from the decking which overlooked the dam. The plan was to then have a limousine drive into the cow paddock, pick up the party and drive them back to where the ceremony was to be conducted, in her mother's front tropical garden. I went to great lengths to plan everything from providing the chopper Pilot with maps and directions to making the helicopter landing pad stand out by marking the area with the large white encircled H using lime. Coloured bunting was placed on any nearby fences. In fact, I was complimented after the flight by the management of the helicopter company for providing exceptional facilities for the Pilot. He explained that normally, the Pilot gets very little pre-flight directions.

As the time of the wedding ceremony approached, guests started asking, where the bridal party was. I kept the charade up by looking at my watch and down the driveway for the arrival of the limousine. At the appointed time the helicopter, a Bell 206, approached low from the south did a couple of circuits of the homestead and then landed in the paddock. After the rotor blades stopped, the limousine slowly drove out, picked up the party and returned to the garden. Everything flowed with military precision.

Our wedding photos were taken at Rockhampton Airport, both in a maintenance hangar and also on the runway. Can you imagine trying to use these venues as a backdrop these days? You would be hauled away by security before you could blink. Back then, we notified the Airport Manager of our intentions and provided the Safety Officer with a carton of beer. We spent close to two hours taking photos of Helen sitting on the wing of an aeroplane in the maintenance hangar, surrounded by tools and a considerable amount of time on the grass at the edge of the runway whilst aircraft were taking off and landing. They were stunning photographs.

Helen's mother was a very strong and highly respected woman. I recall a particular occasion when being my usual, mischievous self, with a devil on my shoulder, a scene flashed through my mind from Faulty Towers where Basil says; 'Have you seen my wife make toast?' Then he mimes a dragon breathing onto the bread. On this occasion, I looked at Helen's mother and said to her; 'I know how you make toast.' I then mimed a dragon breathing onto the bread. Absolutely stunned silence followed for a noticeable length of time. I really didn't know how she was going to react. For a minute, I thought I was in real trouble, again, but then she chuckled, which made me wonder whether it was at my joke or my brazen stupidity. I'd like to think it was at my joke.

As Helen and I were both professional pilots, and from a farming background, we had lots in common. On the Pilot side of things, we understood the pressures around tight timekeeping and frequent roster changes, which included reserve time. A Pilot on reserve must be available to go to work within one to two hours of a call-out. This may be for a flight as short as one hour or as long as two weeks away from home. Understanding these requirements is paramount to a successful marriage for pilots. More than once, we were in planes passing in the night and sometimes we would say a quick hello on the radio to each other. As most international flights land at around 6 am, it was normal for me to get up early, drive an hour from Camden to the airport, to meet Helen when her flight landed. My car had a VHF radio receiver so I could monitor her incoming flight.

At one time, Helen was undergoing B767 training with QANTAS. Due to a lack of QANTAS simulators in Sydney, they used Ansett's simulator in Melbourne. One night I accompanied her to the simulator and after she had finished her training simulator exercise, I was then allowed to sit in the left-hand seat for a free time flight as a guest of the simulator staff. I can't remember the flight circumstances, but without warning, something moved very fast from our high eleven o'clock position, right in front of us, to exit about low four o'clock position. I remember saying something like; 'We'll have him'—meaning I'd chase him to identify him. Immediately I turned hard right, lowered the nose and applied full power, in the direction I thought the object went. Around 10 seconds later, I found the light source (simulator was set for night time) and started to close in. It soon became apparent that I could, when close enough, slow down and formate on the object.

Upon getting closer, it turned out it was the Space Shuttle. The simulator technicians had programmed it into the system. Once alongside the shuttle, the instructor declared; 'Shit, I've never seen that before.' (referring to sighting the Space Shuttle and my flying ability). What an opportunity for an out of work Pilot to be able to have a fun fly. I don't think Helen said anything. Perhaps petty rivalry was starting to appear?

* * *

A lighter side, of a very serious profession, always helps in the day-to-day operations and gives you an overall balance in life. One such notable happening occurs at Adelaide Airport. During the 1989 Pilot's strike, Peter Willoughby (Airport Safety Officer) started the infamous 'Buck Bear' (an old donated teddy bear). One night, Peter placed the teddy bear in an old wicker chair on the airfield as a bit of a joke for Air Traffic Controllers, without telling anyone. Peter consistently denied he had anything to do with it for a year or so. Dubbed 'Buck' by Adelaide Airport staff (allegedly after well-known airline Captain and union official, Buck Brooksbank) the decision was made to see what happened if Peter made him visible to the flying public and the aviation industry at large. Buck and his pet dog 'Mick' have had a lot of adventures over the years including several requests from airlines for Buck to be in the aerobridge when an aircraft Captain completes his last flight into Adelaide. Malaysian Airlines borrowed Buck and took him on a holiday to Kuala Lumpur. Buck has stood guard along the international runway in various incarnations—clutching a beer on Australia Day, riding a bike during the Tour Down Under, Santa at Christmas or dressed up in a Port Adelaide guernsey for the premiership. He has been kidnapped several times but always manages to find his way back home and has participated in fund raising for many charities. He is well known in the aviation industry and when Peter puts him out in the field, it does not take long for the word to get around as pilots start asking where he is. You can follow Buck on his very

From Hero to Zero

own Facebook page[2] Buck Bear (Adelaide Airport Mascot). How marvellous that Adelaide Airport Ltd support Peter and Buck and appreciate how it brings a lot of good humour into such a highly regulated industry.

One of the few times Buck Bear has been caught relaxing instead of his usual vigilant attention to the airfield! (Peter Willoughby)

2   www.facebook.com/groups/27536856685

BACK TO FLYING A DC-3

The DC-3 is a twin-engined, low wing, tailwheel monoplane first flown in 1935. Power is provided by two Pratt & Whitney R1830-92 14-cylinder Twin Wasp radial engines with single stage superchargers, driving three-bladed Hamilton Standard feathering propellers, and rated at 1,200 hp for take-off. As a dedicated passenger aircraft in earlier days the DC-3 only had a single passenger door. The freighter DC-3 has the C-47 Dakota double doors on the left-hand side of the rear fuselage, but these can still serve as passenger doors, by only opening the forward one.[1]

* * *

In 1968, Colonel Keith Hatfield and Major Ron Kerrison took over Casey Airfield at Berwick, Victoria and operated a flying school under the name Group Air Pty Ltd. From what I can ascertain, the company name was 'Group Air Pty Ltd' however, since I was involved with the company, it was referred to as 'Groupair Pty Ltd' so we will continue with that name.

In late 1992 I met with Barry Bell, Geoff Leach (hereinafter referred to as Mr Leach Snr) and his son Mr Nick Leach), in the Essendon Airport car park. The Leaches advised me that they were looking for a Captain for their DC-3 VH-EDC. VH-EDC was in fact a Douglas C-47 Skytrain which was developed from the Douglas DC-3 Airliner. For simplicity, I will hereafter refer to this aeroplane as a DC-3. I took on the position and commenced work to have the aircraft added to the company's Air Operators Certificate (AOC)[2] by submitting the amended Operations Manual for approval to the Civil Aviation Authority (CAA).

On 13th January 1993, I received a letter from a CAA representative approving my appointment as DC-3 Flight Captain for Groupair. At this time

---
1 History of VH-EDC : www.aussieairliners.org/dc-3/vh-edc/vh-edc.html
2 An AOC is similar in definition to a licence to operate a vehicle/machine etc.

the Chief Pilot was not qualified under the terms of the Civil Aviation Orders to hold this position. The letter also stated that 'passenger weights should be based on the advice provided in CAAP 235' (Civil Aviation Advisory Publication regarding standard passenger and baggage weights)[3]. Two months later the Chief Pilot delegated me as DC-3 Flight Captain, together with certain responsibilities applying to DC-3 operations, thus making the appointment official.

In early 1993 another CAA representative conducted a check ride on myself, Geoff Jones and Co-pilot Leach at Camden Airport in NSW. His report stated that I was tested in the left-hand seat including steep turns, stall in the approach configuration, simulated engine fire and simulated asymmetric approach and landing. Circuits and landings from the right-hand seat included simulated engine failure after take-off. The stall in the approach configuration is not a recommended manoeuvre. However, this CAA representative demanded I demonstrate the recovery.

He also observed me in both left-hand and right-hand seat checking a Co-pilot on three circuits and landings. His report also stated that I 'demonstrated a good practical approach and knowledge and handled the aircraft competently throughout.'

In regard to the engine failure after take-off checks, I was carrying them out in accordance with the Groupair Operations Manual procedures. However, this CAA representative was not happy with this, and whilst we were on a taxiway, he told me I had to use the procedure of mixture (auto-rich), pitch (full fine), power (maximum), gear up, flaps up, identify, etc. I remember telling him that what he said was the way light twin-engined aeroplanes were operated, but not the way this class of aeroplane was operated. I carefully followed the operations manual which is an approved procedure. The examiner required me to adopt a different process which I initially declined to do. He then insinuated that he would not pass me unless I accepted the procedures he demanded, so, like most of the aviation industry, I yielded to his demands. He was acting in direct contravention of the operations manual which his department had approved, but this did not seem to bother him.

An important point was that he did not say that I needed further training to satisfy the requirements for approval as Check and Training Captain. He stated that I required further checking on the contents of the Check and

---

3   www.casa.gov.au/files/2351pdf - Civil Aviation Advisory Publication

Back to Flying a DC-3

Yours truly cruising along (Author's Collection)

Training Manual and detailed training programs—a subtle but vital difference in interpretation. The misinterpretation of this paragraph has caused all and sundry to believe I was deficient in my operation of this aeroplane.

The same CAA representative stated that take-off performance charts were discussed, which seemed to be a grey area with DC-3 operators in general, and that he had discussed this subject with another CAA representative. His statement created total confusion within the CAA regulatory authorities regarding the correct take-off performance charts to use for DC-3s. The upshot of this was that this CAA representative was satisfied with my handling of the DC-3 and said I handled the aeroplane competently.

* * *

In late February 1993, I was flown to Hawaii by the Leaches to captain their DC-3 N65388, (later to become registered as VH-SPY) in parachute operations at Dillingham Field on the northern side of Oahu. This was a very interesting assignment. We removed both big cargo doors and loaded 48 parachutists. Once at an altitude of around 12,000 ft, they formed two groups of twenty-four in four rows of six standing shoulder to shoulder facing the left-hand side of the aeroplane. The aeroplane was then brought back to a jump speed of around 120 kt, from memory, before these two groups readied for the jump.

With the aeroplane in this configuration, it was wise not to trim the eleva-

From Hero to Zero

tor forces out. When the first group of twenty-four ran out the door in unison, the aeroplane lost about two tons of weight from the rear. This caused the rear to immediately lift requiring me to pull back on the control column to counteract the sudden weight loss. Within seconds, the second group of twenty-four scurried down the back to adopt the same formation. Again, I adjusted the control column by pushing forward to counterbalance the change of position of weight. Once the second group exited the plane, I pulled the control column back to neutral. It was all good fun.

On 15th May 1993, I was given Check Pilot Approval DC-3s for Groupair.

Sadly, on 11th June 1993, Monarch Piper Chieftain VH-NDU, crashed with the loss of all seven people on board, at Young, New South Wales. That very same evening, Geoff Jones and I crewed 'EDC into Parkes. The weather conditions at Parkes were very similar to those at Young. However, we were in an old DC-3, carried out a monitored instrument approach, with a circling approach, using monitored approach procedures. We conducted a visual left-hand circuit. As I was sitting in the left-hand seat and Geoff was in the right, he flew the aeroplane on extremely basic instruments, mainly with reference to my flight instruments on the left-hand side of the cockpit. My role was to visually and verbally advise Geoff to position the aeroplane onto finals for landing. Whilst flying down wind I told Geoff to maintain circuit height and directed him with heading changes plus or minus five degrees. At

Capt. Geoff Jones and I conducting a pre-flight (Author's Collection)

the appropriate base position, I directed him with angle of bank and descent rate whilst continuing to visually keep the runway in sight. Geoff continued to fly the aeroplane referencing solely to instruments. There was nothing unsafe about it and we carried out an uneventful safe landing.

In January 1994, New South Wales was battling devastating bushfires. Co-pilot Leach was quoting a hire fee on the 'EDC to transport firefighters around the state. He was due for his Command Multi-Engine Instrument Rating renewal, and as an approved person, it was decided that I conduct his test on his other DC-3, N65388 in Cairns prior to us attending the New South Wales bushfires. To ensure he complied with CAA requirements I conducted an exhaustive flight check on 9th January 1994 before signing his form certifying him. It is worth noting that the flight check included simulated engine failures and asymmetric missed approach procedures.

Under the regulations, although I was approved to conduct this test, I was not allowed to certify his logbook, as I was not an ATO. I asked him to get his logbook certified as soon as possible which I was led to believe he did to remain legal. I caught a very early flight (around 5.30am departure) the following day from Cairns to Sydney.

Over the next three days we flew charters out of Bankstown Airport in Sydney in 'EDC. As it was reasonably hectic, I realised when I was filling out my logbook on 12th January that I had not entered Co-pilot Leach's Instrument Rating Test flight of 9th January, so I entered it into my logbook three days out of sequence. A number of entries followed in correct chronological order for the rest of the month of January. Having entered this flight out of sequence would have ramifications after the ditching, as the CAA intimated that Co-pilot Leach and I had been up to something. It is not illegal to enter flights out of sequence. It is just unconventional and I'm sure many others have done it. Why this insignificant fact was picked on by the CAA is hard to fathom when bigger issues were at hand. This was not the first time that I had entered a flight out of sequence. When I was in the RAAF, I realised that I had not entered my wings test flight into my logbook and this was one of the most important flights I would ever make. Although I conducted this highly significant flight on 3rd March 1972, it was the end of September 1972 before I realised and hence entered it into my logbook.

From Hero to Zero

PARKES IS BURNING

In spite of the dramas beginning to emerge, our DC-3 VH-EDC was not without some humorous adventures. On 13th December 1993, Brian Booker, the Co-pilot, and I were bringing 'EDC back from Alice Springs to Sydney with a load of freight. Brian was flying this leg of the night flight and we had to land at Parkes to refuel. The refueller at Parkes had been notified prior to our departure from The Alice that we would be arriving in the evening. On our initial approach onto runway 22, into Parkes, I noticed the amber flashing lights signifying the refueller was awaiting us. I was not happy with the progress of the landing approach and told Brian to go-around and set it up again. This time the approach was fine, and the landing was smooth.

During the landing roll, we started to drift left of the centreline. I looked over to Brian in the right-hand seat and saw him straining to push full right rudder and holding the control column all the way back. We were probably going about 40 kt at this stage.

'Can't you handle it?' I asked him casually.

'No!' he replied in an anguished, higher pitch than normal, voice. A single brake failure on landing is not an abnormal procedure covered in the operations manual. I instinctively realised the situation, and as Captain, I took control from the Co-pilot.

'Taking over', I advised. I expected to use a little right brake to control the aeroplane but on depressing the right brake, the pedal went straight to the stop with a dull metallic 'thunk'. A couple more pumps on the pedal and each time straight to the stop with zero resistance.

With the end of the runway coming up and darkness preventing me from knowing what lay beyond the end of the runway, I decided to ground-loop the old girl. I pulled the tail-wheel lock under the centre pedestal, to release the tailwheel, and applied left rudder and a little brake, to initiate a ground loop to the left, where I knew the surface of the ground was okay. We completed a 180° turn and came to a halt on the grass, engines still running, alongside the runway facing back in the direction from which we had landed.

What I then observed stunned me for a second. There was a line of flame approximately 150 mm (six inches) high, starting back up the runway where we had touched down, and continuing along the runway, curving all the way around and ending behind the aeroplane. My scan then showed reflections of flames on the left inner engine cowl. I checked my wheel but could see nothing.

'Check out your side and tell me what you see?' I asked Brian.

'Shit! We're on fire!' he replied.

'Tell me what you see?' I asked again, as I had no idea where the flames were coming from due to a limited view below the Co-pilot's window.

'The right-hand main wheel's on fire' he replied.

The loss of the brakes on the right-hand side led me to believe that the brake line on the right wheel had become disconnected somehow and this combined with a hot brake/wheel was the source of the fire. Every time the brake was pumped, flammable hydraulic brake fluid was squirted onto the hot brake shoe.

I kept the engines running with as much power over the right-hand wheel necessary to blow the flames away from the landing gear and wheel, without pumping the brake. By having the tail wheel locked and using only brake on the left-hand main wheel, I was able to control the aeroplane. Brian was asked to top up the hydraulic reservoir, situated behind his seat, from the can behind my seat, whilst also keeping me informed as to how the fire was progressing. I also allowed the aeroplane to roll forward ever so slowly as I was concerned that the brake might weld, thereby immobilising us. After a couple of minutes, the fire extinguished itself. I kept the engines running and the aeroplane moving forward for a few more minutes to cool the brakes.

After I was satisfied that there was no further danger, I taxied the aeroplane very slowly to the tarmac and shut down the engines. By this time, the Parkes fire brigade had arrived at the airport, apparently summoned by the aircraft refueller. I thanked the firemen for their attendance and they went back into town. The refueller advised me that there was a fire unit in a shed at the airport, but the rules were that it required two persons to operate it, so he stayed in his fuel truck and possibly would have watched us burn. At least he gave us a lift to a motel in his Subaru Brumby utility. When we got to the motel, Brian seemed in a state of shock, so we dissected each component of the incident in an informal type of counselling session, which was beneficial for both of us.

* * *

Groupair required another Co-pilot, hence Helen recommended Andrew Buxton with whom she had studied aviation subjects at TAFE (Tertiary and Further Education) in Sydney. The first time I met Andrew was in the shopping aisles at Coles supermarket in Camden. We had an official interview sometime later. I had the pleasure of endorsing Andrew on the DC-3 as a Co-pilot in January 1994. This was conducted at Bathurst New South Wales. On one of the night circuits, as part of the endorsement, we were flying downwind at 1,000 ft (305 m) to prepare for landing. Andrew was Pilot Flying (PF), as he was under training, and I was the Pilot Not Flying (PNF) (Support Pilot and Training Captain). It was my task to operate the landing gear levers once asked by the PF. I was totally aware that after the last take-off, Andrew had not called for the gear to be retracted. When Andrew called for 'gear down', I immediately, tongue in cheek, thrust a thumbs-up in his face. The cockpit of a DC-3 is quite noisy hence hand signals are the normal way of in communicating.

'You got it!' I yelled. Andrew was bewildered when I didn't touch any of the landing gear levers. 'Gear down' he repeated. Again, I immediately thrust a thumbs up in his face.

'You got it!' I yelled again. This really threw him. It then dawned on him that the landing gear was showing two greens, indicating that the two main landing gear wheels were already down and locked and that he had not called for 'gear up' after the last take-off. I have always believed that a lesson is well learnt if the person can recognise the fault he has made without my interference if it is safe enough to do so. Funnily enough, Andrew has not forgotten this occurrence, and I don't let him. Andrew became a good friend.

THE DAY THAT CHANGED MY LIFE

Sunday 24th April 1994 was the day when in a matter of 46 seconds, my life changed dramatically. It was a beautiful day with no clouds. The flying conditions were absolutely perfect. As the Captain of the DC-3 VH-EDC chartered to fly the Scots College schoolboy band; their support staff; a few army personnel and members of the media to perform at an Anzac Day Service being held on Norfolk Island, I had begun thoroughly planning for this flight about a week prior. The amount of planning and preparation that went into this charter from Sydney to Lord Howe and Norfolk Islands was extensive and meticulous. We were to fly a long distance across the open ocean with few places to land should an emergency occur. Little did I know that the emergency would occur shortly after take-off.

I was first appointed Captain of DC-3 aircraft in 1979 and had been Captain of this particular aircraft for seventeen months prior to this flight. I had made over 100 flights to Lord Howe Island in other aircraft types, both freight and passenger carrying, including one flight in the very same aircraft.

My crew for the flight was Co-pilot Nick Leach, supernumerary Co-pilot Andrew Buxton and flight attendant Annabel Scott who would manage the passenger compartment. As Captain, I held an Airline Transport Pilot Licence (1st Class) as did Andrew. A 1st Class ATPL permits the operation of an aircraft greater that 5,700 kg Maximum Take-Off Weight (MTOW) as Pilot in Command. The flight attendant was current in emergency procedures required by cabin crew. Co-pilot Leach, as one of the owners of the operating company, had shown me his Australian Commercial Pilot Licence which later was proved by the Australian Government to be invalid although issued by the CAA. All flight crew held a Class 1 Medical Certificate and Multi-Engine Command Instrument Rating.

The operating company had arranged for the passengers to be ready at the Hawker Pacific building at Kingsford Smith Airport where charter aircraft uplift passengers. We were informed early in the day that everything was ready for them to be picked up and the flight could proceed.

As each leg was more than 400 nautical miles (750 km) in distance, there is obviously no opportunity for emergency landing airports en-route and island weather can change unpredictably. It was essential to cover any possible contingencies prior to the departure. Not all pilots go into this depth of preparation, however, it has always been my strong ethics that I support and manage my crew to the very best of my ability.

It is normal protocol for the Captain to undertake all pre-flight and flight planning duties in an operation like this. On the Wednesday prior to the proposed flight, I invited Andrew, who was coming along for the experience, to our house to spend the entire afternoon going through flight planning, fuel requirements, weight and balance calculations, take-off and landing charts, what visual expectations such as clouds or wind were anticipated at the islands and departure times so that last light[1] would not be a problem as Lord Howe Island did not have runway lights. If for some unexpected reason we had to turn back on our way to Norfolk Island, we had to ensure we had enough fuel to return, having prepared for a worst-case scenario of flying on only one engine. As Andrew had no previous experience of flying over long stretches of water, this was a valuable learning opportunity to spend a lot of time going through everything thoroughly with him. Co-pilot Leach was not involved in this session as he had previously flown with me in this aeroplane to Lord Howe Island.

All administrative requirements for over water and international flights were complied with and customs and refuellers at Lord Howe Island and Norfolk Island were notified. Prior permission to park an aeroplane overnight was gained for Norfolk Island. Single-engine fuel was planned to be carried on each sector as was legally required[2]. If an aircraft has an engine failure, it travels slower and possibly at a lower altitude. The consequence of this is a higher rate of fuel usage. Therefore, when planning any flight in a multi-engined aeroplane, we always cater for the worst-case scenario which

---

1 Last light is the time when the centre of the sun is at an angle of 6° below the ideal horizon following sunset. At this time large objects are not definable but may be seen and the brightest stars are visible under clear atmospheric conditions. Last light can also be referred to as the end of evening civil twilight.
2 430 imperial gallons/2,000 litres

for a DC-3 is single-engined operation. In all cases having an engine failure en-route will entail using more fuel than if all engines were operating. This is further compounded if the destination (remote island) has or has been forecast to have adverse weather conditions which could prevent immediate landing. More disturbingly this could entail a diversion back to the mainland.

As Captain of this charter flight, my personal duty is to ensure that the weather is satisfactory for the journey; that flight information is obtained and checked as clear. One of the aircraft's compulsory documents is a valid maintenance release (M/R) which is carried on each flight certifying the maintenance is up to date. The M/R is a document that brings together the flying issues concerning the aircraft. Entries are made by engineers and pilots. Before each flight, the Captain must inspect the document to ensure that there are no defects recorded concerning the engines, radios and airframes. The Captain must then note that he has inspected the aircraft by signing and thus releasing the aircraft for flight. I relied on a review of the previous entries in the M/R, which demonstrated that all maintenance had been carried out. I relied on the engineers to confirm this. I am required to look no further than this document if it shows, on its face, that all is clear. That was the case in this flight. As Captain, I signed off on this. The refueller provided me with a certificate showing my required fuel was uploaded. The company handed me a certificate identifying the passengers and confirming that the total weight of the aircraft is below the MTOW.

A few days prior to the accident, Kevin Wiles of TNT Air Charter (the hirer of the aeroplane) faxed me with a list of 21 passenger names, gender and dates of birth. From this information, a load and trim sheet was completed by me from the data I was given and on which I am entitled to rely. This comprised the load component showing the basic weight of the aeroplane, fuel, passengers and baggage. The trim component showed the calculated centre of gravity of the loaded aeroplane which must fall within a predetermined range. From the information provided and our Operations Manual I could work out passenger approved weights[3] to ensure we were below maximum permitted take-off weight. The CAA directed Groupair to use the standard passenger weights as laid down in Civil Aviation Advisory Publication (CAAP) 235. If any change occurred, I could expect to be informed by the organiser of the charter flight. This included any changes

---

3 CAA Publication No: 2351(1), dated September 1990, Standard Passenger and Baggage Weights

to my load calculations, such as extra passengers. Changes to the weight of aircraft equipment, spares or accessories had to be notified to me by the aircraft owner. In our case, it was the duty of Co-pilot Leach. On this occasion, I was not informed. This is very critical. It is the root of the alleged overweight problem and was concealed from me. As Captain, I must have these certificates before the flight can commence.

I had worked out my figures on the approved weights and the fact that the passengers were going away for only two nights, anticipating their luggage and band equipment would be relatively lightweight. Kevin phoned me at home to say there were now only 20 passengers. In fact, this new information now gave me a greater margin below MTOW.

I invited Annabel, our flight attendant to attend a safety briefing on Saturday 23rd April. Although Annabel was legally qualified and competent to act as Flight Attendant on this flight, she had not gained any experience in over-water flights. Again, I believe in being well prepared for all scenarios. We spent around three hours at the aeroplane which was positioned on the grassed Eastern Park at Mascot Airport, Sydney, going over safety equipment, ditching procedures, survival at sea, etc. This included the use of life jackets; the probable ditching damage to the aeroplane and life-raft launching; passenger and crew evacuation from the aeroplane; cabin and aeroplane equipment to be taken in the life rafts; discipline in the life rafts; keeping the life rafts together and the use of the Electronic Locator Beacon (ELB).

* * *

I have always believed that a good Pilot is a pessimist. This ensures that you are prepared for most eventualities and only a naïve Pilot assumes that nothing will go wrong on a planned flight. I did all this extra safety briefing and preparation with my crew, of my own volition, even though we were all legally qualified and current for safety procedures as required by the Civil Aviation Orders.

* * *

That evening I contacted Co-pilot Leach, as the aeroplane owner and Co-pilot, to advise him that the required number of life rafts and life jackets were not on board. He assured me that they would be on board by Sunday morning as was the case. I had with me on board the aeroplane the CAA approved Operations Manual[4] which contained the aircraft's approved take-

---
4　The Operations Manual is part of the aircraft library which remains onboard at all times.

The Day that Changed My Life

'EDC pictured on the grassed Eastern Park at Sydney (aussieairliners)

off and landing charts. The flight crew carried all the navigation charts we required for the flights. I was satisfied with the standard of preparation and qualifications of the crew ensuring they were well aware of their responsibilities, and capabilities and that they met all legal requirements for the flight.

I had completed all pre-flight planning at home as part of my task as Captain. I reviewed the expected weather, both the night before and in the morning that I'd received by fax. This fax would also allow me to review any special notifications which may have been issued by the flight authorities alerting me to any unusual or unexpected event that may have existed on or near my route to Norfolk Island (Notams). There were no adverse Notams for this flight. I was totally aware that my Pilot licence and Pilot medical certificate were all current and in order.

Andrew arrived at our home early on 24th April and Helen drove us to the airport. We arrived at the aeroplane at 7.30 am to find Co-pilot Leach had arrived earlier and had already commenced the pre-flight duties as he is entitled to do. These consisted of a normal walkaround inspection, including checks of fuel and oil quantities, caps and drains, plus control locks, pitot covers[5] removed and a thorough visual inspection of the external components of the aeroplane as permitted by the operations manual. To check the fuel for contamination, a small quantity is drained from each tank prior to

---

5 A pitot cover is a simple device to protect dust, moisture and insects entering the pitot tube (air speed probe) when the aeroplane is not being used.

the flight for the presence of water. If water is present, further draining is required until all water is eliminated. I inspected the safety equipment on board.

I checked the fuel docket and passenger manifest of my expected passengers. Apart from operating the aircraft, Co-pilot Leach's duties, under my direction, was to oversee the loading of passengers and baggage and attend to any minor matter that may arise prior to the flight. His responsibility was directly to me. I was aware of what were minor changes concerning life-rafts, but the overall alteration was small and I accepted the change. After receiving notification of one less adult passenger the night before, we were still under the MTOW. My initial calculations showed we were 127 kg under the MTOW, for which this aircraft was licenced, therefore with one less female passenger this brought us to 196 kg under MTOW. I was not informed of extra weight having been loaded in addition to my load sheet. I was not happy with the way the extra life rafts had been secured, so I re-tied them down near the right over-wing emergency exit, in such a way that they could be released at a moment's notice if required.

During this time, Co-pilot Leach carried out the pre-start checklist which entailed checking and positioning appropriate controls, systems and switches prior to engine starting. This is all done complying with a written checklist. He then started the engines and conducted the engine run-up check. An engine run-up check is a series of last-minute checks by pilots of an aeroplane prior to take-off. This entails running the engines independently at a medium power setting and checking the magnetos and exercising the propeller feathering system. He did not advise me of any abnormalities with the engine run-up. There was no hint of any abnormality by sound or vibration. This is normal procedure. There is no legal requirement for the Captain to conduct the pre-start checklist and engine run-up. The engines were then shut down whilst we carried out further preparation.

At 8.30am, after entering the cockpit, I started the engines and taxied the aeroplane some 300 m to Hawker Pacific's apron, the concrete area immediately outside the office and hangar. As this was a general aviation flight, we did not have the luxury of baggage loaders. Therefore, I engaged the services of Helen and Andrew to assist me in loading the baggage onto the aeroplane. The weights of this baggage had already been taken into account in the loading document calculations. The passenger manifest was completed by the flight attendant who unexpectedly allowed an undocumented extra adult woman aboard without my knowledge or approval. As per normal procedures, it is not a requirement for the Pilot in command to check the manifest names against the passengers on board. I was still only aware of a flight crew of three, a cabin attendant and only twenty passengers—not twenty-one! At no time was I advised of anything to the contrary.

Once on board, the passengers were seated by our flight attendant, Annabel. The seating configuration of this DC-3 was two abreast both sides of the fuselage with a centre aisle. Running lengthways down each side of the fuselage, above the seats, were open hat racks for small lightweight items.

As Captain, I occupied the traditional left-hand seat and as Co-pilot Leach, the right-hand seat. After removing the landing gear locking pins, which are inserted when the aeroplane is on the ground to negate accidental, unintentional landing gear retraction, Andrew climbed on board and after closing the main cabin door, took up his position on the jump seat (this is a fold-down seat between, but a little behind, the pilots' seats). We strapped in and with rudder pedals adjusted to suit we were ready to start engines.

The forward windows are not very large by today's standards but are adequate and incorporate a square sliding section as a storm window for use in limited visibility to obtain direct vision. For a larger aeroplane, the two pilots sit in relatively close proximity, and each Pilot can reach all the controls and switches. As with most heavier 1930s and wartime vintage aircraft, the controls are dominated by a standard, semi-circular control wheel. Full flight instruments are on the panel in front of the left-hand seat and the right-hand seat has basic flight instruments only. Between the pilots is a central engine control pedestal at knee height on which are mounted throttles, pitch levers, mixture controls, tailwheel lock, fuel selectors, carburettor heat knobs, autopilot selector and fuel cross-feed selector, parking brake knob, two trim cranks for aileron and rudder plus the elevator trim wheel.

Above the Pilot's heads on either side are two roof (or eyebrow) electrical panels, containing many toggle switches for the various services used and a propeller feather push button. This was the location of the feather button which was activated during the emergency. There is one for each propeller. Between these two panels, centrally mounted just above the point where the two windshields meet as a V is a small circular panel containing the master ignition switch and the two individual engine ignition wingnut switches, each with four positions (Off, Left, Right & Both).

There is a system of hydraulic controls. The panel for this with its various selectors is located behind the Co-pilot seat. An electrical junction box is in the compartment aft of the cockpit on the left, just rearwards of the small baggage door opening out to the left side. Firewall shutoff valves, CO_2 fire extinguisher controls and the associated engine selector are all found under a floor panel between the two seats. The communication and navigation radios on board are mounted in the racks behind the hydraulic panel, on the right side. Standard flight and engine instruments are found on the main instrument panel, plus the required radio-navigational instruments. Above the Co-pilot's knees, on the right-side cockpit wall, are the two hydraulic pressure gauges, the forward one showing undercarriage downline pressure and the rear gauge showing system pressure.

After receiving the all clear from the ground crew, and after all the necessary preparations of switches, levers and selectors had been made, the No 2 (right) engine was cycled through nine propeller blades with magneto switches off and mixture in ICO (idle cut-off) using the starter. After the ninth blade[6] had been completed with no hesitation of the propeller blades, indicating no hydraulic lock of the engine cylinders, the ignition was switched on, the booster coil and primer were then activated. The big radial then roared to life amid a clatter of conrods, shaking cowls and a puff or two of blue smoke, all very normal for a radial engine. The starter and booster were released and at this point, the mixture control was moved up to the Auto Rich position. Engine speed was stabilised at 1,000 rpm, as it must not be exceeded until the oil temperature gauge reads at least 40°C and a check was made of fuel pressure, oil pressure, suction and hydraulics all within limits. The procedure was repeated for the No.1 (left) engine. After start checks for both engines were completed, which included turning off the fuel boost pumps, placing the hydraulic selector to the rear, turning on inverters and radio equipment plus lighting as required.

The aeroplane taxied at 9.00am for take-off—right on schedule.

---

6   This is to check for what is called a hydraulic lock (as some of the cylinders are inverted, engine oil can leak into the cylinder head). If an engine was to start with this condition it could blow the cylinder head off the cylinder.

ENGINE FAILURE—LEFT ENGINE

Co-pilot Leach flew the aircraft from the right-hand seat and taxied the aeroplane for the north-south runway known as 16 (one-six) for a Bravo 3 intersection departure allocated to us which gave us an available runway length of 11,000 ft (3,330 m) for taking off. This was more than enough. At this time there was only one serviceable north/south runway due to the new runway construction being incomplete.

The Co-pilot's take-off briefing to me was: 'Take-off weight is 11,757 kg, call V_1/V_2 at 81 kt. Any malfunction before V_1 call STOP and I will abandon the take-off. A malfunction at or after V_1, I will nominate—you will feather after my confirmation. I will continue to fly the aircraft until such time as you call Taking Over.' As we were about to take-off on runway 16, we discussed that in the event of an engine failure after take-off, we would anticipate returning to the airport for a landing on runway 25 or as dictated by circumstances.

After all the required checklists were completed, we obtained line-up clearance and checked the runway was clear, we lined up on the centreline. We then, along with other items, closed our sliding cockpit side windows, tailwheel lock in, landing gear latch to spring lock position, and received take-off clearance, thereby completing our line-up checklist. The Co-pilot smoothly and steadily applied take-off power. As is normal, I made fine adjustments to the throttles and confirmed that the take-off power of 48" MP (manifold pressure)[1] and 2700 rpm was set. I consistently monitored all engine instruments and airspeed whilst observing the runway ahead. At around 45 kt a gentle push forward on the control column causes the tail wheel to leave the ground. The aircraft remained straight by use of the rudder pedals which controlled the large rudder.

---

1 Also referred to as MAP (Manifold Absolute Pressure)

From Hero to Zero

Near impossible to reach (Mike Milln)

The take-off roll appeared normal. Engine instrument indications confirmed MP and rpm were correctly set, which was my responsibility as Pilot Not Flying (PNF). V_1/V_2 of 81 kt was called[2] and simultaneously confirmed by holding up two fingers horizontally in front of the Co-pilot's face. As the noise from the two big powerful radial engines prevent normal conversations on the take-off roll, we use hand signals in addition to verbal communication and we gave the usual take-off signals. The lift-off was normal and the aircraft climbed out at the correct speed[3] of 81 kt. The landing gear was selected up as soon as we were safely airborne. It is virtually impossible to reach the levers required to retract the landing gear of a DC-3 whilst strapped into the seat with the shoulder harness, as was supplied in this aircraft. This is a time critical period on take-off and gear retraction must be initiated as soon as possible after lift-off. A Pilot cannot afford the time to loosen his shoulder harness and bend down to activate the landing gear safety latch which then allows the landing gear lever to function. It is common practice for pilots, at this time, to fasten the lap belt but not the shoulder harness, thus allowing freedom of upper body movement. It is not unusual for one landing wheel in a DC-3 aircraft to retract before the other. Under these circumstances, normal retraction, for both wheels, can take anything up to 20 seconds to fully retract with both engines activating their own hydraulic pump. Maximum power must be maintained during this procedure. Landing on one wheel can be disastrous and I was confronted with this possible risk shortly afterwards. On this occasion, however, at approximately 20 seconds after taking off and

---

2 On a DC-3 V_1/V_2 are both at 81 kt (knots) —most multi-engined aeroplanes have different values for these speeds. V_2 is the speed which an aircraft may safely be climbed with one engine inoperative.
3 Take-off Safety Speed—the minimum speed to which an aircraft must be accelerated in establishing the take-off distance required.

Engine Failure—Left Engine

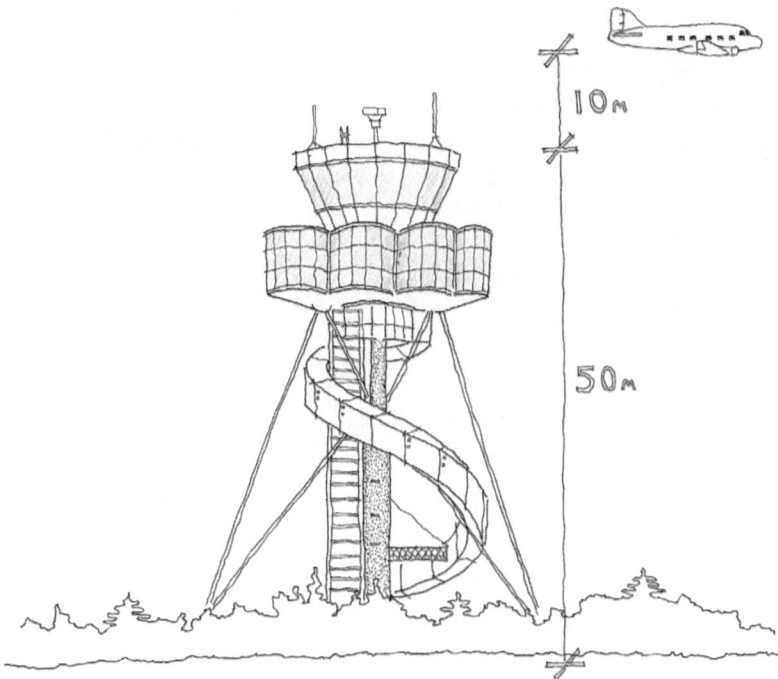

We only climbed approximately 10 m higher than Sydney Control Tower (Nickola Ramsey & Edward Ramsey)

an estimated altitude of 200 ft, whilst travelling in excess of 100 kt, we heard two bangs in quick succession as the left engine failed which was called by the Co-pilot who was flying the aircraft.

'Engine Failure—Left Engine' he confidently called out. I then confirmed, as required by our procedures.

Within my flying career, I had undergone hundreds of simulated engine failures after take-off both in multi-engined aircraft and in simulators covering the DC-3, as well as the anti-submarine P-3B Orion aircraft, Boeing 747, DC-9, AW650 Argosy Freighter, Learjet 35, Cessna Citation Jets and Beechcraft Super King Airs plus numerous other light twin-engined aeroplanes. In fact, on checking my logbooks I have in excess of 500 hours in simulators alone. Simulator time is almost exclusively emergency and abnormal procedures. I believe that a good Pilot is a pessimist, not an optimist. Being a pessimist allows one to be prepared for what could possibly go wrong and anticipate. If a Pilot is not anticipating an engine failure on take-off, then he is not doing his job. Therefore, when the Co-pilot called 'engine failure—left engine', being mentally prepared for such an event, there was

From Hero to Zero

Showing one landing gear retracting quicker than the other (Richard Harris)

no surprise factor. A good analogy is cricketers fielding in the slips position. These fielders are in a crouched position constantly expecting the ball to come off the bat directly to them with their cupped hands ready to catch instantly. If they just stood in position, similar to the outfielders, it would be virtually impossible for them to mentally prepare and then physically position themselves to take a catch.

The aeroplane drifted slightly to the left which is a symptom of the right engine continuing to operate whilst the left engine has failed.

The engine instruments and aircraft's reaction confirmed failure of the left engine and the Engine Failure or Fire (in flight) checklist for flying the aeroplane was carried out as per the company Operations Manual. We had memorised and practised this procedure as there is no time to read a checklist in the initial phase of flight. Phase One (memory recall items) was called by the Pilot Flying and confirmed and actioned by me as Pilot Not Flying, then Phase One (for a second time) and then Phase Two was read, confirmed and actioned from the Operations Manual Checklist. This completed the left-hand engine shutdown. I then looked at the engine to confirm that the propeller had stopped and it appeared to be in the feathered position (but it wasn't). I thought about landing straight back on the same runway we had just taken off from, but my thoughts were that the operations manual states it is mandatory that the Pilot must proceed with the take-off and then add to this the fact that I did not know the position of the landing gear.

'Echo Delta Charlie's got a slight problem. We'll just ah ... standby one' was my radio call to the Control Tower Operator who had sighted something unusual with our aircraft after we took-off.

'Echo Delta Charlie, confirm operations normal?' he radioed back.

'Ah negative, we've got ... just shut down the left engine we'll be returning ah ...' I replied. The aircraft was about 200 ft above the runway and I was presuming that the aircraft could fly under control and return to the airport.

It was during this communication that my 'press-to-talk' thumb switch, positioned on my control wheel stuck 'live' in the transmit position, so the control tower were able to hear and record[4] all further radio transmissions and cockpit conversations.

The flight had lasted just 40 seconds from lift-off, including raising the landing gear and identifying the left engine failure, shutting down the engine and feathering the propeller in sequence and carrying out emergency checklist procedures. When time allowed, I was also advising ATC of my progress though I could hear nothing from them as my microphone was jammed in the 'on position'. As it was, I had been placed in a very challenging situation which demanded my complete attention.

At this stage I fully expected the aeroplane to continue climbing and intended to position it for a left-hand turn, which would have allowed us to return for a safe landing on the east-west runway. All my aircraft performance charts and training indicate that the DC-3 aeroplane should be expected to continue climbing to enable normal management of the aircraft on one of its two engines.

In this emergency, altitude is your friend. At Sydney Airport I was particularly aware of obstacles and the risk of large populations of people in structures such as high-rise buildings. There were also cranes on nearby wharves. The Kurnell Oil Refinery, approximately 5 km to the south, was in my direct line of flight. Therefore, flying at an expected 91 kt meant we would have arrived at Kurnell in approximately 1.5 minutes. If I were able to achieve 50 ft per minute rate of climb, as much later, suggested by the CAA from the safety and security of being behind a desk, I may still have been less than 100 ft above the water. I also took into account the cliffs on the southern side of Kurnell, which are around 200 ft high, to which could be added the height of the Cape Bailey Lighthouse.

Flying straight ahead was an inconceivable option for me and I rejected it whilst considering what I might do.

---

4 In the 1950s a Cockpit Voice Recorder (CVR) was invented to facilitate the recording of cockpit and radio communications of aircraft. This is one component of the two 'black boxes' that aircraft crash investigators seek immediately following an incident. At the time of the ditching this equipment was not a legal requirement.

When flying for optimum performance with a stricken engine, it is essential to slightly bank towards the good engine whilst still flying straight. When the aircraft turns, performance is even further degraded. Lack of height, but more serious, lack of aeroplane performance, as in our situation, can be a recipe for disaster. We were to the left of the runway centreline caused by failure of the left engine. I approached the flight, at that point, as one which was under control, although with limited options.

I TAKE OVER

Suddenly everything changed to being a critically dangerous flight with an unforeseen set of life-threatening circumstances. The aeroplane was not climbing and airspeed was beginning to decrease. The aircraft would not climb even though I was looking at the instruments and seeing all of the *indications* of take-off power which I had previously set for the take-off. The aircraft ought to have been capable of climbing with even lower power than that already set (i.e. full power) and yet it was not doing so.

That is when reality kicked in and the gravity of the situation became clear. The expected power and performance were not there. I immediately reassessed the suddenly changed circumstances. The aircraft was performing as if a drag parachute had been deployed and we were going nowhere but down. Fast! I was mystified as to why the operating right engine wasn't producing full power. The aircraft ought to have climbed away in the configuration we had set, that is wings level, appropriate rudder position and full power being indicated. And yet, the aircraft wouldn't maintain height. This led me to realise I had a partial loss of power on the right engine coupled with a total loss of power on the left engine making it an un-flyable aircraft.

The Co-pilot was flying exactly as I required.

About 50 seconds had passed since lift-off. At this point, every second was crucial and my mind was racing as I tried to weigh my options.

Up to this point, I planned to climb to a safe height and return to the airport but now, I was coping with the fact that the power setting on the right engine 'indicated' take-off power, but the aircraft would not accelerate. In fact, the aircraft was now decelerating and descending. In a situation such as this, maintaining safe airspeed was critical. By now, I estimate approximately 10 seconds had passed during which we identified and shut down the engine, feathered the propeller and told ATC we would be returning. But this was now impossible. Airspeed had decreased alarmingly and I was going to have to make an emergency landing. In the front of my mind was the overpowering recollection of the tragic loss, at this very point on the runway we were departing from. Fourteen years prior a Super King Air[1] had crashed and all 13 people on board, including a one-*week* old *baby, had perished only metres from our current position.* I was utterly determined this was not going to happen to my passengers. The risk of catastrophic fire and immolation were also at the front of my mind. I could envisage this happening with all the fuel in the wing tanks, the oncoming large rock-strewn end of the runway, capable of ripping the fuel tanks apart, plus the position of the retracting wheels being unclear, left me with the safest option of landing in the water under control.

'Taking over,' I declared to Co-pilot Leach and took over the flight controls as the airspeed decreased towards 80 kt while the right-hand engine continued to rotate at indicated full speed but with less than full power. This was not a matter for anyone other than me. It required one hundred percent concentration.

We could not afford to lose more airspeed, so I continued a descent from our low altitude, which was the only option I had to maintain a safe airspeed. I had to trade altitude for airspeed as the aeroplane was not going to stay in the air. Performance was decreasing, and if I lost control of the aeroplane, by allowing it to slow to below controllable airspeed, I was at risk of having the aeroplane roll uncontrollably to the left and nosedive into the water. This would have been a catastrophic manoeuvre.

My first option was to land back on the runway. The landing gear had been selected up after take-off. The DC-3, in normal operations, has one engine-driven hydraulic pump per engine and the landing gear is not mechanically linked together. As the wheels are not directly connected to each other on a DC-3, one wheel will almost always retract or extend before the other. It takes a long time for the cycle to operate and that is with two engine-driven hydraulic pumps working. Right at this time, we were down to one engine-driven hydraulic pump. Could I get both main wheels down and locked and land on the remaining runway without nosediving over the edge? Extremely improbable! The edge was constructed of huge rocks, as large as 1.5 m long,

---

1   Advance Airlines Flight DR4210, Super King Air, registered VH-AAV

The numerous sharp big rocks at the end of the runway (Author's Collection)

arranged so as to break the sea swell and preserve the seawall. Some of these rocks protrude above the level of the runway. This was not a good option for a plane loaded with fuel. If the aeroplane had gone over the edge, it would have been ripped open and fuel tanks probably would have ruptured and exploded. You can imagine the devastation. We had neither the altitude nor performance and therefore no capability to turn around and make it back to any runway. Had I attempted this, we would have crashed well before reaching land.

The second option was to try and make it to the new third runway. We were not aligned with this. The aeroplane did not have the performance to reach it, and as it was still being constructed, it was nowhere near a suitable landing ground. There were vehicles and mounds of dirt/sand, and equipment everywhere. This most certainly was not a viable option.

My third and last option was to carry out a controlled ditching. The aeroplane's altitude and airspeed were still decreasing. Remember, this was all happening in a matter of seconds. I was extremely conscious of the fact that I must maintain control of the aeroplane. To lose that control meant the risk of a fatal crash.

My brain was analysing 20 plus years of flying experience together with other aircraft accident reports and outcomes within literally milliseconds. At this point, because of my Orion flying experience, it became obvious that the safest outcome was a controlled ditching, for which I had received extensive training in the RAAF.

Having made that decision with a silent left-hand engine and an incapable right-hand engine, at less than 100 ft (30 m) above the water, I then totally concentrated on a positive outcome after selecting a suitable ditching site, configuring and positioning the aeroplane. This required me to ensure that the aircraft touched down at the absolute slowest safe speed possible, just above 60 kt^2. Lowering flaps allows a slower approach speed whilst at all times making sure of my use of the right rudder pedal to maintain wings level. These two factors were also directed not only to slow speed, which would allow me to retain as much control as possible until we made contact with the water, but also to control the rate of descent onto the water to the lowest possible amount whilst maintaining the nose of the aircraft clear of the water until after the body of the aircraft had touched down. I applied aileron on the control wheel to allow gentle manoeuvring of the aeroplane to avoid a small watercraft which was in my pathway by initially veering left, followed by right to align with my chosen ditching path.

If I lost control by losing airspeed, the left wing would drop, hit the water and the aeroplane would cartwheel. Again devastation; certainly serious injuries and more probably loss of life. I was astounded at the rate of loss of airspeed and altitude.

Andrew, quite rightly, remained silent during the emergency. I directed the Co-pilot to lower the flaps. This all happened fast. I was totally preoccupied at this stage of the emergency with maintaining control of the aeroplane. There was no time to direct our flight attendant or passengers to adopt the brace position, nor to advise the tower with a mayday radio call. I relied on the fact that I had left the seatbelt sign in the 'on' position and expected our flight attendant to require the passengers to prepare for an emergency landing. Andrew turned and signalled the flight attendant with a thumbs down to signify the severity of the situation.

Once the aeroplane was ideally set up only a few feet above the water, I closed the throttle, raised the nose slightly to arrest the rate of descent, readying the aircraft attitude for impact. I remember thinking to myself that the

---

2   The laws of physics determine that the force of impact increases with the square of the increase in speed. If you double the speed you increase the force of impact four times.

Sketch depicting aircraft attitude just prior to ditching (Author's Collection)

aeroplane perspective was very low. Normally prior to landing, the cockpit would be around 15 ft (4 m) off the ground and we were now a mere 6 ft (2 m) off the water. We splashed down an astonishing 76 seconds after take-off. Out of those 76 seconds, only 46 seconds were available after the engine failed. To put this timeframe into perspective, the average person takes 45 seconds to brush their teeth. I reiterate I had only 46 seconds from the engine failing to landing on the water.

The aircraft, in fact, touched down at the optimum speed and rate of descent and came to an abrupt halt within just a few metres. It did not skip nor sink. The aeroplane slewed around to the right as the spinning propeller acted like a huge disc dragging in the water. Remember, as the left propeller was feathered, it offered very little drag in the water.

My head struck the windscreen on impact. Andrew suffered a cut to his left ear. The Co-pilot fortunately did not sustain any injuries. A bow wave came up over the nose, windscreen and along the top of the cabin causing water to flow down past the cabin windows affording the illusion that we had submerged. The aeroplane swung approximately 90° to the right and settled on a westerly heading with the tail less than 50 m from the western side edge of the new runway which was at that time under construction. The fire warning bell was ringing as was the landing gear warning horn. I completed the relevant shutdown and evacuation checklist, silenced the fire warning bell, but felt frustrated that even by turning the battery master switch off I could not silence the landing gear warning horn. The Co-pilot advised it was because the aeroplane's electrical system had shorted out.

I turned around to look back into the cabin to check how our passengers had

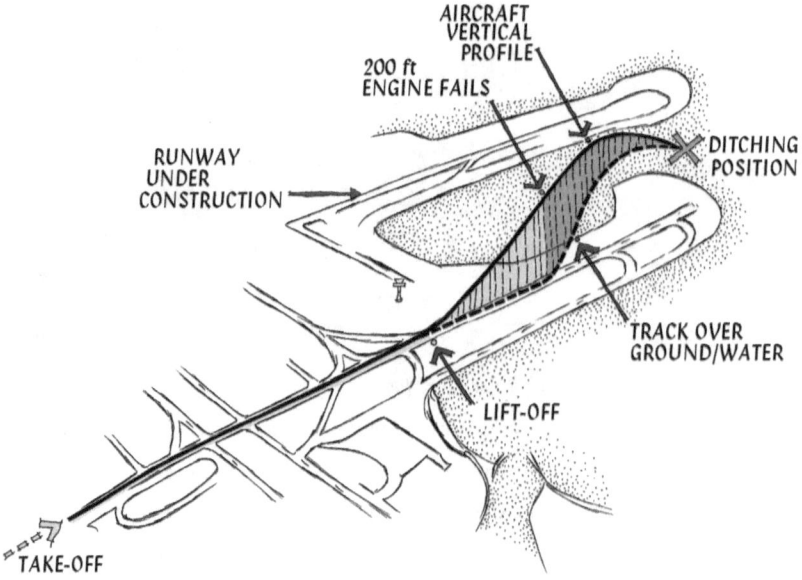

3D presentation of our track and flight path (Nickola Ramsey & Edward Ramsey)

faired in the ditching expecting to see carnage; bodies and limbs strewn everywhere. Instead, I saw the passengers standing up and calmly putting on their life jackets. Some of the boys were even laughing as if it was all a big adventure! I experienced an overwhelming feeling of relief. Only seconds before I was reliving within myself the tragic devastation of the Super King Air crash that had occurred nearby. To be able to see my passengers up and mobile and so very calm, was the most rewarding sight I could have wished for.

Contrary to all media reports, Co-pilot Leach exited the aeroplane via the overhead hatch, as was captured in this book's front cover photograph. He walked along the top of the fuselage onto the right tailplane and was taken off by a pleasure boat without even getting wet. He took with him the red aeroplane flight folder containing the aeroplane's maintenance release form, charter documents and other non-operational paperwork. Though under my command, his decision to leave was his own initiative and thankfully I had a very capable supernumerary Pilot, Andrew, to assist me in the evacuation of passengers and crew in his absence.

I then turned my attention to assist the passengers. I ordered Andrew to 'get out, get everybody out' he immediately proceeded to the cabin to help the passengers and ensure they were donning their lifejackets correctly and prepared them to exit the aeroplane via the main cabin doors on the left side.

I Take Over

Passengers evacuating the ditched aircraft (Newspix)

By that time the passengers had positioned themselves towards the rear of the aircraft and had begun to inflate the life rafts. Thanks to their quick thinking, the life rafts were now ready for use. Small pleasure boats soon arrived from everywhere—greatly assisting us by caring for the passengers and taking them safely to shore. I was delighted to see that some of the boys did not even wet their feet.

I remember looking out the left side cockpit window and seeing some engine cowls (covers) ripped back or missing. The top of the right wing was well above the water level. The right engine had been ripped from the airframe during the impact and the aeroplane, due to the imbalance of weight, was sitting in the water, left wing low.

Once it appeared that all of the passengers had alighted, I then proceeded through the cabin to the rear door, double-checking that nobody remained onboard. At this stage, I was becoming concerned at the rate with which water was entering the cabin. There were times when pleasure craft could get close enough to the passengers to allow them to just step straight into their boats, but by the time Andrew and I had completed our duties, none were in close proximity. As we were now concerned that the aeroplane was on the verge of sinking, we jumped into the water and swam to a nearby vacant life raft which had been deployed by passengers. By then, all the passengers had been picked up by pleasure boats, so the life rafts were unoccupied. I would estimate that it was less than 2 minutes before all passengers had evacuated the aircraft. I must commend all the passengers, Andrew and Annabel for their coolness and purposeful actions in a genuinely life-threatening environment.

Although we made sure that the passengers had donned their life jackets prior to exiting the aeroplane, the flight crew had not, due to time constraints and our primary concern had been the passenger's safety. A funny thing I remember from my Pilot training is that when you carry out a wet dingy drill that involved life jacket use and life raft competency, it was always fairly hard to get into a life raft. Not so in the real-life situation. I believe I would have put a performing seal to shame.

Andrew and I were in the same raft and I commented to him that this would be just my luck to be stuck in a raft with only him. We have a similar sense of humour. It was only a short time before a pleasure boat took us on board and proceeded, at lightning speed, in a westerly direction to get us across the bay for medical attention. All of the other crew and passengers had been taken in an easterly direction to the new runway. My four-bar epaulettes should have made it obvious that I was the Captain as I protested loudly that as survivors of an air crash, we had to stay at the accident site as a group until all were accounted for. The driver appeared to not understand English too well. Eventually, one of his crew convinced him to turn around and take us back to the new runway where rescue equipment and personnel awaited us.

In the meantime, Andrew had procured a mobile phone and calmly called his wife, Stacey, to let her know the situation. After the call, Andrew told me that Stacey had a premonition about the flight and begged and pleaded with him many times not to go. I have since told Stacey that her begging was wasted on Andrew; she should have told me!

* * *

One of the reasons I ditched where I did was that I thought the survivors could make their way up the seawall of the new runway to safety. It was only when our boat took us in that direction that I realised the seawall was a 3 metre vertical concrete wall. It also has another horizontal section protruding out over the sea acting as a wave deflector. Pity the poor survivors of an accident, especially anyone incapacitated. In fact, the firemen who were waiting to attend to us once we arrived had to anchor their ladders and then put them over the edge for us to climb up out of the rescue boat. At the time

I Take Over

The gracious lady gives a final salute (Newspix)

there were no crash boats in operation at Sydney Airport. I believe that years before there had been at least one.

The aeroplane did not sink immediately as it took significant time for the air inside the huge wings to be displaced with seawater. This combined with little damage to the underside of the entire aeroplane, gave us the time we needed to evacuate. I estimate the plane floated for around 15 to 20 minutes before giving one final salute, with her right wing raised vertically, prior to slipping below the surface.

Although it appeared that 'EDC had failed, it was the system that failed her.

It was so sad to witness the end of one of the majestic DC-3 aircraft, which has such a central part in the history of air travel.

* * *

Earlier, after seeing us taxi out, Helen had proceeded to drive home to Camden. When almost home, she heard a newsflash on the radio that an aeroplane had crashed at Sydney Airport. Obviously, on the law of probability, she deduced that it was probably our flight. She then drove to Camden Police Station asking if they would drive her back to the airport as

The old girl peeks from below the surface (Andrew Buxton)

she felt too distressed to drive. They declined, so Helen drove herself back and eventually tracked me down at the St George Hospital where the flight crew had been taken. I feel compelled to mention that all emergency services were fantastic, as were the hospital staff. One of the nurses prepared me for an injection.

'But I'm not injured' I protested.

'No, but you've been in Botany Bay,' she replied before proceeding to jab me.

Helen drove me home that afternoon. Before leaving the hospital, we tried to see Annabel, who had suffered a broken wrist, but were not allowed as she was being treated at the time. Although I am in no way religious, during the drive home my thoughts were that I had just carried out my purpose in life. It sounds strange to say it, but it was the only way I could sum up my feelings. I cannot bring to mind what we discussed during that journey, but it was on the way that Helen provided the words for *Rod's Swan Song* to the tune of Jimmy Cliff's I Can See Clearly Now. You can read the lyrics on my website (www.FromHeroToZero.com.au).

My divorce to my first wife Leone had been extremely bitter and unpleasant and I had not seen my children for at least five years. You can imagine my surprise and pleasure when my two eldest children, Gary and Kylie (in their early 20s at this time) turned up at my home to see me that very evening. They stayed for around an hour and then left. I was extremely hopeful that as I'd come close to death, they may reassess our relationship and wish to be close to me again. Unfortunately, this was not to be, not for want of trying on my behalf. Too much influence had been bestowed upon them without my

I Take Over

Emerging from her watery grave (Andrew Buxton)

'EDC recovery (Fairfax Media)

side of the story ever being told or asked for. Their visit had not been the time to discuss this and I was never given another chance.

Late evening, approximately 12 hours after the accident, Mr Leach Snr, John Lymbery and Bruce Ibbotson visited our home in Camden to inform us that, due to this accident, they had been to their hangar to get the paperwork ready for the investigation.

I was astonished, and to this day, cannot understand how Geoff Leach the 'EDC Co-pilot's father, and one of the owners of the aircraft, had literally witnessed his own son crash, only to then leave the Hawker Pacific departure area immediately afterwards. At no time did I see him visit his son in the hospital.

The following day my two younger children, Mark and Kris rang me. It was a brief but very much appreciated phone call.

A PILOT'S EYE VIEW OF FAILED ENGINES AND A DITCHING

I had reviewed the engine documentation, which was presented to me before the flight. That was all I was required to look at and review. There was nothing on that report which could have alerted me to the double engine failure that was about to occur. The Captain of a flight is required only to be presented with signed current maintenance documentation indicating all is in order. That was the case for this flight. The problem lay hidden behind documents, which I was entitled to accept on face value. I had no option but to accept the engineer's release of the aircraft for flight.

The problem that arose came from two sources: the left engine which obviously failed, compounded by its propeller that had failed to feather. This provided a windmill like dragging effect, which caused a braking or drag effect on the airframe. On the other side of the aircraft was an engine, which was simply not delivering the power which it ought to have done. Although the instruments indicated normal operation and the controls for the engine were all correctly positioned, the fact was that the engine did not deliver the power that could be expected. This immediately indicated that the engine had something wrong with it. It was defective.

* * *

Three years after the accident I obtained documents from the Bureau of Air Safety Investigation (BASI—now called the Air Transportation Safety Board (ATSB)) investigation stating that numerous spark plugs were defective. These documents even admitted that the spark plugs were tampered with before being tested. A spark plug requires to be both clean and the gap over which the spark is to travel, set at a particular distance, even though it is only a few millimetres. For the plugs to have been cleaned and reset by

BASI to the manufacturer's recommended distance for sparking, prior to testing, whether they worked in an engine or not, interfered with any proper test of that spark plug's capacity to ignite fuel in the engine. As it happens, after alteration and testing, eleven of the twenty-eight spark plugs so tested were still found to be defective on the right engine. It is unknown which of the others would have failed for being too dirty and/or not properly opened to the required gap for the spark to jump. This clearly points to the fact that the engine was incapable of delivering the horsepower necessary to hold the aircraft in the air.

Implausibly the official public BASI report states: Right engine—'With the exception of the propeller governor, no pre-existing abnormalities were found.'

The DC-3 aircraft operates by use of a propeller system known as variable pitch or constant speed. Both words refer to the same activity, namely the capability of the blades of the propeller to turn towards the oncoming air. As the aircraft gathers speed the air approaches the aircraft faster and faster and so the propeller turns towards the onrushing air to force the air backwards and drive the aircraft forwards.

The instruments which the Pilot sees tell only of the fact that the propeller pitch angle can vary, not what the limits of variability may be and those limits can stealthily arise because of engine limitations such as ineffective spark plugs. In fact, there can be quite serious power shortfalls which do not show up on any of the instruments available to the Pilot, even with the pre-flight checks where the engine will undergo settings of increased power and speed. Those increased power settings have only limited effectiveness. In this case, they revealed nothing. They can only be identified by mechanical testing.

The left-hand engine failed and the propeller did not move to the feather position as it is designed to do. The subsequent report concerning the left-hand propeller showed that it jammed, partially feathered. A feathered propeller is one where the Pilot causes the propeller blades to move as far as practical to stand parallel to the airflow which drastically reduces the drag on the airframe. That did not occur in this case with the left-hand propeller, despite the fact that I had pushed the appropriate feathering button. It later transpired that there was a mechanical failure preventing this from occurring.

The aircraft at best, when it was slightly above the height of the Sydney Control Tower on its track above the runway, was plainly unable to do more

A Pilot's Eye View of Failed Engines and a Ditching

than reach a landing point within a few hundred metres. Height was frighteningly low and power was astonishingly weak.

The site of the horrific King Air crash on the seawall where 13 people lost their lives was only a few hundred metres from where we ditched. I had actually landed at Sydney Airport about an hour or so after that event and the sombre atmosphere at the airport at that time was overwhelming. I presume that is why it had such a lasting effect on me and was so influential in my thought process when preparing to ditch. I was deeply moved and felt a great sense of relief that I had managed the aircraft and saved the lives of all onboard.

Recently I located a copy of 'Pilot's Flight Operating Instructions C-47 Airplane' (the military version of the DC-3) issued by the United States Army Air Forces in 1942. Interestingly it states:

> 'The first impact of the tail can be mistaken for the shock against which they (crew) are on guard, but it will be followed by greater shock as the nose strikes the water after a correct three-point tail-down ditching.' We complied with this.

> 'Use of Flaps. - The flaps should be lowered to reduce the speed at which the airplane can approach and touch down. It is better to use a medium setting and not to lower them fully …' After the aircraft was recovered, the flaps were found to be lowered to approximately 22° which was very close to optimum lift of 18°.

> 'Touch down. - Apart from choosing the best point at which to ditch, the Pilot should hold off until he loses all excess speed above the stall and so strike the sea at the normal three-point landing attitude.' This was achieved.

There was no way I knew what position the landing gear was in after the gear has been selected up. In this case only one engine-driven hydraulic pump was operating. In this timeframe I was not afforded the time to go through the visual checks—I was hoping they were fully retracted, but uncertain.

When events do not go according to expectation and option analysis removes access to conventional pathways, advice such as the following extract from a flight manual may become more relevant:

> 'This manual provides the best possible operating instructions, however, on occasions, these instructions may prove to be a poor substitute for sound judgement. Multiple emergencies, adverse

weather, terrain and other considerations may require modification of the procedures.'

All the ditching practices I carried out in the RAAF as a Pilot on Orion aeroplanes came flooding back. At opportune times, when I was Captain and the workload deemed it suitable, I would instigate a practise ditching. I would do this by calling over the public address system on the Orion, 'Practice, practice, practice, ditching in 5 minutes!' The whole crew of around 12 to 13 members would then prepare by carrying out their individually allocated duties. In the cockpit, we would simulate the sea level at an arbitrary figure of as low as 500 ft. This way we would configure the aeroplane in the proper configuration of landing gear retracted, full flaps, heading to accommodate wind and sea state conditions with an airspeed of 1.1 x Vs (10% above stalling speed). More often than not, we would have one engine shut down to conserve fuel and if so, the aeroplane would be asymmetrically powered with one engine operating on the left and two operating on the right. This training was invaluable.

Due to the age of DC-3s, it was not required to be fitted with a Flight Data Recorder (black box) or cockpit voice recorder. Pushing either propeller feather button activates an independent electric oil pump, via an electrical solenoid, which then produces high-pressure oil, pushing against a piston in the propeller hub. This then causes the propeller blades to rotate parallel (edge on or feathered position) to the air flow reducing their drag to a minimum. Visually I had checked that the propeller had stopped, and it *appeared* to be in the feathered position. This proved subsequently not to be the case. Due to the circumstances of this engine failure, time did not allow me the privilege of spending precious seconds evaluating the blade angle.

Pilots are taught from initial stages of training that the order of priorities in an emergency is to Aviate, Navigate, Communicate. This can mean the difference between life and death. My radio transmissions to the control tower were, to say the least, brief, concise and to the point. I did not make a mayday radio call due to time constraints, but I was well aware that the tower operator knew the nature of our emergency.

The last airspeed reading, I noted prior to impact, was just above stall speed and I remember being very pleased with it. Impact forces are directly related to impact speed. For example, one half of the impact speed equates to one-quarter of the impact forces. The slower the speed on splashdown, the lower the impact force. I believe the point of splashdown was abeam the southern end of the new incomplete third runway on the western side, approximately 50 m from the edge.

In the final BASI report, released in March 1996, nearly two years after the crash, BASI on numerous occasions, reported events in an intimidating way by using the phrase 'unapproved charts' after the CAA admitted that the charts in the Groupair Operations Manual were approved (as per its letter dated 22nd April 1993).

From Hero to Zero

THE RISE TO HERO STATUS

Obviously, immediately after the accident all media coverage portrayed me as a hero for having saved the lives of everyone on board. I never saw myself as a hero—just a Pilot doing what I was trained to do. I was dealt a set of circumstances that were never envisaged—a ditching immediately after take-off. I was quietly pleased that the media acknowledged these exceptional circumstances and very proud of my actions that day in such a time limited incident. This acknowledgement was totally unexpected but appreciated.

We may have landed safely and without physical injury, but the time following the accident is when I felt the full brunt of the emotional turmoil that was to torment me for many years. Chief Inspector Kevin Rafferty of Mascot Police Station handled himself and the situation extremely professionally. His media interviews were accurate and watching a person of this calibre supporting my efforts was very rewarding and comforting, especially when everybody else was trying to blame me. I am eternally grateful for his words of support.

After any air crash, there are always armchair critics (self-appointed experts) who will presume pilot error without knowing the full facts. I was extremely disappointed to hear that a well-known aviation insurance broker suggested I had shut down the wrong engine. How these people feel they can make judgements with such unfounded remarks, but without accountability, astonishes me.

I received a phone call about two days after the accident from a government health service asking if I required counselling[1]. I declined, stating I felt fine but asked if they could send someone to see my mother in South

---

1 Counselling in this reference is understood by the psychology industry to mean assisting people with trauma and emotional issues, whereas counselling within the CAA means correcting a Pilot's misdemeanours and ensuring the Pilot understands and can comply with its requirements i.e. correct use of take-off charts, weight charts etc.

Australia. The afternoon of the accident I rang my Mum, who was 81 years old at the time, and told her what had happened. She said something like; 'That's nice, dear.' So, I knew the seriousness had not sunk in, but once the news was all over the TV and newspapers, I knew it would impact her then, so it was prudent that she received help. When the health service went and visited her the morning after, I was very appreciative.

THE FALL TO ZERO STATUS

As urged by Tony Hannam's foreword at the beginning of this book, I also strongly suggest you read the testimonials at the end of the book before reading any further. It is very important for you to know and understand my aviation reputation before I was attacked and ruined.

* * *

Obviously after the ditching, I, more than anybody, wanted to know the reasons behind the aeroplane failure. I initially cooperated to the fullest with both the CAA and BASI. I answered all of their questions to the best of my knowledge. It only took a few days to comprehend that these departments were being very selective in the information they chose to report on. I kept reiterating how I couldn't work out how the aeroplane would not climb on one engine as it should have. These authorities would not even contemplate this avenue.

The aeroplane's documentation including, but not limited to, the flight plan, load sheet, trim sheet and passenger manifest, ended up in the possession of the BASI investigators as is protocol. At the BASI interview that week, when I was asked about time compression, I commented that in the period of the emergency, time did not appear to slow down, in fact just the opposite, it appeared to accelerate. It all just happened so fast.

Prior to take-off on the day of the accident, I believed we were carrying only twenty-four people in total for this flight. The Scots College band leader's wife had been allowed to board without my knowledge or permission and her name was not listed on my passenger manifest. As Captain, I was in the cockpit when the passengers boarded. It was only later in the evening of the ditching, after media reports started surfacing, that I was made aware that we had actually been carrying twenty-five people. On 18th December 1995, some nineteen months later, BASI requested Hawker Pacific, Sydney Airport to compile a passenger list which was sent to them via facsimile. What was very interesting is that passenger number twenty-five had an annotation alongside her name stating 'not on passenger list'. This is a fact that I have been adamant about since the time of the accident. All television footage and interviews showed me talking about the total number of persons on board to be twenty-four. As this book goes to print, twenty-five years later, I still do not know who authorised her passage, why my permission wasn't sought and why I wasn't informed. My task, as Pilot in command, is to conduct the flight within the parameters of the information given to me, whether it be passenger manifest, actual aircraft weight, weather briefings and appropriate notice to airmen (NOTAM) which show any en-route conditions which may affect the flight. It was the responsibility of the person in charge of passenger loading to advise me of the extra passenger. This did not happen.

In addition to this and unbeknown to me until after the accident, Co-pilot Leach had loaded extra tools and equipment onto the aeroplane. This compromised my calculation of 127 kg below MTOW to the Bureau of Air Safety Investigation's claim of weight being 562 kg above MTOW. The BASI report claims that the total passenger weight was 221 kg above the standard weights I was permitted to use by the CAA. It was also estimated by them that the fuel weighed 83 kg more than I had calculated. These two facts alone were unsupported errors in the report—my calculated fuel weight was the amount I was planning to carry out to sea to Lord Howe Island: it was accurate.

My passenger weight calculation was a wholly permitted and normal process authorised by the CAA[1] and used for flights with multiple passengers. This prevents the inconvenience of individual mass weighing at embarkation when the passenger load and its consequences would require to be obtained and calculated. Taking these errors into account, more than 300 kg of the BASI's alleged weight has been added without justification. It must also be noted that the flight simulation carried out in the Netherlands, some twenty years later, demonstrated that in a single engine (take-off power) flight, the alleged overweight had no negative impact on flying ability. However, due to 'EDC's seriously compromised right-hand engine, adequate power could not be delivered to hold the aircraft in the air.

---

1 CAAP 235

From Hero to Zero

'EDC back on dry land (Fairfax media)

The initial BASI interview was held on 27th April 1994, at the Novotel Hotel at Brighton Le Sands. Sydney. It was conducted by Barry Linard (BASI) and in attendance was Wing Commander John Thynne who was at the time Directorate of Flying Safety, RAAF. The interview was tape recorded with my consent. However, I never received a copy of the interview. I remember commenting numerous times that even JATO (Jet Assisted Take-Off) rockets would not have kept this aeroplane in the air. When the engine failure occurred, it just felt like a drag parachute had been deployed, pulling us down to earth and then the aeroplane became 'un-flyable', so drastic quick action was required to ensure passenger safety and survivability.

John Thynne told me outside the interview room that he had listened to the control tower tape, which was quite informative, (as my microphone 'press-to-talk' thumb switch had stuck in the live position), allowing what was said in the cockpit to be transmitted over the radio. I guess you could say that this was the DC-3 equivalent of a CVR (cockpit voice recorder). John, who was obviously involved with numerous air crashes/incidents, commented that this recording contained the best example of crew resource management (CRM) he had ever heard under these unique circumstances.

It was a pity that John Thynne was asked to leave the investigation on the second day. I questioned John about the BASI investigation and he said that his line of thinking about the cause of the accident had not agreed with

The Fall to Zero Status

BASI's. I felt so alone. John had studied the facts of the case and concluded that my decision was both timely and accurately carried out. This was a great help to me in what appeared to be a disbelieving CAA response.

After the ditching there was total disarray and utter confusion within the CAA regarding the question of take-off charts, Civil Aviation Orders (CAOs) and Airworthiness Directives (ADs) applicable to the DC-3 aircraft. Particularly, the directive in question had not been issued to pilots at that time and in fact one CAA staff member stated that he was not even aware of this directive until after the accident.

Colin Torkington, Manager Airworthiness, sent an electronic memo to George Macionis, head of CAA Safety, on 26th April 1994 confirming details of the DC-3 involved in the accident. He acknowledged the Extended-Range Twin-Engine Operational Standards (ETOPS) were conflicting.

Further confusion within the CAA arose over the subject of ETOPS. They admitted that operators could believe that it did not apply to DC-3 operations, even suggesting that the CAA take up a position stating that this was not a factor in this particular accident.

They admitted there was a communication problem between Flying Operations and Airworthiness as to what the correct performance charts were.

Barry Linard, BASI Investigator, was supportive in his investigation when he wrote that he believed the flight planning and preparation had been thorough and further went on to say that he would not like to level any criticism at the crew as in his book they had done an outstanding job. He also could not explain why the aircraft could not climb away even if slightly overweight—this was a view shared by a particular CAA representative conversant with DC-3 aircraft.

Four days after the accident, Andrew indicated he wanted to get back on the horse. He hired a Beechcraft Duchess, a small four-seater twin-engined aeroplane, which he piloted, and invited me to go along for the trip. To get back and enjoy the feeling that we gain from flying was fantastic therapy for both of us, and just what we needed. We had a great time. Later that day I was asked to deliver a Navajo aeroplane from Sydney Airport to Bankstown Airport, and so naturally invited Andrew to come along. We caught the train into town which was a little noisy so when I said something to Andrew, he couldn't hear and leant towards me pulling his ear to indicate he couldn't hear me. Immediately, his face showed he had caused himself excruciating pain. He had forgotten about the stitches on the top of his ear from the injury he sustained in the accident. As he pulled himself off the ceiling of the train, I was literally rolling with laughter. Isn't that what friends are for?

The following day, I was requested to attend another interview with the CAA representative. I had accurately suspected that our interview was secretly recorded, as later I would see his transcript of our meeting though a copy was never afforded me. I was accompanied by another experienced Pilot. At this interview, I distinctly remember this CAA representative saying that he was not concerned if it was within 10% of MTOW (BASI allege that I was 4.7% above the MTOW). He was paranoid over the fact that I could not remember doing the normal things accomplished in a flight such as the normal checklists, the pre-take-off briefing, raising the landing gear after take-off, etc. I could recall the abnormal events of the flight, but most of the normal procedures I had trouble recalling, although I was confident and can assure the reader that I complied and actioned all checklists. The aggressive way he behaved in this interview was out of all proportion. A major disaster had been averted and he was badgering me about procedures that are deeply embedded in my flying technique. In further retrospect, I know that I carried out all the appropriate actions, even if in the heat of an aggressive disbelieving atmosphere, I could not identify them item by item. Throughout my entire flying career I have never cut corners in aircraft operations in any shape or form, including for monetary gain, to save time or even when requested by high level CEOs. Safety has always been paramount to me.

Sometime later, I chatted with a clinical psychologist over this matter, and she reassured me that it was quite normal to not remember the repetitious actions we do in life. It was the unusual that stood out.

* * *

Although I had been kept up to date in regard to Annabel's condition, Helen and I visited her at the hospital the Friday afternoon following the accident. She was improving but I thought I would try and cheer her up, as only I could do. During our visit, Annabel told me that Co-pilot Leach, who was a long-time personal friend of hers, had told her that as soon as we were airborne she could undo her seatbelt, which, unfortunately, she did! Annabel's relay of this action shocked me as I was not aware that safety procedures in the operations manual were not being adhered too. If I had been made aware of this, I certainly would have immediately rectified this unauthorised and dangerous

The Scots College presentation (Author's Collection)

advice. In retrospect, after being catapulted over some rows of seats as the aircraft impacted the sea, she was very fortunate to have only suffered a broken wrist. All others wearing their seatbelt were fortunate to have only suffered minor cuts and bruises as described in the multiple television media coverage. Annabel was the only one to sustain what BASI considered a serious injury, in its report. Annabel's mother was also visiting at that time, so it was appropriate for us all to meet up to support her.

That evening, our crew, sadly minus Annabel, were invited by the members of The Scots College to attend a barbecue given in our honour. We were presented with commemorative plaques which made me feel very proud of what I had accomplished. I took the opportunity to explain what actually happened in the cockpit, from the Pilot's point of view, in this unique event. I felt this was imperative due to the gravity of the situation. Had I not explained, then the misinformation that was circulating in the media would have overridden the truth of what really happened. There was criticism that ranged from my not giving the 'prepare to brace' command to being accused of being the one pictured on the tail of the aeroplane leaving the aircraft immediately after the accident. As previously mentioned, I was actually in the aeroplane meticulously concentrating on my first duty which was to ensure passenger safety. This was followed by the safe and orderly evacuation of all my passengers and crew before I even considered leaving. That evening was the one and only personal contact I ever had with The

Scots College since the ditching even though on numerous occasions I faxed them with further details which were not ever acknowledged. On reflection over the years, recently exacerbated by the 'Sully' ditching in the Hudson River and the subsequent portrayal of that event, it has always saddened me that my relationship has been so remote from my passengers. However, I take great comfort knowing that they all survived to go on to have families of their own.

* * *

The emotional isolation I felt was probably the hardest thing to deal with. Well-meaning friends, who had no clue as to what I was experiencing, could only offer the most thoughtless, insensitive, not to mention infuriating, glib such as; 'You'll get over it'. Under no circumstances should these words be uttered to anyone who has suffered a traumatic experience, be it a family tragedy, accident or whatever. Believe me, you don't get over it! A good and supportive friend just listens and doesn't comment. Advice isn't what you need at this time. Support, without judgement, means everything. I've learnt to control my thoughts, but you never get over it and it takes its toll on your family and friends. My wife Helen supported me throughout the court proceedings, but it finally took its toll when she finally said: 'Can't we go a day without you mentioning it?' I'm sure the accident and the maltreatment by the bureaucracy in the aftermath was a factor in our marriage breakup.

Sadly, I'm sure the CAA had no comprehension or acknowledgement of human factors. This then continued when they totally disregarded my reputation, integrity and self-worth by completely ignoring the personal side of an accident. Such pressure has to take its toll somewhere—more often than not it comes down to your personal relationship with your partner as they are living the nightmare with you. Here am I telling the truth and expecting to be believed and understood, and instead they dissected, twisted and selected the facts. I felt I had been thrown into a pack of wolves and was now fighting for my survival.

COUNSELLING/SUSPENSION

Counselling is generally understood to be a discussion with a person with psychological or other training to deal with the stress or aftermath of a worrying event. The aviation industry uses the word with a different meaning, namely that the person is assumed to have done something wrong and a government officer will conduct some form of fault-based interview. Thus, when I was invited to engage in counselling, I declined because I was, and remained convinced, that there was nothing that I had done in the entire flight that justified any form of reprimand dressed up as counselling.

Five weeks after the ditching, I received a letter from a CAA representative, requesting, that I contact them to arrange a counselling meeting as a matter of urgency. It came across that the counselling meeting was not out of concern of my emotional state after the accident, but to see whether during the counselling it became apparent that there was clear evidence that serious regulatory breaches may have occurred, hence I may incriminate myself. The CAA representative also stated that, in his opinion, if I attended the CAA version of counselling, I would be admitting liability! Hence, I sought legal advice from Laurie Gruzman QC who advised me that as I had nothing to account for, I should not attend. Although this was in agreement with the CAA representative's opinion, he later advised me that if I didn't attend the counselling session, they would have to consider suspending my licence thereby terminating all current and future employment related to flying. On the other hand, he was saying he could fully understand why I didn't want to admit liability. As far as I was concerned, there was no liability. I had done everything right and everybody had lived to tell the tale. The CAA representative himself felt that the CAA letter to me could have been framed better. I personally considered this to be bullying, harassment and intimidation. To report that I had been counselled would have informed every Pilot and bureaucrat that I had done something wrong.

Early in June on a Channel 9 Newsbreak, the presenter stunned me when he reported that the preliminary BASI report found that there had been no engine failure. This was soul destroying and upset my family and friends enormously. In their final report, nearly two years later, they confirmed a substantial power loss to the left engine. This again shows the casual and chaotic way BASI reported.

In mid-June 1994, a CAA representative sent a memo, in part, to the CAA Investigator stating that he was prepared to make a positive statement that he was fully confident in my professional competence to safely exercise the full privileges of my licence under the condition that I be counselled on the use of performance charts on the DC-3 aircraft and the method of calculating all-up weight on the DC-3 aircraft. The only area where he disagreed was whether or not to give me another chance at counselling.

This memo and its contents were never forwarded to me. Had I been made aware of the memo perhaps I would have agreed to speak to the CAA and delve a little further into its intentions—it was some years later before I sighted a copy of it. It became up to me to prove otherwise and of course I was on the spot. The CAA were not. It is a very unpleasant position to be in when I emphatically deny any wrongdoing. Had the subsequent allegations been upheld using untruthful reasoning, punishment could have resulted in the suspension or cancellation of my licence, hence I would have lost my livelihood and my reputation. Had this happened, I would never have worked as a Pilot again (my chosen and passionate field). This borders on guilty until proven innocent. No amount of counselling could change the outcome—as what I carried out on the day was correct—there was nothing to answer for. The inept CAA representatives, the prejudiced investigators, the failure to conduct a proper mechanical enquiry, the amazing behaviour of the Co-pilot, the naivety of the CAA, the bias against the Pilot and the lack of organised care for me and the crew should be remarked on. It is terribly concerning that the CAA was spending so much time on blaming the pilots, an easy target, when a clear, untainted and fresh mind would see that the first thing to settle, obviously, would be to make sure that the aircraft was operating properly. This is what should be expected, particularly in light of the fact that I had constantly reiterated that the aircraft could not continue flight.

The pilots can only react to what they are given. In this case it took years for anyone to actually find out the real cause, but the question of blame on the pilots got underway very quickly.

* * *

After approximately two months laying on the seabed after it was torn off in the impact by the rotating operating propeller, the right engine was recovered from Botany Bay. It should have been raised immediately after the accident as the proof of this engine's condition was crucial to the cause of the accident and why the aeroplane lacked performance. Remember, this is the engine that should have kept us in the air.

* * *

It was 24th June, nine weeks after the accident, when the CAA sent a fax to my home late on a Friday afternoon notifying me of the suspension of one of my Pilot's licences and DC-3 endorsement and advising me of a requirement to undertake a written examination and flight test in the interests of the safety of air navigation. What I cannot understand is that if I was such a danger that it had to suspend my DC-3 licence, why was I still permitted to fly Boeing 747s, Learjets and other aircraft? This action made a mockery of the entire CAA administration. It saw fit to allow me to fly an aeroplane carrying over 300 passengers yet disabled me from flying an aeroplane capable of carrying up to 32 passengers! This felt like more intimidation and harassment.

This was by far the worst day of my life. I believed that my flying experience, skill and ability had saved twenty-five lives from tragic results, and this was the way the Authority thanked me.

After reading the letter of suspension, I was feeling such anger, despair and disbelief, that I walked outside our house just shaking my head and staring at the ground. I felt at such a low point, I could have ended my life then and there. The contemplation was very real. How could these chair-bound, after-the-fact management critics, with the luxury of sitting in air-conditioned offices, drinking coffee, taking all the time in the world, dare judge and condemn me. They discarded my recall of factual events which took place in just 46 seconds. I was in the aeroplane, they were not! They chose to ignore the status of the engines, the management of the aircraft (with what were obviously paper overhauls by the owners) but preferred to believe the easy option, without any evidence, that I was mis-handling the controls thus disregarding my vast experience in simulated and real engine failures previously. They also implied that I applied inappropri-

From Hero to Zero

Showing inappropriate aileron blocking the air speed indicator from view (Mike Milln)

ate aileron[1] and insufficient rudder never taking into account that my application of aileron was to turn the aeroplane to avoid a collision with a pleasure boat. The physical ditching of the aeroplane had no lifelong mental or emotional impact on me, unlike the handling of the entire botched investigation.

I did not want to be hailed as a hero. All I wanted was recognition as a Pilot doing his job. A Pilot does not get paid for what he does, he gets paid for what he might be called upon to do in extreme circumstances. This is all I did. I called on my decades worth of knowledge, skill and experience to avert a tragedy. The four reasons it gave for suspension were (quoted directly from its letter):

'(1) You were, or may have been, above Maximum Take Off Weight (MTOW) on take-off from Sydney International Airport, thus casting doubt on your ability to accurately complete aircraft weight and balance calculations;

'(2) Following the loss of power, you may not have conducted the emergency procedures in accordance with the Engine Failure or Fire on Take Off After V_1 procedures at Section B1.3 of the Groupair Pty Ltd DC-3 Operations Manual approved by the Authority;

'(3) you may have allowed the First Officer to continue flying the aircraft after the power loss, despite his apparent use of sub-optimal technique (involving insufficient application of rudder

---

[1] I had applied slight aileron to a avoid a small pleasure boat. Had I applied inappropriate aileron, my most critical flight instrument, the air speed indicator, would have been hidden from my view. At no time did this occur.

and compensation by use of an inappropriately large aileron deflection), resulting in the aircraft not realising its performance potential; and

'(4) you may have so long delayed taking control of the aircraft from the First Officer that ditching became inevitable.'

I categorically deny all these baseless allegations as they are pure speculation and unfounded.

The Aviation Bulletin Number 1 from 1992, Courts to suspend licences:
'The Authority's power to suspend or cancel licences as a punitive measure is to be removed under proposed changes to the Civil Aviation Regulation (CAR).'

'The only grounds the Civil Aviation Authority wanted to suspend or cancel a licence was competency, said Peter Ilyk, the Assistant General Manager of the Legislation Development Branch.'

'Under the Regulations as they stand the Authority can suspend or cancel someone's certificate or licence if they have committed an offence,' Mr Ilyk said.

'What's been decided now is that the Authority really isn't here to provide punishment, that's a job for the courts.'

'We want to at least try to help people in only looking at whether they are safe to fly, not whether they should be punished for a breach of the law.'

'What you want is an objective, impartial body taking away licences on those grounds and that body is a court of law.'

'The associated amendments to the Civil Aviation Regulations removing the Authority's power to punitively suspend or cancel someone's licence or certificate will be made in due course.'

Unfortunately, I was unaware of this information until well after my suspension. At this time, only major airline pilots were members of unions, so I didn't have the commercial, personal, institutional or financial support to help me along the way.

* * *

I have never been charged with an offence and yet this mismanaged behaviour by the CAA effectively ended my professional flying career. Again, CAA appear to choose when and where it uses which regulations it wishes to impose.

* * *

The CAA representative's process was flawed after gaining information from its (CAA) **unamended** operations manual. They are required to amend their copy of an operations manual whenever the operator provides an amendment. This they did not do, which explains why I could not find the *'Engine Failure or Fire on Take Off After V_1'* procedures he mentions in his Affidavit submitted to the Administrative Appeals Tribunal (AAT) months after the ditching. In a CAA electronic memo a staff member confirmed that the CAA copy of the Group Air Operations Manual had not been amended (available on my website is the emergency checklist referred to by the CAA and deleted by Amendment B4 dated 8th December 1993).

I purchased a photocopier for our home, as it became apparent this was going to be a long and drawn-out process, but never envisaged it would take more than 25 years. In July 1994 I produced a 62-page booklet consisting of my records, qualifications, experience and professional references to try and right a wrong. Approximately twenty-five copies were produced and posted to various people whom I thought may be able to help me. These included, the Commonwealth Ombudsman, the Hon Laurie Brereton (Federal Minister for Transport), the Hon John Sharp (Shadow Minister for Transport), General Peter Gration (AC OBE Chairman, CAA), and the AAT.

In July 1994 the CAA responded to one of my letters by stating that the lack of single-engine performance could have been caused by the right engine not developing normal power. This was the one and only time I ever saw the CAA mention this in regard to the right engine. This highly plausible avenue should have been thoroughly explored, but again for some unknown reason, they chose to ignore it.

I stated on the day of the accident, when we lost the left engine, it felt like the right engine was not producing the power and that was my thought as we were going down. The left engine showed various signs of failure. At least two audible backfires, a perceived small swing to the left, engine gauge instrumentation confirmed loss of power and flight control input was adjusted to correct the upset caused by the left engine failure. At this stage with the right engine gauges indicating take-off power, I intended the aircraft would continue climbing and be able to return for a left circuit to land at Sydney Airport. If the right-hand engine had been developing take-off power, the aeroplane would most certainly have climbed away on that engine alone. As performance (air speed and altitude) declined rapidly, the

'EDC in the old East/West Hanger at Sydney Airport after the ditching (Author's Collection)

only sensible conclusion was the fact that the right-hand engine was not developing take-off power. In the light of the fact that I had mere seconds to evaluate the problem, assess the situation and analyse the options, the CAA still expected me to conduct a fault-finding operation. Its opinion was that I had the time to find the cause of this lack of performance—time did not permit this. Although in the letter quoted above at point (b), where the CAA stated that it was one of the probable causes of the ditching, no further reference was made to this statement.

The CAA and BASI have completely ignored and omitted the crucial fact that the right engine was not producing the rated power required to remain in the air.

Towards the end of July, a BASI representative faxed me with details of BASI's weight calculations, and in this stated that 'A weight and balance summary was compiled from known and estimated data.' I rang BASI over this and challenged it on how it could include this in 'the factual information section of BASI's report' when in its own terms, it is estimated! I witnessed BASI weighing the passengers' baggage while it was dripping wet, on a set of analogue bathroom scales on a hangar floor and then they 'factored' it. The starting weight, or basic weight, of the aeroplane is under considerable doubt as the aeroplane was weighed in a non-approved configuration prior to the ditching. They did not weigh most passengers' personal items but asked them for 'guesstimations' via a questionnaire. Therefore, take-off weight, as constantly claimed by both the CAA and BASI, is in no way actual.

By law, aircraft must be re-weighed at regular intervals (3 yearly) and at that time had to be weighed twice to confirm accuracy. Unbeknown to me, when the aeroplane was last weighed in October 1992, it was weighed on Road and Traffic Authority (RTA) truck scales, not approved by the CAA. The aeroplane was weighed in the open, in the tail down position instead of the level flying position as required by the CAA. This process should have been conducted in a hangar. The aeroplane was weighed in a non-approved environment, in a non-standard position and on non-approved scales. This re-weigh was witnessed by an impartial aviation expert. The empty weight and centre of gravity for the aeroplane were unknown. It was certified by an authorised Weight Control Authority officer of the CAA. It is quite probable that this re-weigh was highly inaccurate. It is highly plausible that the basic weight of the aeroplane would have been in error, therefore the BASI calculated final MTOW would also be in error. They accused me of being an amount overweight to the exact kilogram. How can that be when there were so many dubious statements concerning the weight? Another interesting fact of this weighing in 1992 was that the resulting figures from both weight records were identical—8158 kg. Each of the three jack-point figures showed identical weight readings as well—what are the chances of this? Impossible! The probability of this occurring is infinitesimal and when I have discussed with other aviation personnel, in their field of expertise, they are just dumbfounded, (but in its wisdom the CAA did not question it)!

I applied to the AAT for Stay of Decision of my licence but was refused (www.FromHeroToZero.com.au).

As I was leaving the Tribunal hearing in July 1994, I was approached by the CAA's Legal Officer who was quite rude, abrupt, and intimidating in her line of questioning of me. I indicated to her that I was going to the USA to take my FAA Airline Transport Pilot flight check in a DC-3 as I couldn't be assured of an unbiased test by the Australian authority.

The Office of Legal Counsel CAA wrote to my solicitor on 1st August stating that a CAA representative requested that my flight test be observed by a CAA representative who was currently in the USA. The expense of this was to be borne by me. This was totally unnecessary, not to mention a huge cost to me.

By passing this flight test in the USA, with or without a CAA representative's attendance, the CAA was compelled to re-issue my licence in Australia under Civil Aviation Regulations (CAR) rules. They were also directing me to withdraw my application with the AAT to ensure they 'saved face'.

The CAA greatly misled me and for this, I can never forgive them. They were manipulative, devious and deceitful. They had not made it clear, nor was I aware, that once gaining the FAA Airline Transport Certificate in the USA, I automatically, under CARs, would be re-issued with my CAA Air Transport Pilot Licence in Australia. How these people can sleep at night never ceases to amaze me. On the strength of gaining the FAA Airline Transport Pilot Certificate, this would have entitled me to the Australian equivalent licence under CARs.

The CAA were not content with me just undertaking a flight test, it also wanted me to undertake an examination to prove I continued to possess the aeronautical knowledge appropriate to holding an Air Transport Pilot Licence. In fact, the CAA told me that a person was writing an examination especially for me in Canberra. Did they really think that I came down in the last shower? I knew an examination that was being written especially for me would be written in a manner that ensured I didn't have a snowflake's chance in hell of passing. Had I sat and failed its exam, their actions would have been vindicated. I am not that naive. I was quite prepared to close my navigation bag and walk away from aviation. This I would do with pride. I would not give the CAA the satisfaction of failing me, thereby justifying its actions.

* * *

My wife, Helen, had been an enormous support to me. It was commendable and greatly appreciated. In a fax to our friend Boyd Munro, she stated:

'His FAA Airline Transport Pilot Certificate had been organised quite some time ago and he agonised whether to go or not. I pretty much packed him off telling him, firstly he needed to get away from all the dramas going on here and secondly to prove to himself and everyone else that he's still one of the best (if not *the* best) DC-3 pilots around. This is a very expensive business and the only people that win are the lawyers. But we still maintain Rod has done nothing wrong and we'll fight long and hard to prove it. As he says, 'they can take away his

From Hero to Zero

licence but they'll never take away his professionalism or his pride'.'

* * *

In February 1993, I had travelled to the USA and passed my FAA Airline Transport Pilot Certificate written exam with a requirement that the check flight portion be completed within two years. This written examination consisted of questions from Airline Transport Pilot FAA Written Exam First (1991-1993) Edition, a 650 page book which I wrote a note in the back: *purchased on 22nd February 1993, passed my test on 23rd February 1993.* Yes, I had approximately twenty-four hours to study that book before the examination. Something I was very proud of.

After my licence suspension, I travelled to the USA again in August 1994 to undertake the FAA Airline Transport Pilot Certificate check flight in a DC-3 N7500A (previously owned by John Travolta) out of Clover Field, Santa Monica airfield in California. This is the same airfield that the first DC-1 lifted off on 1st July 1933. The FAA had been fully informed of my circumstances and licence suspension prior to my trip. A suitable time was prearranged with an FAA examiner, Mr Gerald E Parrott of the Van Nuys Flight Safety District Office and I passed my flight check and hence gained my FAA Airline Transport Pilot Certificate No 2504175 on 9th August 1994.

On returning to Australia, the CAA requested to see my certificate and then lifted my suspension. They had also requested from Mr Kevin Moore, the Civil Aviation Representative at the Australian Embassy in Washington DC, information on my FAA Airline Transport Pilot Certificate test flight. Mr Moore provided the following response:

'Mr Aarvik and the FAA operations inspector who conducted the ground and flight test for issue of Mr Lovell's Airline Transport Pilot Certificate and DC-3 type rating. Mr Parrot were both aware of the accident in Sydney, as Mr Lovell told them about it before he began his flight training in preparation for the FAA test. The flight training comprised 3 hours DC-3 flight time, much of it under actual asymmetric conditions (engine closed down, propeller feathered) after a simulated failure of the critical engine at 500 ft after take-off and including an asymmetric ILS approach. Mr Aarvik felt Mr Lovell's ability to cope with asymmetric conditions was without question. He added that the asymmetric sequences, particularly approaches and landings were well planned and well flown by Mr

Counselling/Suspension

DC-3 Santa Monica (Author's Collection)

Lovell. In preparation for the test and during the test (Mr Aarvik acted as Co-pilot during the test), as FAA policy precludes inspectors from any flight crewmember role during flight test, which are conducted and observed from the jump seat.

'The FAA test was particularly thorough because of the inspector's awareness of the Sydney accident. The flight test was preceded by a two-hour oral test and the flight test lasted three hours instead of the usual hour and a half. The FAA inspector who conducted the test was able to recall it and remembered the result was a pass. Like all regulatory authorities the FAA does not grade candidate performance during flight test but simply records a pass or fail assessment.

'A failure in any one aspect of the Airline Transport Pilot Certificate and type rating flight test results in a failure of the whole test.'

* * *

I was now starting to question what licences and aircraft endorsements I had left. I contacted the CAA. Their response and its gobbledygook answer can be read on my website: www.FromHeroToZero.com.au Be prepared to take a cup of tea, a Bex and a good lie down after reading the response—your head will spin!

The lifting of my DC-3 licence suspension was not only expensive, but bittersweet when I received the following correspondence from a CAA representative:

'The acceptance by the authority of your recently acquired overseas Airline Transport Pilot Certificate and DC-3 aircraft endorsement, does not in any way signify acceptance or support of any actions undertaken by you in your capacity as the approved DC-3 check and training Pilot of Groupair Pty Ltd, or in your capacity as the Pilot in command of Australian registered DC-3 aircraft VH-EDC, which aircraft was involved in an accident near Sydney International Airport on 24th April 1994.'

After my three-hour flight check in the USA, and two-hour oral test, and consequential written report (as above) by Mr Kevin Moore (CAA representative, Australian Embassy in Washington DC), the above statement is beyond belief and I am astonished.

* * *

Another example of the types of insults I was subjected to by CAA representatives, who came across as having very little knowledge of DC-3 operations, were statements saying that there was a strong possibility that no trouble check had been carried out and that we (the crew) had unnecessarily placed ourselves in a single-engine situation because of poor training/ Crew Resource Management (CRM). Remember, I had a conversation with a CAA representative in February 1993 regarding trouble checks not being applicable to this class of aeroplane and therefore contravened our operations manual. We had emergency checklists, as laid down in our operations manual, and we followed them scrupulously. Secondly, I had 46 seconds from engine failure to being in the water and these so-called experts believed I should have carried out a very time-consuming trouble check which is not done in this airline type flying.

A CAA representative was obsessed with rudder trim not being applied after the engine failure. Trim tabs are used by the Pilot to relieve the requirement of maintaining continuous pressure on the controls. These are small control tabs fitted to the rudder, elevator and ailerons which can be positioned by mechanical means, normally via a wheel or handle. This small action of applying trim can be very time consuming as the DC-3 were not fitted with electric trim actuation. It shows how little he appreciated the gravity of the situation. Within my extremely limited timeframe, the thought of applying rudder trim never entered my mind. These so-called trouble checks and application of rudder trim would have taken up at least 10 of my precious 46 seconds! Time I obviously did not have. A couple of years prior, this same CAA representative had demanded that I carry out a non-recommended manoeuvre in the DC-3 to which I objected.

The CAA representatives showed their lack of knowledge and ignorance in DC-3 operations by making these ludicrous statements.

* * *

The question of the legality of Co-pilot Leach's Pilot Licence is discussed after the ditching.

> 'It appears that Mr N W Leach presented himself to Licencing staff at Bankstown and on the basis of log-book entries relating to a US registered DC-3 and a US Commercial Pilot Licence ... was then issued with a DC-3 endorsement on his Australian Licence.
>
> 'The problem we now have is that Mr Leach is currently flying the DC-3 out of Cairns and there is serious doubt over the validity of the endorsement. The Civil Aviation Authority issued the endorsement on the information that Leach provided, then the DC-3 endorsement on his Australian licence is invalid. [person named] has recommended that we suspend Mr Leach's DC-3 endorsement, but we did issue the endorsement.'

I relied on the CAA who issued Co-pilot Leach's Pilot's Licence. I am not required to look behind this document which was issued by a government department.

* * *

On 12th October 1995, I received the draft final investigation report. This was soul destroying. It was the second most devastating day of my life. The report basically alleged that I was less than competent in my supervision of Co-pilot Leach's aircraft handling and administration of records, as well as not physically taking the controls until it was too late. I responded to this report in December advising them that I disputed and disagreed with many findings and that it ignored vital evidence which I provided, resulting in them opting for the much easier cause of pilot error.

When the final BASI report[2] was released to me in March 1996, it was extremely disappointing, but not unexpected, in its findings. The only changes it made were the ones I pointed out that had made them look negligent.

---
2 www.atsb.gov.au/media/24341/aair199401043_001.pdf

Over two years after the ditching, the CAA/CASA[3] was still contemplating charges against me probably on some minor perceived breach. Sometimes, I wished I had been charged so that I could have had my day in court and blasted them out of the water. However, in July 1996 the Acting Director's view was that a prosecution would be unsuccessful. Accordingly, he decided that 'Mr Lovell should not be prosecuted'.

In July 1996 Jim Thorn, Editor of the Australian Aviation magazine invited me to write a response[4] to the authorities to their article on the accident in a previous edition. Macarthur Job assisted and guided me in writing this response as he believed that I had carried out an incredibly safe ditching under the circumstances. He also believed that I was wrongly accused. Macarthur Job was a highly experienced and respected Australian aviation writer and air safety consultant. He published nine books on aviation; was formally a Flying Doctor Pilot and until his death in 2014, held a Pilot Licence. Job was a Senior Inspector with the Air Safety Investigation Branch of the Australian Department of Civil Aviation and for fourteen years was Editor of the Department's Aviation Safety Digest. In 1972, the magazine won the US Flight Safety Foundation's Publication of the Year Award. In 1981, as a member of the Guild of Air Pilots and Air Navigators, he was granted the freedom of the City of London.

CAA chose irrelevant information to report on. The decision to make observations about me for these matters seemed paramount to its report. These critical CAA factors include its failing to oversee the poor condition of the engines—lack of CAA supervision of maintenance. That is where its focus should have been directed.

It will not admit that it is responsible for letting this situation deteriorate and thus put people's lives at risk—a complete opposite to what its charter states. To deflect the critique away from itself gives all of the appearance of a major effort to ensure that the department is not liable in any way. This is a commonplace understanding in industry, it is referred to in one enquiry after another but nothing ever changes.

---

3 As of 6th July 1995, the CAA became known as The Civil Aviation Safety Authority (CASA)
4 http://FromHeroToZero.com.au/The-Plane-Truth.php

THE PAPER WAR

The Aftermath—all of the following events concerning the ditching occurred on the ground, after the event, with plenty of time to decide the decisions for which I only had 46 seconds.

Another CAA staff member (known to me) stated:

'No matter what ultimately happens to the company or Captain, the Captain's final skill and situational awareness in keeping control and ditching the aircraft without loss of life or serious injury should be kept in mind'.

I wrote to General Peter Gration, AC OBE, Chairman CAA Board in July 1994 asking for his assistance in correcting a gross miscarriage of justice. I believed he was in a position to review the situation I had been forced into. Two weeks later, I received a two-page letter from General Peter Gration in which he stated:

'You will appreciate, therefore that I cannot interfere in the process currently underway.' He further went on to say, 'I can assure you that the Authority has not made any automatic assumption of pilot error in this matter.' and 'The procedures, to which I refer, are designed, together with an appeal process, to ensure that gross miscarriages of justice do not occur. I am satisfied that the procedures, in this case, are being adhered to, and you have, and are, exercising your rights under the appeal process.'

On 1st November 1994, he addressed the Aviation Press Club, Sydney.

'It is important for Australia to have a strong and competent administration of aviation. There is a real job to be done and I believe I can make a contribution to getting it done. Part of that task of a Chairman of the Civil Aviation Authority is doing what I am doing here today: making the record of myself and the Authority subject to public scrutiny. It is right and proper that those responsible for the administration of aviation in this country be answerable for their actions.'

Around July 1994 I made contact with Jonathan Charles of the Commonwealth Ombudsman Office, who obviously then made contact with the CAA prior to responding to me.

The CAA organised to discuss a strategy in regard to me prior to its meeting with the Ombudsman in early September 1994. I had always believed that the office of the Ombudsman was independent.

Mr Charles confirmed on 11th November 1994 that he had met with the CAA personnel and discussed my case at length and the fact that I had reported that the left propeller had not properly feathered. The CAA stuck to their guns by stating that they had no evidence that the left propeller had not feathered correctly. Not true—a BASI investigator informed the CAA representative, a week after the ditching, that they were looking at the possibility that the left propeller had not fully feathered.

A letter, in late November from CAA's Legal Counsel to the CAA representative stated that they had approved a draft letter to be sent out to me from the Ombudsman's Office. To say that Legal Counsel was arrogant was an understatement as they boasted that it was favourable to them and then finished off by stating that it was another victory. Another victory! Yes this had become an 'eliminate Rod' scenario.

What arrogance! Let's get this perfectly clear. The Office of Legal Counsel CAA approved a letter from the Ombudsman to me. Silly me. I thought the Ombudsman was impartial!

March 1995 saw me meet with Jonathan Charles of Commonwealth Ombudsman Office, along with Capt Jim McGowan, DC-3 Check and Training Captain, Aircruising Australia (refer testimonial at the conclusion of this book). The purpose of this meeting was to put my case forward in person (which seemed a better option), and to refute the CAA's allegations. I had presumed this would be with an impartial arbitrator. Again, to no avail.

Again, in January 1997 I wrote a multi-page letter to the Commonwealth and Defence Force Ombudsman (CDFO), previously known as the Commonwealth Ombudsman Office, requesting a review of his findings and presenting additional evidence. None of their responses led me to believe I was being heard fairly.

After preparing my case and the lengthy correspondence that followed, it wasn't until July 1997, three years later, that I received notification from John Sharp's office stating that he believed CASA had handled all my claims and allegations in a competent and thorough manner. I persisted with further letters to him and also the CASA Board. I still felt determined to clear my name and status no matter how long it took.

In August 1997 I again wrote to John Sharp, I advised Sharp of the reply I received from a CASA representative, in a dismissive seven liner, stating in part 'a competent and thorough investigation' was carried out without any investigation into my ten-page official grievance. Minister Sharp's words summed it up beautifully 'there is nothing that I can usefully add'. I was flabbergasted with this weak and inadequate response.

My wife Helen and I had twice visited BASI in Canberra, meeting with three senior BASI officers, to discuss the numerous inaccuracies in the report and attempt rectification. It had been an abject waste of our time and our money. They appeared to have listened, and in fact agreed verbally, that the charts in the Groupair Operations Manual were approved but they would not rewrite the final report. They agreed that the left propeller, by not fully feathering, would increase the drag. Yet again, I was left rotting on the heap. The fact that the right engine was not delivering full power (unproven at this stage) was not discussed as I was concentrating on other known factors at this time. It left me feeling extremely disappointed with the way BASI had conducted this investigation. In my opinion, it was perverting the course of justice.

Again, I asked Sharp for help in this matter, and was again disappointed. I put it to him that the suspension of my licence was in direct contravention of its own 'Compliance and Enforcement' manual.

After I conducted a radio interview on Alan Jones' program, Sharp rang me immediately afterwards chastising me for not acknowledging his help and support. I'm still waiting for his support. I told him that I wasn't going away, nor remain quiet until the wrong his departments had done to me had been righted; compensation paid; and, even more importantly, a full public apology made by them.

I sent an official eight-page grievance, in December 1996, to the Manager, Corporate Relations, Civil Aviation Safety Authority—this can be seen on my website (www.FromHeroToZero.com.au) 'Grievance Procedures'.

As a last resort, dealing with the Ombudsman's Office, I wrote to the Director of Investigations on 18th November 1997 with regard to the CAA, stating that their actions were most certainly unreasonable, unjust, oppressive or improperly discriminatory and also based on speculation alone. My professional ability, qualifications, experience and standing were not even considered. Again, I stated that I believed the investigation carried out by the Sydney office of the Commonwealth Ombudsman was incomplete and indifferent. The Commonwealth Ombudsman's office had advised me that CAA admitted that they had egg on their face regarding my case. He also advised that the CAA had said that the CAA representative in Adelaide, who did not approve me as Chief Pilot, was not proper and it should have been given due consideration. This was confirmed by John Pike, Assistant Director of Aviation Safety Regulation in his letter dated 22nd March 1995.

In 1997 I wrote to the Attorney General advising them that I had become aware of the Ombudsman Office sending draft copies of its own letters regarding my situation to the Office of Legal Counsel, CAA, seeking its approval before responding to me. I expressed my shock to learn that the help I sought from the Ombudsman, who I believed were there to assist victims, was putting me at a disadvantage by colluding with the CAA. I requested a review of the investigation and that I be kept informed and involved in all aspects. The response I received was that The Office of the Ombudsman came within the responsibilities of the Prime Minister and hence they would refer my letter to the Hon John Howard MP, for consideration. The Office of the Prime Minister replied that since The Commonwealth Ombudsman was an independent statutory office, neither the Prime Minister nor any other Minister could direct or review her Office's actions. There was a wall wherever I turned and any hope was quickly dashed.

The failings of the system never cease to amaze me. As a 'coal face' member, with lots of hands-on experience, one would think that this would be valued by various government inquiries, especially considering the millions the government had spent training me to fly in the RAAF. I took the time to respond to some of the inquiries regarding aviation and aviation safety. Some of these consisted of:

- A submission to the inquiry titled: The 1996 Standing Committee on Transport, Communications and Infrastructure—Plane safe: Inquiry into aviation safety—the commuter and general aviation sectors

- A 44-page submission to the BASI REVIEW 1999
- In 2012, I made a 73-page submission to the Senate Standing Committees on Rural and Regional Affairs and Transport.

DESERT DICK

Dick Lang, along with his wife Helen, ran two businesses based out of Adelaide. Their company is known as Desert-Trek which is Australia's oldest 4WD safari company and Desert-Air which is Australia's oldest air safari company. Dick was also favourably referred to as 'Desert Dick' by those in the industry.

Let's now back-track ten months prior to the ditching when, in June 1993, Dick rang me to ask if I would meet with him to discuss DC-3s. My wife Helen and I flew to Adelaide on 2nd July, to meet with Dick and his wife Helen. After a successful meeting, Dick formally asked me if I would accept the position of Training and Checking Captain for his company. That very same day I faxed Dick with my acceptance. On 21st July, I was given Check Pilot Approval DC-3 for Desert-Air Safaris by the District Flight Operations Manager, CAA, Parafield.

At this time I was heavily involved in DC-3 operations. I was eager to keep up to date on all aspects of DC-3s, therefore on the 22nd July, when the CAA held a DC-3 seminar at Bankstown Airport, I attended with ears and eyes wide open. One of the speakers was referred to as 'Mr DC-3 Australia' by senior CAA staff—this accolade was not shared by other DC-3 pilots.

In October 1993, I had the pleasure of assisting Dick ferry DC-3 P2-005 (ferried as VH-PWN) from PNG to Cairns, Queensland and on to Adelaide. It was a great flight with an almost as-new DC-3. This was an immaculate aeroplane built in 1943. It had very low airframe time (approximately 15,000 hours) in its fifty years of service and had been well cared for. It was ex-United States Air Force, A65-63 in the Royal Australian Air Force, Papua New Guinea Defence Force before Dick Lang purchased it. (In the year 2000, it was dismantled for parts in Sydney. A crying shame.)

Dick and I had many enjoyable flights together during my employment with him. There were flights to the outback where his yarns always entertained everybody.

After the ditching, I could no longer act for Dick due to my licence and endorsement suspension in June 1994, so his DC-3 operation was grounded, resulting in a further loss of income to us both. In August 1994, Dick was forced to take on an Ansett Pilot to replace me as Check and Training Captain.

In February 1995, since my licence and DC-3 endorsement had been reinstated. Dick mentioned that he would like me to return to the position of Training and Checking Captain on DC-3s and relayed a discussion he'd had with a CAA representative in Adelaide who had said that he could not consider that I be appointed to this position because of my reluctance to present myself or communicate with the CAA in the past. A CAA representative does not have the power to make that judgement. Therefore, it was clear that it had now become a very personal matter aimed at me and nothing to do with regulations.

I received a call from Dick in March 1995 asking if I would consider accepting the position of Chief Pilot for Desert-Air Pty Ltd. I advised Dick I would be more than happy to accept. Dick, in a fax to the CAA representative, offered to stand aside as Chief Pilot for his company and nominated me for that position. The CAA representative advised Dick that after due consideration he had rejected my application as charges were pending with the Department of Public Prosecutions (DPP) against me—all news to me! I then sort clarification from upper level CAA management re Chief Pilot requirements and was informed that if I met the laid-down requirements I should have been approved. The local CAA representative later denied his comment regarding charges, however a copy of his file note dated 6th March 1995 (obtained via Freedom of Information) refers to matters being referred to the DPP. For the next four months Dick and I were intimidated and harassed, so much so, that at the end of June I decided to tender my resignation to Dick. The CAA representative had caused unfair, increased commercial and personal pressure on Dick and his business. Ultimately, Dick reluctantly accepted my resignation which meant he, like many others in the industry, had to buckle to do exactly what the local CAA representative had wanted all along and sadly I did not fly for Dick again.

THE PLANE TRUTH

After the ditching, I sought factual reasons, answers and the truth as to why the DC-3 became un-flyable. I became an amateur aircraft crash investigator as this was my only means to get answers and hopefully justice. In the BASI report into the ditching, I found that its conclusions were inaccurate, incomplete, superficial and in certain areas, plainly untrue. It was obvious to me that both government departments (CAA and BASI) were trying to create a diversionary smoke screen by alleging an overweight aeroplane and mis-handling by Co-pilot Leach, and not acknowledging the real factual reasons the DC-3 would not fly. Major findings were conveniently omitted as reported after the examination of the unserviceable and unapproved right-hand engine spark plugs. Was this perverting the course of justice? When I found out the appalling mechanical state of the engines, I was devastated that this aeroplane was allowed to fly. To my knowledge, no action was ever taken against the owners, who were responsible for the maintenance of this aeroplane. I now know why it would not stay airborne—the right engine was not producing sufficient power. Now to prove it!

Another book could be written highlighting the negligent maintenance deficiencies on this aircraft. Some, but far from all, have been published in the BASI report—'Technical Examination of the Wreckage' commencing on page 11. However, BASI have not included significant factors such as the overall condition of the spark plugs in both engines.

In its Investigation Report 9304023 into accident De Havilland DH-104 Dove VH-DHD, (3rd December 1993) they did, however, conduct flight tests[1]. BASI conceded that an aircraft with less than 6,000 airframe hours, had a 27% reduction of single-engine climb performance probably attribut-

---

[1] www.atsb.gov.au/media/25019/aair199304023_001.pdf

able to age of aircraft and engines.

Prior to that accident in May 1975 Department of Transport Aircraft Accident Investigation Summary Report into the Bristol Freighter registered VH-SJQ[2], which unfortunately crashed into the sea. Here the department stated the aircraft involved in the accident could not climb after an engine failure in flight. They stated that the remaining engine produced 26% less power than normal maximum power. Nothing at all to do with Pilot's handling ability. Talk about a contradiction of allegations and accusations thrown my way.

In the Aviation Safety Digest 108/1979[3], the investigation into a light twin-engined aircraft accident estimated that degradation due to the 3,400 airframe hours, reduced the single-engine climb gradient by about 100 feet per minute.

'EDC had in excess of 40,000 airframe hours and two engines both on CAA approved engine overhaul time extensions, which showed signs of 'mechanical distress' and marginal cylinder compression, yet was given zero percentage performance degradation.

On reflection, due to these factors, I believe that when the left engine failed, I lost the more powerful of the two leaving me with a crippled aircraft.

The 'EDC BASI Report states (in part):

Left engine

'During dismantling of the left engine, the following abnormalities were noted: On removal of the no. 3 cylinder inlet valve pushrod cover, pushrod and tube, excessive wear of the pushrod and of the cylinder where the pushrod enters the valve rocker housing was apparent. Further inspection revealed that one of the thrust washers which are fitted either side of the rocker arm on the rocker shaft was not fitted to the shaft. The thrust washer subsequently fell out of the valve rocker housing. The loose washer was oval in shape, having sustained impact damage during engine operation. At the last time of fitting, the shaft was installed but failed to engage the washer which subsequently was left within the rocker housing.

'The rocker arm end of the pushrod contained heavy rub marks which penetrated the pushrod to about 25% of the wall thickness. The curved

---

2 www.atsb.gov.au/media/24618/197502854.pdf
3 www.atsb.gov.au/media/5774804/asd_108_79.pdf

From Hero to Zero

BASI pushrod (BASI)

edges of these wear marks matched the deformed washer. There was also a curved depression within the rocker housing, adjacent to the inlet pushrod tube, which matched the shape of the deformed washer.'

Wow, that poor old girl's fate was sealed for some time!

The report also stated that the AWI expressed the opinion that both engines should not operate on the overrun period at the same time, however, the CAA did not have a policy on this. When the left engine hour overrun approval was granted, the AWI had assumed the right engine had been changed. There was an entry dated 24th April 1994 (the morning of the accident) in the VH-EDC Aircraft Logbook that the right engine had been changed. Incredibly, sometime later this entry had subsequently been crossed out and noted as an 'incorrect entry'. How can an engine be removed and replaced and be recorded as an incorrect entry? Duplicity?

The lack of performance of the aeroplane and hence the inability of it to fly on one engine was not investigated or analysed. They preferred to create scenarios which better fitted in with their consensus, to ensure any criticism being deflected onto other parties rather than have to explain their own operational behaviour—maintenance and regulatory supervision—which was criticised in the BASI report and are more likely the culprits.

As a matter of interest, when in the DC-3 simulator in 2018 in the Netherlands (referred to later in this book), I had to bring the single-engine power back to approximately 850 bhp on one engine, before which the aeroplane would not climb, proving that 'EDC was struggling desperately with climb performance as I suspected when I previously reported it to BASI.

When the left one of those two engines failed, combined with the drag of the propeller not fully feathering which was pretty much swept under the carpet in the BASI report, there was nothing that any Pilot could have done to achieve at least level flight, let alone climb—proven in the simulator. Even though this was reported to BASI, it was, amazingly, ignored in the investigation, instead of being recognised as the most likely cause of the accident! The aircraft was no longer capable of asymmetric flight, and the fate of it and all on board was, from this point on, in the hands of the Captain. The BASI have not acknowledged the vastly increased drag caused by the left propeller not going to the fully feathered position. This fact alone may have destroyed any chance the aircraft had of maintaining height on one engine. With reference to degradation of engine/airframe performance, which BASI failed to address in 'EDC's investigation, the Aerodynamics for Naval Aviators[4] page 149, shows a pertinent graph. This shows that the parasitic drag from my propeller, stationary at 65°, was more than the drag from a windmilling propeller.

Let's analyse that drag. Any physical body being propelled through the air has drag associated with it. In aerodynamics, drag is defined as the force that opposes forward motion through the atmosphere and is parallel to the direction of the free-stream velocity of the airflow. Drag must be overcome by thrust in order to achieve forward motion.

With DC-3 'EDC, the engine cowl flaps were in a fixed slightly open (Australian modification) position, rather than the trail position of the RAAF aeroplanes. Individually, the enlarged left aileron trim tab and associated aileron, each 24 ft (7.5 m) long, the bubble viewing window on the right side of the fuselage, the mis-fitting doors and hatches, the flaking and peeling wing walk, may not seem much, but collectively they added enormous parasitic drag.

The fixed tab on the left aileron had been replaced with a much larger one. The CAA Safety Deficiency Manager, on 23rd August 1994 stated that there was no documented evidence to support the report that the fixed tab on the left aileron had been changed whilst the aircraft had been operated by South Pacific Airmotive. South Pacific Airmotive was the name used for the operational and invoicing side of the Leaches business. Blind Freddie only had to

---
4 ISBN 9781619540170

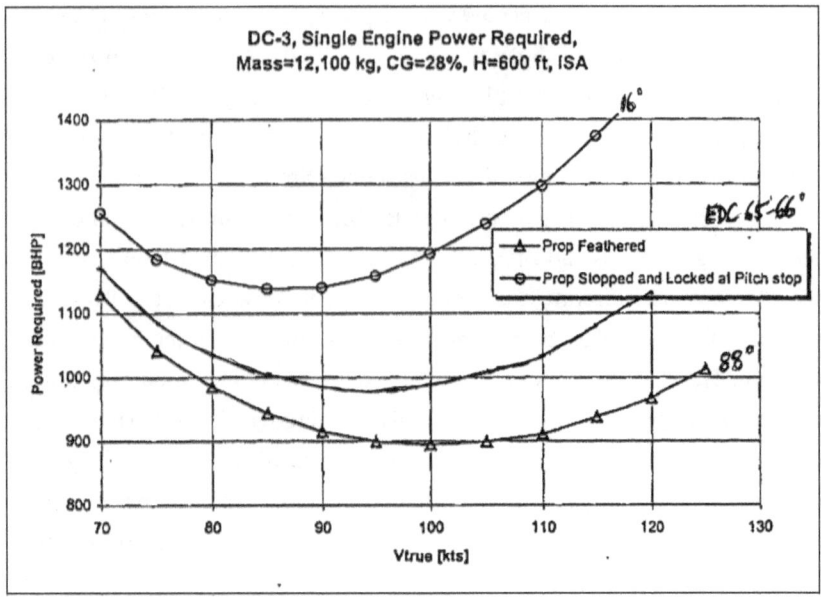

Pitch Graph (Author's Collection)

look at the aileron to see that the trim tab had been changed. This is not the only instance of changes being made without being documented.

But what about the left propeller which was of potentially enormous drag contributory significance? The BASI report states that the left propeller was at 65-66° of pitch instead of the 88° pitch of the fully feathered position. On page 37 of this report it states this caused 'negligible' (zero) increase in drag (no degradation in aircraft performance). However, on page 49 they admit that the aircraft performance was degraded due to the propeller not being fully feathered. Again, a total contradiction. I consulted a retired aerodynamicist who believes the use of the word negligible in this context is irresponsible.

Surely, the BASI report loses its integrity when it contradicts itself in such a significant way. But what is worse is that there was no further mention anywhere in the report of any scientific investigation or tests

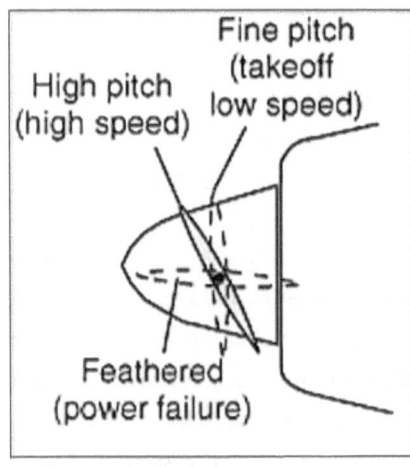

Various propeller pitch angles (Author's Collection)

to understand the likely effect that an improperly feathered propeller would have on the performance and ability of the aircraft to continue flight in this configuration. A specialist examination concluded that the propeller had not been able to operate to the full-feather position for some time. As part of the engine runup procedures, the feather button for each engine is activated momentarily. This is merely to check that the electrical circuitry and feather pump are working. As soon as the blades move slightly to feather, there is a reduction in engine rpm and at that stage the feather pump check is concluded so as to not put undue loads on the engines. At no stage are pilots required to check full feathering pre-take-off. Full feather checking is a maintenance procedure. A video taken of the aircraft on the bottom of Botany Bay before recovery operations commenced showed clearly that the propeller was not in the feathered position.

And that, my friends, is where the BASI report left it!

Having recovered, stripped down, examined and established a major problem with the left propeller no further interest in establishing the detrimental effect of such a huge potential problem was ever considered. The contradictory statements were dismissed without question or explanation and never reared their ugly heads again. The aircraft wouldn't fly so it was immediately deemed a mis-handling problem by the Co-pilot flying when the engine failed. I can assure you that as soon as that engine failed the aircraft was doomed and no Pilot on the planet could have done anything other than crash into the water or surrounding land. I took over the controls from the Co-pilot within seconds of completing the engine shutdown procedure, and there was no mis-handling, with all flight controls being applied correctly as the speed decelerated from 100 kt to the required 81 kt and it still just would not fly. It had to be ditched within the next 25 seconds as it turned out, and I was criticised in the BASI report for delaying taking control until a ditching was inevitable.

And this is supposed to be an aircraft crash investigation report?

'EDC was fitted with what is called needle or toothpick propeller blades as opposed to paddle blades. It is widely accepted that the former provided less performance than the latter. It is believed that the toothpick or needle-nosed blades are not used in the United Kingdom due to their limited performance. All companies operating DC-3 type aircraft in the UK, USA, and South America advise that single-engine performance with paddle blades is far superior. VH-EDC had needle blades. BASI make no reference as to what

From Hero to Zero

Propeller blades: paddle (left) and needle (right) (Author's Collection)

blades were fitted.

So now we are flying only on the right engine which is indicating full power. But are we?

From the final BASI report (page 14):

'Right Engine. This engine was subjected to strip examination along with an inspection of the engine records and SOAP (Spectrometric Oil Analysis Program) analysis submitted for the TBO (Time Between Overhauls) extension. With the exception of the propeller governor, no pre-existing abnormalities were found.'

Really? What about the spark plugs?

In another report from BASI (not released to the public and details not in the final report):

'Left engine: On removal of the spark plugs from the left engine it was noted that there was a mixture of massive electrode and fine wire type plugs fitted. The electrode 'gap' settings were noted to be inconsistent between plugs and the majority showed evidence of electrode wear beyond normal life.

'These plugs were subjected to post recovery examination and testing. After cleaning and re-gapping 5 plugs either did not fire or were found to be electrically breaking down on test.

'Right engine: Twenty-five spark plugs which were recovered from the right engine were similarly cleaned gapped and tested. Of these 11 were considered to be unserviceable, either failing to fire or from electrical breaking down when being tested.'

Examples of fouled (left) and new (right) spark plugs (Author's Collection)

This report also found that of the fifty-six spark plugs, only thirteen per engine were deemed to be of the approved type of plug.

How convenient that this was omitted in the final BASI report and why on earth weren't they tested as found instead of being cleaned and gapped first? Any backyard mechanic knows that a spark plug with too big or small a gap will not be efficient or not work at all and is always the first thing you go to when your lawn mower or your old outboard won't start.

Why wouldn't they test them as they found them (appalling procedural error)? Is it illogical to presume that BASI, in other accidents, have repaired parts prior to testing them or did this only occur in my investigation? Even after cleaning and resetting the gap, they still found eleven to be unserviceable. Can we speculate how many would have been found to be unserviceable if they were tested as removed from the engine?

The right engine was examined after it had spent approximately nine weeks in saltwater as it had detached from the aeroplane on contact with the water. There was no evidence to prove that the engine was developing full power prior to the accident, even though the engine instrument gauges suggested it was.

BASI maintain without any explanation or proof that this engine was producing the appropriate power output with just over half of the spark plugs working correctly. Unbelievable! If both the CAA and BASI still maintained that the right engine was producing full power (impossible) then why won't they release test data to me under the Freedom of Information Act as I have requested and have been denied? To this day, I'm still waiting for this information.

From what I can work out, as I am not an Aerodynamicist or expert on aircraft performance, but from my calculations and approved simulator test flights in Amsterdam, I believe both engines had been producing significantly less power than required and indicated. Following considerable research, 'EDC's climb performance on two engines was nowhere near the claimed and expected power of a normal DC-3. The right-hand engine had a higher time in use than the left engine, and according to BASI, the right-hand engine had eleven unserviceable spark plugs, whereas the left-hand engine had five that were unserviceable.

For the aviation and technical people, who are probably asking why wasn't this picked up in a pre-take-off engine run-up, Pratt & Whitney Aircraft Manual of Engine Operation, page A10, sums it up by saying:

'It is difficult to see any tangible value in running the engine up to take-off rpm and manifold pressure as a routine pre-flight check. While it may give great satisfaction to the pilot to see these quantities registered on the instruments, a little analysis will show that this achievement is no guarantee that the expected power is being produced and delivered to the propeller.'

I firmly believe that neither of 'EDC's engines had been tested by a recognised method to ascertain whether they were delivering full power prior to the accident and there is absolutely no way a Pilot sitting in the cockpit can measure power output, he can only set the levers to provide the nominated instrument indications in MAP (Manifold Absolute Pressure) and rpm that are supposed to provide it.

As engines get older they lose power. Although correct power settings are indicated to the Pilot by the instruments, it may not in fact exist. Pratt & Whitney, the manufacturers of the engines say, in a publication, that although correct power may be indicated to the Pilot by manifold pressure and revolutions, the engine may in fact have one or even two cylinders inoperative causing a great reduction of power. This is partly because the variable pitch propeller will absorb variations and maintain steady rpm. In 1997, a CASA Senior Airworthiness Inspector agreed that this was in fact correct. The only reliable measurement of power is by use of a test club propeller (TCPs)[5] or by causing the engine to run a generator or similar motor of known capacity. A TCP is basically a single set pitch that cannot be altered. They are usu-

---
5   www.casa.gov.au/files/003pdf-13

Wooden Test Club Propeller: Diameter 254 cm (100 in), Chord 33 cm (13 in) (Motoart.com)

ally made with square tipped blades of laminated wood construction. The blades are made wide to provide maximum power absorption and airflow with minimum tip diameter.

Did either engine get tested accordingly before or after the accident? Both were, amazingly, operating in the over-run of their maintenance schedule beyond 1000 hours because the CAA, remarkably, did not have a policy to this effect! The CAA approved permits to over-run, issued on 6th July 1993 (right engine) and 4th February 1994 (left engine) despite the indications of mechanical distress together with marginal cylinder compression recordings known to the CAA and detailed in the BASI report, only because the CAA believed (mistakenly) that the right engine had already been changed.

At the time of the left engine failure precipitating the ditching, the time since overhaul was 1027.56 hours and the right engine time since overhaul was 1085.53hours. The pilots do not have these details at their disposal and rely on maintenance schedules to provide them with reliable and well-serviced equipment and regulatory authority (CAA) surveillance to ensure that this is the case. As does the travelling public.

From Hero to Zero

As Captain, I was handed what I believed to be the valid maintenance release. This is the only maintenance document I am required to sight and sign prior to any flight. The maintenance release records the current legal airworthiness status of the aircraft. It is the document an approved person issues which certifies that all required maintenance inspections, maintenance manuals, airworthiness directives, system of maintenance and maintenance schedules have been performed in accordance with approved maintenance data. The aircraft is then considered airworthy at the time this document is issued and therefore should remain airworthy for the period of maintenance release. This then allows the Pilot to make informed decisions about the aircraft's condition and suitability to operate. As to the deficiency of maintenance, this is an area that I, as DC-3 Flight Captain, had no control over. Had I identified a deficiency prior to the flight, I would have acted on it immediately. I was employed to fly the aircraft[6], not oversee maintenance. Other people were employed by Groupair for various maintenance positions.

BASI made a comment regarding the aircraft maintenance release that the maintenance being carried out on the aircraft was not compliant with the category of maintenance as required by the certificate of airworthiness.

---

6 Responsibility of Pilot in Command—www.vfrg.casa.gov.au/general/pilot-responsibilities/pilot-in-command/

BELOW ZERO

The power base between Helen and me shifted over the years. After she had gained her captaincy, I eventually became a 'handbag'. A contributing factor to the breakdown of this marriage has to be attributed to the ditching. I was having to resort to doing menial jobs at this time, as CASA's opinion of me was putting prospective employers off as they considered possible repercussions against their company. Helen was going up through the ranks as a QANTAS Pilot which caused us to drift apart. The pressure we were both under started to show. Our relationship had been great in the beginning—so much in common—but for some reason, she thought the grass was greener elsewhere. When we divorced, a year later in Brisbane, we passed each other in the public common room of the court. When she glanced at me, she had the saddest eyes I have ever seen.

In 2000, I met Marilyn when we were both working for Security Monitoring Centre at Ashfield, in New South Wales. After dating for a short while, Marilyn swayed me into marrying her. She said she wouldn't just live with me. It had to be marriage or nothing. On the morning of the wedding, I remember thinking I should call it off. My inner voice was trying to warn me that it just wasn't right. Like a lot of naive people, I thought it would get better later on, but it never did. It became very clear to me that, unfortunately, this had been a rebound marriage. Certainly not Marilyn's fault.

* * *

As my aviation career was being torn to shreds by the powers that be, I had to resort to various other roles to ensure my financial stability whilst not being employed as a Pilot. These roles varied from taxi driver, security guard, coach driver, semi-trailer transport driver, casual mobile library driver and warehouse team member. Though these roles kept my head above water financially, they certainly were not part of my planned life. As a coach driver in Sydney in 2001, I felt honoured to have been chosen to transport all the Australian Governors and their wives from their hotel to the venue for the Centenary of Federation celebrations held at Centennial Park.

After separating from Marilyn in 2003, I realised I needed therapy, so I went out and bought a 1961 Mack B61 Prime Mover—as one does! I can't tell you much about the marriage, but I can tell you all about my Mack. Over the next few months, I restored and road registered it. This truck had a very slow pair of differentials and top speed was 35 mph (60 kph). The old girl revved away happily but with no insulation on the firewall the heat in the small cabin could sometimes be distressing—as was the noise! On a trip from Camden to Toowoomba, I had a 20 litre drum of engine oil on the seat beside me for company. This prime mover bumped and jiggled along, as there was no trailer or load on it to steady its movement. I often talked to myself on long trips just to pass the time. Then I came up with a brilliant idea. The oil drum became my 'Wilson' from the movie Castaway. I would tell a joke and look at Wilson, the oil drum, and he would be nodding away over the bumps laughing at my jokes. I finally found a friend who really appreciated my sense of humour!

* * *

Whilst at an interview for the role of storeman/packer at a major supermarket distribution centre, I was asked what I had done previously in life. I replied that I had been in transport all of my life (which was not untrue). I did not inform them of any of my previous aviation experience nor about the accident, as I feared this may go against me. Experience has taught me to adapt to my surroundings like a chameleon. If I had taken the time to talk about my career as a Pilot, I would have been made to feel like a tall poppy and ridiculed for wanting to apply for what some people may think a menial position. The question that would no doubt have followed would be why I would want such a role, and I imagined a rejection due to being over qualified. By downplaying, I received notification that I had been successful in my application but working for a major supermarket chain turned out to be the most depressing and demoralising experience I have ever endured during my working career. Even when previously applying for general aviation Pilot positions, I never admitted I could fly anything bigger than what that company operated—those hiring did not want to know, therefore Boeing 747s and the like were never mentioned.

My therapy—my B61 Mack Prime Mover (Nick Bielby)

After some time during this same employment, I applied to be a Team Leader but was unsuccessful as they deemed they didn't know how I would react to a stressful situation. When I was told that, I had a lot of trouble trying to suppress my thoughts and laughter. Funnily enough, even as a lowly team member, quite a few trainers would ask me how I operated certain pieces of equipment, such as high-reach forklifts, as I had far more experience operating these machines than they did. Frequently, newer team members would ask me questions on either operational or personal issues, something that I thought should have been directed to their team manager. I felt honoured that they had such faith in my abilities and opinions that they sought me out.

One day, a potentially serious incident occurred in the distribution centre. Whilst I was stationary picking cartons on my pallet truck, a forklift drove past, struck and dislodged one of the vertical supports for the numerous horizontal beams above and lodged itself under the nine-metre-high warehouse racking. This racking held a lot of pallets, some weighing over a tonne. The heaviest pallets were normally placed on the uppermost level, which always surprised me. Peter, the forklift driver, wanted to immediately back-up his forklift by removing it from under the racking. I immediately told him to stop what he was doing, get off the forklift and walk slowly to the centre aisle. Another driver was about to enter this aisle and I advised him to block off the aisle with his machine and not allow anyone else through. I then told Peter that he and I would walk to the Manager's Station in the centre aisle to advise him that this was a very dangerous situation that required urgent attention. The Manager immediately came down and started taking statements from Peter. He asked me whether I was involved in the incident and when I replied that I wasn't he promptly told me to get back to work. There was no compassion or asking if I was alright considering Peter and I could have been killed. Had Peter backed up his forklift, he would have brought down the whole storage rack of pallets with the tonnes of supplies crashing down on top of us. It's a shame we didn't have CCTV to replay the incident so that management could then see how I reacted to a real time stressful situation!

As it turned out, in the most ironic way, we didn't need CCTV at all because around 2009, I was quite unexpectedly approached by the producers of the TV series 'You Saved My Life'. They invited me to appear in a segment of the show revolving around my ditching of the DC-3. Dr Andrew Rochford was the show's presenter and an amazing gentleman who I found easy to talk to, especially considering how very uncomfortable I felt talking about myself, particularly on camera. Andrew put me right at ease and into a position where I felt quite comfortable talking about the accident. We filmed the interview on the beach at Sans Souci on the western shore of Botany Bay. For those who have never seen the program, it was based on a surprise meeting of a hero and the people he/she saved. This was an extremely emotional time for me. Knowing the program format, I had an inkling of what was to follow. One of the passengers, Brad Lovett, a student at The Scots College at the time of the accident, approached me during the on-camera interview and thanked me for saving his life. You can only imagine the rush of emotions I felt at this moment. The filming, of course, was never discussed with my workmates at the supermarket distribution centre, as again, I don't like 'big-noting' myself. I thought nothing more of the episode until, many months later, unbeknown to me, it went to air, at around midnight. At that time our shift finished at 11.30 pm so most team members would go home, have a coffee and watch a little TV to wind down after work. The next afternoon, when I arrived at the centre, I was treated like a movie star! At first, I couldn't understand what all the fuss was about as I had not watched television the previous evening. People came out of the woodwork to shake my hand and admit that they had no comprehension of my past and achievements as I never discussed it with anyone. My intentions of staying low key were blown out of the water that day.

Previous to this program going to air, whilst I was Acting Team Leader, one of the managers told me that my managerial skills were sadly lacking and that I should start ordering people around. I replied that I'd held positions of rank with numerous people reporting to me, but I had never, ever ordered anyone around, and I never would. By the look on his face, you could tell that the training he'd received by the system did not allow him to understand my way of thinking, though it was very clear to me that his managerial skills were sadly lacking. I hoped he had watched *You Saved My Life* when it aired as I would have loved to have seen his face when he realised my background history. Funny though how the uncovering of my extensive experience didn't boost my career prospects at all.

* * *

The most degrading part of my employment in the distribution centre was being ordered around by young, ambitious managers who were hell-bent on climbing the corporate ladder, yet had no real life experience. They relished ordering around mature-aged, intelligent staff, without ever wanting to know or appreciate the qualities of their previous professional background. We were made to feel that they didn't want people like me—contributing to an increased efficiency of the company, as they appeared to see us as a threat to their career goals. Certainly, in my case, they had no clue as to the level of experience I had, the millions of dollars spent on my RAAF training, and what was more insulting was that they were too indifferent to be interested in their staff's past professional or personal life.

It was incredibly belittling, demoralising and soul destroying. To retain my sanity and a balanced lifestyle, I reverted to buying and restoring classic cars, trucks and tractors as a hobby.

* * *

It was during my employment at the distribution centre that I met Pauline, who was a very successful event promoter and organiser. We hit if off straight away and not long afterwards she moved in with me. We spent five wonderful years together before we both found different interests and our personal life together faded away, so we parted company. Pauline remained a very dear friend and confidant until sadly, in late 2018, she passed away. Pauline was instrumental in restoring my confidence by making me see the value in myself, a little like one of my classic vehicles. She recognised that I had a different way of doing things and would comment to my friends that, 'Rod marches to the beat of a different drum.' It was a fair comment. Her advice to start the healing process was to summarise what I had become compared with what I used to be.

'You've become totally mindless, like a robot. You've lost your incentive and certainly your confidence.' She once said to me and then later said, 'I remember when you were asked to write for a car club magazine, under a member profile segment. Everybody was quite astounded that you had such a diverse career. It took quite a few steps, but after a period you started to emerge as an enthusiastic but modest man. You felt life held more for you than just distribution centre work.'

* * *

In 2003, when I started working in that distribution centre, staff were expected to pick up 120 cartons per hour. Ten years later, the pick up rate had almost doubled to around 220 cartons per hour. These cartons ranged from small lightweight boxes up to the size of those holding eight bottles of 2 litre soft drink that weighed around 16 kg per carton. Suppliers normally deliver their products on pallets which consist of numerous smaller packages suitable for the supermarket workers to unpack and display. When the supermarket places its order, a picker goes around and assembles the order and then places it on a pallet or roll-cage to be delivered to the supermarket. I believe I was the oldest team member who picked cartons every day. State and national managers would visit and I would quite often confront them by asking 'How would you like your father doing my job?' Needless to say, that question was never answered.

Making the maturing team members work on the more physically demanding labour-intensive jobs, was their way of encouraging us to depart the workforce. The younger team members were given the less labour-intensive jobs and office positions. Most of the older workforce had good work ethics and a vast range of experience that could enhance the company enormously, but management created a culture which was no longer appealing to the ageing workforce. If our pickup rate was not at an acceptable level, we were confronted by management and our short-comings were written down on their report. How humiliating!

At one stage, some Human Resources bright spark initiated introducing a group hug at the commencement of each shift. Every shift started with a briefing and it was at this meeting that the new initiative was instigated. We were then told to form up, in our already set teams, and meet in our designated areas for our group hug which produced raucous laughter. Needless to say, we all boycotted the group hug, got on our assigned equipment and did what we were being paid to do—we got to work. It was no surprise that we were never asked to do that again!

Management treated us with utter contempt. They used to preach values and behaviours which was laughable. Talk about the pot calling the kettle black. We were treated as androids (a person regarded as lifeless or robotic). Managers passed us in the aisles, or even on walkways and would look the other way. We were in constant fear of losing our jobs. New managers were never introduced to the workers. Was it because we were not worthy? Managers were always negative and derogatory and only extremely rarely said thank you. When asked to remain for a further five minutes after our shift, without additional pay, we would not comply on the basis that we would be docked pay if we were even one minute late clocking on at the start of the shift.

Did I feel a valued and worthwhile team member? Not at all. We were always walking on egg shells, never sure when one of us might be marched out the door.

* * *

My aviation career post ditching was completely ruined thanks to two government departments—CAA and BASI. As previously explained, a Pilot loses pretty much all his credibility after he suffers a licence suspension. When it happened to me I was gutted. After only eight weeks my licence was reinstated after great personal expense, but by then the damage was done and continued to affect my opportunities to gain employment in a flying capacity of any sort. The stupidity and sadness of this suspension is that it was unfounded and based on pure speculation, some of which was provided by an outside source which had no substance. The proof of this was demonstrated by the reinstatement of the licence only eight weeks after it was suspended, with no charges being laid. However, the threat of those charges lingered on and eventually stopped any possibility of me returning to DC-3 check and training, ultimately causing me to leave my beloved aviation industry altogether. I was held in high esteem as an operator by not only my peers but also certain members of CAA/CASA. Unfortunately, this was not sufficient to overcome the prejudicial outcome of perceived intimidation of those who wanted to employ me. The thought of having to tolerate interference from the regulatory authority was enough to put any employer off. It would be just too hard for them. Hence, the CAA/CASA aftermath was to effectively cause the cessation of my current and future employment in my area of expertise in DC-3 check and training. This horrified me!

I guess the passion never leaves as in 2008, whilst still employed at the distribution centre, I felt it was time to try and reinstate my flying career in a branch of aviation that I have always considered a noble pursuit. I applied for a Pilot's position with the Royal Flying Doctor Service (RFDS) based at Mascot Airport. On my initial application for this position, I made them fully aware of my 1994 ditching. As my application progressed, the RFDS Melbourne office rang me to ask if I would attend an interview to be conducted in Sydney.

'If you are sending up some twenty-year-old, with just a university degree, you can forget about it. I won't be attending. But, if you are sending up some experienced pilots, who have been there and done that, I will gladly attend' I replied. The young girl laughed.

'Don't worry, it's the experienced Chief Pilot and Senior Pilot who will be interviewing you' she assured me.

I thanked her and confirmed that I would be happy to attend. The interview was low key, more conversational than set questions and answers, and thoroughly enjoyable. I specifically remember them saying as the interview concluded that I was just the type of Pilot they wanted. Besides the interview, I passed all their requirements which included the simulator check ride and the aircraft technical refresher course. You can imagine my elation when the RFDS were about to hand me a letter of offer of employment. The last step was obtaining approval from New South Wales Health, who contract the RFDS to provide aircraft, maintenance and pilots at their Mascot Airport base which came under their jurisdiction, RFDS was required to obtain their approval of any pilots they hired. Imagine everyone's shock and disbelief when my appointment was denied.

I made enquiries as to why New South Wales Health had made this decision by writing to the Chief Health Officer and Deputy Director-General, Population Health. I went further, writing to The Hon Reba Paige Meagher MP, Minister for Health, but all to no avail. She replied with the same old story that there had been concern over the BASI report into my ditching of

DC-3 VH-EDC into Botany Bay.

Even 14 years after the event, the final BASI report, which took one month short of two years to be published in a form which had so many question marks over it, had yet again stopped me gaining valuable employment. I stress yet again, no formal charges of any kind were ever laid against me over any findings or conclusions whatsoever with regard to an utterly inadequate, incomplete and inconsistent report that continues to haunt me to this day. At the time of writing this book, 25 years have passed which has allowed me the opportunity to dissect almost every conclusion drawn in the report. New evidence already mentioned in the previous chapter, The Plane Truth, has come to light as the result of my research which proves that the investigation was seriously flawed and should be reopened and corrected. Never mind the monetary cost of losing employment opportunities, it is impossible to quantify the dollar cost of the mental anguish that I have suffered.

My reputation with people, even those who did not personally know me, was irreparably damaged. When viewed as a detached, isolated incident by a third party, the BASI report criticism has overwhelmingly cast a shadow of doom out of all proportion to the incredible outcome of the ditching due solely to the manipulative skills of the Pilot faced with controlling an unflyable aeroplane. This seems to elude those who make retrospective judgements. The incorrect, adverse and defamatory BASI report has been posted on numerous aviation accident websites and forums around the world. This can never be undone or rectified. Thankfully, my friends and fellow aviators have been incredibly supportive. For this I will be forever grateful.

VERIFICATION AND VINDICATION FINALLY OBTAINED

For many years I attempted to discover unbiased and unquestionable proof that the aeroplane's flight performance on 24th April 1994 was credible and could be verified.

This finally came to fruition in December 2017 when I contacted Dick Verburg, President and CEO of Multi Pilot Simulations (MPS) in Groenekan, Netherlands. This company had designed, developed and certificated the world's first DC-3 simulator, after the tragic crash of the Dutch DC-3, PH-DDA.

You can only imagine how elated I was when Dick agreed that his company would conduct some test flights in their European Aviation Safety Agency (EASA) Certified DC-3 simulator whilst configured with the performance characteristics of the Botany Bay aircraft. Dick said, 'We are committed to assist you to investigate this situation as the Dutch crash was my main drive to develop the DC-3 simulator.'

I'd appreciated all the support I had received from friends and peers, but now for the first time, I had a DC-3 simulator to fly—equipment that is authoritative and measurable. Finally, someone who could help me prove my cause. I will never forget the feeling of jubilation that came over me. After nearly a quarter of a century of continuously trying to find someone who had the capability to support my synopsis, the powers that be aligned the planets for me. After many discussions, Dick later invited me over to the Netherlands to recreate my ditching conditions in his simulator to experience first-hand my scenario with his full support which would also further the comparison of analysis of the two ditching experiences discussed. He advised that they had received a request from Luchtvaart Nieuws, an avia-

Verification and Vindication Finally Obtained

Flying the DC-3 flight simulator at NPS in the Netherlands (Reismedia—Klaas-Jan van Woerkom)

tion publication company, to come to the simulator and film me and tell the DC-3 Botany Bay story.

This once in a lifetime opportunity could not have come at a better time as it coincided with ANZAC Day and I was able to combine two hugely significant events into one trip to Europe. The plan was to fly to France to participate in the 2018 Anzac Day Dawn Service which was commemorating the 100th Anniversary of the Battle of Villers-Bretonneux—a pivotal battle in WWI and one of Australia's great military triumphs. This is where my father fought in the 48th Battalion, Australian Imperial Forces, exactly 100 years prior, to the day.

It was a very emotional and rewarding trip. To walk on the soil where my father fought 100 years ago was an unbelievable experience that I could not even begin to describe. As I was going to be in the vicinity, I was asked by a friend, Owen, to take a photo of his uncle's gravesite at the Crucifix Corner Cemetery. It was such an honour and pleasure to be able to do this small task that meant so much to him. When I was growing up, Dad showed me a German Iron Cross that he said had been given to him by a German soldier whom he saved from drowning.

Soon after the Dawn Service, I caught a train from Amiens to Paris Nord and then boarded their high-speed train (300 kmh) from Paris Nord to Rotterdam Centraal which took two and a half hours, transferring to a slower train and then on to Utrecht Centraal, in the Netherlands where I met Dick.

The following morning we drove to the simulator factory where I met quite a few of the staff and also Tom van Hoorn, who is a Captain on Boeing

777/787 at KLM Royal Dutch Airlines and Head of Training and Chief Flying Instructor for DDA Classic Airlines, who operate a DC-3.

Tom took up the right-hand seat of the DC-3 simulator and after a couple of normal circuits, we went straight into the re-enactment of my ditching. Remembering that I had not flown a DC-3 in well over twenty years, I was initially a little rusty with my flying skills and had lost some of the finesse of my previous years. Attention to detail and the natural feeling of an aircraft, are some of the qualities it takes to be an outstanding Pilot. It's amazing that, after so many years absence, this return to flying a DC-3 fell back into place within minutes. I just felt like I had come back home.

The simulator was configured with the exact BASI alleged conditions on that fateful day from being over-weight at 12,446 kg (27,440 lb) for take-off, and the same weather conditions with wind and temperature, etc. The simulator was set to cause a left engine failure at 200 ft above ground level, and the left-hand propeller blade angle would move to 65° rotation of the pitch angle of the blade to the direction of the aircraft's flight, instead of 88° of pitch angle, which is the expected movement of the propeller blade when the feather button was pressed.

When the programmed engine failure happened, and we carried out the Phase 1 Emergency Engine Shutdown actions and checklist, I could not believe what I experienced. The aircraft (simulator) flew, as I could have only hoped it would on the day, and we kept flying and climbing. I was so elated, and I called out to Tom, 'This is nothing like my aircraft ... it's flying!' There was absolute triumph in my voice. This was verification that had my aeroplane only suffered a left engine failure and an incomplete feathering propeller at the same time, with the right engine producing full power, as claimed by CAA and BASI, then my aeroplane should have performed similarly. This simulation was remarkably and unbelievably different from what I experienced, yet the conditions were as close as a simulator could match to the real thing.

We continued to operate the simulator for a single-engine circuit at Botany Bay and performed an uneventful single-engine landing on the simulated runway at Kingsford Smith aerodrome, which in 1994, had been my original plan. This flight was incredible. I mentioned to Tom that when my aeroplane had the engine failure, it felt like a parachute had been released from the back of the plane. The speed bled off so quickly that if I had not reacted the way I did, the aeroplane would have stalled and we would have crashed into

Verification and Vindication Finally Obtained

the sea or the runway with tragic and devastating results.

Again, this reinforced and finally confirmed, beyond reasonable doubt, my beliefs about the ditching. The accident had nothing to do with Pilot technique or aeroplane weight, but all to do with the combination of mainly the tired right engine not producing maximum rated power combined with the amount of parasitic skin airframe drag and a mechanically incompletely feathered propeller.

Having recreated the original scenario which demonstrated the aeroplane could have kept flying if all other aspects of the aircraft and engines were operating properly, we then performed another exercise using another single-engine scenario with a lesser power setting. This entailed reducing the right engine power from the full 1200 brake horsepower (bhp) nominally available to me to 1050 bhp (a 12.5% reduction) and simulating our Maximum Except Take-Off (METO) power with the aircraft treated as loaded with the alleged BASI overweight. To our amazement, the simulator climbed yet again!

In the next exercise, we reduced the power even further to Climb Power (approximately 850 bhp—a 30% reduction), again with the same overweight calculation as before, to simulate the conditions at the time of the ditching. Even at that power setting, I was able to control the aeroplane although it now necessitated a slow rate of descent flying it for approximately 3 nautical miles (6 km) which was approximately five times the distance afforded me, to carry out a controlled ditching.

In my opinion, so far as the actual right-hand engine of the crash aircraft is concerned, whilst the engine performance dials available for me to read on the instrument panel were supplying me with the indications of take-off power, the engine, in fact, was producing an estimated 850 bhp (some 30% reduction in power).

After my actual ditching, the investigation revealed that in the right engine, eleven out of the twenty-eight spark plugs were unserviceable. No wonder 'EDC with one engine shut down and the other not producing rated power, could not stay in the air.

The Executive in charge of the test on behalf of Multi Pilot Simulations, Tom, reported the following:

'Also there is no doubt in my mind that the crew did a very good job of maintaining aircraft control and flying the aircraft to a controlled ditching, instead of trying to maintain level flight at all costs and stalling the aircraft in the process—we all know how things would have ended in that case.'

On 25th September 1996, the Dutch Dakota Association, lost their DC-3 (PH-DDA[1]) which crashed into the Wadden Sea about 35 miles north of the Dutch capital, sadly killing all 32 people on board. The crew had reported engine problems five minutes after take-off from Texel Island on return to Amsterdam, 89 km away. They too shut down the left engine and its propeller also mechanically failed to feather correctly, flying at an altitude of around 500 ft they tried to position the aircraft for an emergency landing but lost control and crashed onto a flooded sandbank covered by just chest-deep water, around nine minutes after take-off.

I owe my sincere gratitude to Dick, Tom, Ewout and staff for their cooperation and incredible assistance in providing this very unique opportunity. This simulator ride was a long-awaited life-changing experience for me. I found it to be uplifting, supportive of my claims and eliminated a lot of questionable reports.

Following the simulator ride, I rang my close friend Tony Hannam, retired Cathay Pacific Captain, as I was so elated with the simulator outcome. I just needed to share the great news with my good mate and the one who supported me through so much and encouraged me to tell this story. We discussed the tragic Netherlands accident at length and both saw parallel circumstance of the two crashes.

Both aircraft had suffered a failure of the left engine just after take-off; mine occurring at about 200 ft, whilst theirs was at 800 ft. In both cases, the Pilot had shut down the failed engine, and the left propeller failed to fully feather. The Dutch aircraft was higher above the sea and thus had more altitude and more time—approximately four minutes. I had just 46 seconds.

If ever there was a comparable state of affairs it was this one. Both pilots were faced with the risk of sacrificing the aircraft in an effort to save the lives of passengers.

I knew the impossible judgement required in such a short time frame. It is and was horrifyingly demanding because of the risks of losing both aeroplane and passengers. That was too appalling to contemplate and yet both of us were faced with that problem in our separate cases.

It's bad enough to lose an aeroplane, and importantly, there is no guaran-

---

1 Coincidentally my Tiger Moth was registered VH-DDA, only one letter different.

Verification and Vindication Finally Obtained

Ever grateful thanks to (L-R) Ewout van Wijk, Dick Verburg, Tom van Hoorn, self (Reismedia—Klaas-Jan van Woerkom)

tee that a ditching will be even partially successful. For both of us in those days, there was no DC-3 simulator to experiment with. To flight test an aircraft in actual flight with a fully loaded aircraft, with the same situation and configuration, would have been too dangerous.

The Netherlands Aviation Safety Board Final Report 96-71/A16[2] (under the heading of Human Factors) expanded into such areas as cognitive functioning whilst handling multiple emergencies in a short time-frame, experiencing a high workload whilst relying on the false hypothesis that the flight crew believed that the aircraft will always fly on one engine if the other one fails.

Even the cockpit layout of the DC-3 was considered sub-optimal as an ergonomically challenging aviation workplace (such as the flight crew having difficulty operating the landing gear retraction sequence whilst wearing the shoulder harness).

I later phoned Andrew Buxton that day, who was the supernumerary Pilot on the ditching, to confirm with him if he remembered the rate at which the aeroplane lost speed and performance. He totally agreed with my assessment.

The Botany Bay Ditching report does not anywhere, within its narrative, place the words human and factors together, let alone even consider what my

---

2   https://Reports.aviation-safety.net/1996/19960925-0_DC3_PH-DDA.pdf

crew were up against. There was nothing human written into the BASI report.

By contrast to the Dutch report, which took account of these critical factors, the scant recognition of the positive outcome of the ditching of VH-EDC was the BASI Report statement on page 48 which stated: 'The success of the subsequent ditching by the Pilot in command resulted in minimal injuries to the passengers and crew.' In my ditching, there was only one physical injury, being a broken wrist suffered by Annabel, our Flight Attendant.

Technically the Dutch report focussed on hard demonstrated facts—again, streets ahead! For example, they requested Hamilton Standard, manufacturers of the propellers, to produce drag figures for a range of blade pitch angles. They discussed flight crew performance and human factors stating that the pilots were confronted with multiple mechanical failures i.e. a combination of engine and propeller failures. Also concluded was that due to the unpredictable variety of combinations, these emergencies could not be and therefore were not foreseen in the training syllabi. The Netherlands Aerospace Laboratory generated a DC-3 computer simulation program in which drag figures, pertaining to a locked propeller were incorporated to reconstruct flight parameters.

The Dutch report was an example in so many areas of how my BASI accident report should have been presented! The technical investigative analyses were deep and thorough and content tabulated with graphical representation of engine power versus propeller drag at varying blade angles was illuminating. Information provided by such authoritative sources as the propeller manufacturer (Hamilton Standard) and the Netherlands Aerospace Laboratory as well as demonstration flights made with a DC-3 of Air Atlantique at Coventry Airport in the UK, coupled with analysis by the Air Accidents Investigation Branch (AAIB) in Farnborough, indicate how professionally the Netherlands Aviation Safety Board conducted themselves compared with our own CAA/BASI counterparts. No such technical analysis was offered by BASI—it used unsubstantiated opinion. Due to the right engine not delivering indicated maximum power, 'EDC had suffered effectively a double engine failure. Neither CAA nor BASI acknowledged or attempted to explore this obvious and genuine avenue.

The concluding remarks from the Netherlands Aviation Safety Board (NASB) Report of PH-DDA (which unfortunately killed all 32 souls on board:

'It is assumed that the level of skill and experience of the flight crew was adequate for normal operations, however not adequate to cope with the difficult control and performance conditions as occurred in a short period of 3-4 minutes. This, together with the high workload situation, resulted in the degradation of performance of the crew in such a way that they did not maintain flying speed and lost control of the aircraft.'

Given the circumstances, PH-DDA and VH-EDC are incredibly similar incidents, as in an engine failure followed by that propeller failing to feather properly. This is where the likeness ends. I maintained control and used my available options to bring the inevitable ditching to the most useful spot, namely, near the end of the new unfinished runway all within a 46 second timeline. This required rapid assessment of available options, aircraft management followed by a controlled flight without stalling, up to and including the ditching point.

The concluding remarks then go on to say 'A factor to be considered is hypothesis of the pilots that a twin-engined aircraft like the DC-3 is able to be safely operated with one engine inoperative and is capable to maintain altitude and a safe air speed. This hypothesis is built and strengthened during their airline Pilot career. In this case, with a not fully feathered propeller, it was a false hypothesis. In a high workload situation realising that it was a false hypothesis takes time, which was not available.'

* * *

Further technical reports have surfaced since the ditching, such as Professor Dennis Pearce's 'Inquiry Into Civil Aviation Safety Authority's Actions Relating To Reports of Deficiencies in Certain Engines', when in 1998 he was asked to investigate claims that CASA did not act properly in following up a number of complaints involving Mr AG Leach and his son Mr NW Leach (the Leaches) and a number of organisations associated with them, namely California Airmotive, California Airmotive Pty Ltd and Groupair Pty Ltd. This report is available on my website www.FromHeroToZero.com.au

In 1998, The National Institute of Airworthiness Surveyors Australia, (NIASA) wrote to The Chairman and Members of the CASA Board, expressing grave concerns over a series of events surrounding the illegal and improper overhaul of one or more aircraft piston engines by California Airmotive Pty Ltd (this letter is also available on my website).

On 26th October 2013, on the Crikey Website[3], Ben Sandilands, aviation journalist, is quoted as saying:

> 'One feature of the NTSB Investigative process in the US, which is lacking in Australia and Europe, is its transparency and openness. There is none of the disgusting collusion and suppression of embarrassing disclosures as seen between our safety investigator, the Air Transportation Safety Board (ATSB), and our safety regulator, CASA, over the 2009 Pel-Air crash, ... It is examples like this, moved by the NTSB that shows the difference between competent, diligent and fearlessly open disclosure of air safety problems and issues in the US today, and the rotten performance in this respect of our own air safety bodies.'

---

[3] https://blogs.crikey.com.au/planetalking/2013/10/26/ntsb-to-hold-asiana-crash-hearings-on-automation-issues/

ADDRESSING BASI

NOTE :
- In Australia, the MTOW of a DC-3 is normally 11,884 kg (26,200 lb)
- However, it is interesting that on two occasions prior to the ditching this DC-3 was given approval by the CAA to operate at 12,200 kg (26,900 lb)
- The DC-3 was certified in the United Kingdom for 12,700 kg (28,000 lb) MTOW
- In World War II the DC-3 was approved for 14,061 kg (31,000 lb) MTOW
- This equates to the DC-3 actually being capable of carrying some 2,177 kg more. Therefore, the BASI claim of 562 kg above being such a consequence is illogical

Although I am critical of the BASI report in its condemnation of me as Captain, the factual evidence they have produced in relation to the lack of maintenance on this aircraft is condemning on the owners. It must be categorically stated, yet again, that as Captain, my job was to fly the aircraft, after being provided with a valid maintenance release—not oversee any maintenance.

The following is a precis of parts of the *Technical Examination of the Wreckage* section of the report:

1. *Left Engine*: One thrust washer, which should have been fitted on the rocker arm, was not fitted to the shaft and in fact, on this take-off had lodged in the valve rocker housing causing No. 3 cylinder inlet valve to remain open. This caused the fuel/air mixture in the common induction system to ignite, thereby causing loss of power to the engine.

2. *Left Engine - Left Magneto*: The splines of the accessories' driving gear were worn well beyond service limits. The left magneto had a different serial number to that recorded in the engine logbook.
3. *Left Engine - Propeller Governor*: The propeller governor pitch control cable pulley block securing bolt was excessively worn. On the alleged inspection, four hours prior to the accident, this was certified as serviceable.
4. *Left Engine*: No. 12 cylinder—Out of the sixteen base studs of this cylinder, two were found to be sheared and missing. On the alleged inspection, four hours prior to the accident, this was certified as serviceable.
5. *Left Engine - Spark Plugs*: It was found that the electrode gap settings were inconsistent and the majority of plugs showed electrode wear beyond normal life. On the alleged inspection, four hours prior to the accident, these were certified as serviceable.
6. *Left Propeller*: The propeller blades stopped at 65-66° of pitch instead of the 88° of the fully feathered position. There were numerous indications of worn and unserviceable parts in this assembly. There was no certification to indicate that the left propeller had been de-sludged as required by Airworthiness Directive.
7. *Both engines* were granted an extension to their overhaul times. It is inconceivable that a government authority would issue extension on both engines, concurrently and, in particular, when the oil samples indicated abnormally high wear metals of iron, lead and aluminium. BASI stated that despite the indications that the engine was suffering mechanical distress together with marginal cylinder compression recordings ... the CAA still approved the extensions. Considering the right engine had in fact flown more hours than the left, it is highly probable that it too was suffering from mechanical distress. The BASI report also states that the Airworthiness Inspector assigned to the company had been verbally advised by the company on 26th April 1994 (two days after the ditching) that the right engine had been changed. There was an entry dated 24th April 1994 in the aircraft logbook, that the right engine had been changed. This entry was subsequently crossed out and noted as an incorrect entry.

8. *Emergency Locator Transmitter*: The owners advised that the battery had been changed on the alleged inspection, four hours prior to the accident. The report stated that the battery pack had not been recently renewed.

9. *Aircraft Category*: The certificate of airworthiness for the aircraft was issued in the Transport Category, requiring it to be maintained to Class A standards. However, the aircraft continued to be maintained as a Class B aircraft according to maintenance records and the CAA. The Class A system of maintenance is more structured and accountable than is the Class B system. Amazingly all DC-3 aircraft on the register ... were in the transport category and, with the exception of VH-EDC, were being maintained as Class A aircraft.

* * *

In early August 1994, a BASI representative spoke to a United States Instructor who indicated that 'EDC Co-pilot Leach flew a DC-3 in the United States for less than one hour. This instructor indicated that it was not a command check and for someone of the Co-pilot's experience would require a minimum of 10 hours ground school and significant flight training followed by an FAA examiner observing the flight before he would be able to be endorsed as a DC-3 Pilot. None of this occurred.

The CAA admitted, against its own policy, that they had issued a DC-3 Type Rating to Co-pilot Leach without ever substantiating the overseas completion of the required training. It was not my job nor my responsibility to confirm his overseas rating.

It would not be unfair to say that our own regulatory authorities published a report that was inadequate, incompetent and embarrassing in its admissions of ineptness.

It should be the case when new evidence turns up and is sufficient to re-open the investigation and do it again, properly, then this should occur. I would imagine that the authorities are obliged to do so under the terms, not only of the Transport Safety Investigation Act 2003 (TSI Act), but also for Australia to fulfil its obligations of the Chicago Convention. In my case there is no new evidence as such, just evidence that was swept under the carpet.

The travelling public must have confidence in the regulatory authorities doing their job correctly and anyone in the aviation industry in this country would be high-fiving Senator Nick Xenophon for his comments after the 2013 Senate Committee Inquiry into Aviation Accident Investigation and Reporting[1] when he said 'the general industry attitude towards both the ATSB and CASA is incredibly concerning; it is a mixture of fear, suspicion, disappointment and derision.'

It is important to point out that the convening of this Senate Committee in 2012 had nothing to do with my own ditching investigation and report, and yet it had everything to do with it.

A Westwind business jet operated by Pel-Air VH-NGA conducting an aerial ambulance mission was flying from Apia in Samoa to refuel at night at Norfolk Island en route to Australia with a stretcher patient and spouse, nurse, doctor and two flight crew on board. The pilots attempted four landing approaches in poor weather then, running almost out of fuel, the Captain elected to carry out a controlled ditching into the rough sea whilst they still had fuel to power the engines. Miraculously, all on board survived. Its accident report, published by the Australian Transport Safety Bureau (ATSB—replacing BASI) was the subject of an ABC Four Corners report because it raised more questions than it answered and it was fundamentally the reason why the Senate Committee was convened—to investigate the investigators!

Selfishly perhaps, the Senate Committee Inquiry was manna from heaven for me because everything that could ever be published about a poorly conducted aviation accident investigation and report that the Inquiry uncovered in the Pel-Air investigation, had happened to me. Could it be that my Botany Bay BASI Report became the template for all further reports on ditchings? Why not, from the BASI point of view—it worked in 1994 so let's do that again. Thankfully I can now direct your attention, item by item, from the Committee's findings on the Pel-Air investigation and report, to prove that I am not making any of this up (in my own experience), as it is a direct parallel of what happened to me some 15 years earlier.

The committee received considerable evidence suggesting that the ATSB did not comply with ICAO (International Civil Aviation Organisation) guidelines and standards in completing its investigation and report on the Norfolk Island ditching. One of the recommendations made was that the investigation be re-opened by the ATSB with a focus on organisational, oversight and broader systemic issues. Senator Edwards said that he had heard that this

---

1 https://www.aph.gov.au/Parliamentary_Business/Committees/Senate/Rural_and_Regional_Affairs_and_Transport/Completed_inquiries/2012-13/pelair2012/report/index

Pel-Air report would be a joke in international standing. He then asked Mr Dolan if he was proud of this report to which Mr Dolan replied that he was not. I couldn't agree more, and I hope they will do the same for Investigation Report 9401043 Douglas DC-3 Botany Bay NSW 24th April 1994 Ditching.

You may remember earlier in the book I chose not to be counselled by the CAA after the ditching. There was good reason for this as the Senate Enquiry Committee found out.

Part of the Executive Summary states: 'Finally, the committee notes that many submitters and witnesses provided evidence 'in camera' due to fear of retribution, particularly from CASA, were they to go public with their concerns. The committee also notes that this reticence to speak in public has been apparent for each inquiry this committee has conducted in this area over several years and finds this deeply worrying. There is an obligation on CASA to allay these concerns that retribution could follow speaking out, which appear to be widespread within the aviation industry.'

Therefore, had I chosen counselling I would likely have been even worse off as independent legal advice, as well as that from a CAA representative, advised me not to at the risk of wrongly admitting liability—unsurprisingly. Even though I chose the alternative pathway of not attending, my flying career was still shot to pieces. Did the Pel-Air Captain choose to be counselled which would have proved this other route was a bad idea too—maybe even worse? Either way, the Committee got it in one with its assessment of what is rife in the industry once a Pilot in command publicly offers an opinion.

The committee was understandably troubled by allegations that agencies whose role it is to protect and enhance aviation safety were acting in ways which could compromise that safety.

Again, in the Committee's Executive Summary it states:

'It is regrettable that a Senate inquiry has had to make recommendations which should have been made by the ATSB.' 'To simply focus on the actions of the Pilot and not discuss the deficiencies of the system as a whole is unhelpful. It is disappointing that CASA and the ATSB continue to assert, in the face of evidence to the contrary, that the only part of the system with any effect on the accident sequence was the Pilot.'

'Because of the unbalanced nature of the ATSB report, the only conclusion that a reader could plausibly reach is that the accident in question was caused by pilot error. In turn, this appears to imply that the suspension of that particular Pilot's licences by CASA was the only action necessary to enhance safety and reduce future risk.'

'The ATSB investigation could not be anything but flawed.'

'Evidence received by the committee would appear to suggest that senior ATSB staff may have intervened to alter the final report in order to secure a desirable outcome for both the ATSB and CASA.'

An excerpt from an internal email outlining an early discussion reads: 'We discussed the hole that CASA might have got itself into by its interventions since the ditching, and how you (Mr Martin Dolan, ATSB Chief Commissioner) might have identified an optimum path that will maximise the safety outcome without either agency planting egg on the other agency's face.'

Given the ATSB's central role in improving aviation safety by communicating lessons learned from aviation accidents, the committee is surprised by the agency's near-exclusive focus on the actions of the Pilot and lack of analysis or detail of factors that would assist the wider aviation industry.

Had my ditching caused a fatality, I suspect that the former, highly respected, NSW State Coroner, Derrick Hand (who investigated the Seaview accident) would likely have come to an entirely different conclusion as to the cause of the accident, than that published by the CAA/BASI.

After requesting information, I received an interesting package of documents from Alan Stray, Manager Major Investigations and Quality Assurance, BASI in early 1997, containing numerous revealing facts.

- Of the 28 left engine spark plugs, once they were cleaned and even re-gapped, five did either not fire or were found to be electrically breaking down.
- Only twenty-five spark plugs were recovered from the right engine (which had been immersed in salt water for two months). They were also cleaned, re-gapped and then tested and of these eleven were considered unserviceable for the same reasons.
- Of the fifty-six spark plugs, only 26 were deemed to be of the approved type of plug.
- BASI Comments: 'Considering that this aircraft had been certified as completing a 100 hourly periodic inspection for maintenance release issue 4-6 hours prior to this accident the visual condition of the spark

plugs suggests that little attention had been given to the inspection and setting of the spark plug gap, or the worn condition of the electrodes.'
- As I had queried how an engine is test-run under a known load, an ATSB representative insinuated that I was misunderstanding the operation of supercharged engines and to back up his assumption, he had the audacity to quote an article written by Mr Leach Snr himself, owner and maintenance engineer of 'EDC at South Pacific Airmotive.
- A senior BASI representative also stated that there was confusion over the issue of FOI allocations as Groupair was a Victorian based operation and I was a New South Wales based Pilot. These were two entirely separate regions with separate administration duties. This confusion reigned due to the fact that I also had my own charter licence in New South Wales.
- BASI and the CAA infer that Co-pilot Leach had not undertaken a check flight. However, on 9th January 1994, three and a half months prior to the accident, I conducted an instrument rating renewal test on Co-pilot Leach, at Cairns, Queensland, which he passed as a Co-pilot and I verbally told him I considered his aircraft handling was above average. According to the Groupair Operations Manual, Section C2 'In the case of pilots employed as Co-pilots only, the flight test required for the renewal of his instrument rating (Capt or Co-Pilot) is deemed to satisfy the requirements of one of these checks.' It is interesting to note that in September 1993 Laurie McIver carried out a flight check on Co-pilot Leach and expressed a similar opinion by writing on his report 'Well above required standard'.

I can now confirm that 'EDC's climb performance on two engines was significantly less than the climb performance on a normal DC-3. This was verified by my simulator ride in late April 2018. It also accounts for the fact that when we lost the left engine, which I now believe was the more powerful of the two engines, there was no violent swing to the left, as would be expected if the right engine was producing 1200 bhp.

* * *

In the first week of June 2018, I applied to the Australian Transportation Safety Board, under the Freedom of Information Act, to access documents in relation to engine, propeller and airframe findings. Some four months later, I was advised that they had rejected my application and would not be providing me with anything at all. They stated that as opinions were involved in the manuscripts, they could not issue any documentation. I thought it strange that the BASI report is full of opinions and yet acceptable. I told them once again that I was not interested in opinions, I just wanted the findings and facts of the investigation. To date, they have still refused my request for further information. How strange, as I am now even denied access to the documents that I was freely given in 1997 and have in my possession. What are they hiding?

ROD'S FINAL THOUGHTS AND EXPECTATIONS

Aviating has given me enormous pleasure in life. I have travelled extensively with a bird's eye view of the world that is simply breathtaking. Whilst flying Orions I can claim to having sighted all of Australia's coastline from a height of three hundred feet or below. I also consider myself privileged to have some of the finest aviators in Australia as personal friends. Most pilots aim to become a Captain with a major airline. Due to circumstances beyond my control such as age, vacancies, economic climate, references, experience, official reports and records, etc, I was never in the right place at the right time, and an inappropriate or inaccurate incident summary of investigation is not something that would further my career. This was disappointing for me. However, now reflecting upon my aviation career, I would not have swapped it for the world. Having experienced both airline and general aviation flying, general aviation is entirely different from airline flying and the challenges and tasks it produced were more gratifying than one could ever hope for. Sometimes I have flashbacks as to how well off financially some of my peers are because of their airline careers, but I accept and am very content with my life now. I'm a firm believer that there are only two types of people in the world: victims and survivors. I know I'm a survivor. I've learnt from the negative incidents in my life that it doesn't matter what is thrown at you along the way, it is how you face and deal with it that counts. Overall, I consider myself one of the luckiest people in the world. At seventy years of age, I have no major medical issues, I have a roof over my head and food on the table. I am lucky enough to live in one of the most beautiful areas in this country. Obviously, winning the lottery would significantly ease my financial situation, but in the big picture I am very content in life.

I consider myself to be a safe, competent, professional and experienced aviator. I am very fortunate to have been trained and checked by some of the most highly respected military and civil aviation organisations in the world. During my flying career, I've had a number of engine failures or precautionary engine shutdowns including two in 'EDC. The outcome of all of these were uneventful. Testimonials in Appendix 1 will bear witness to my professional ability.

Over the last few years, my hatred and anger has diminished as I realise that the government authorities are untouchable. After all, I would never take them to court knowing I had little chance of winning, but I will defend myself to my last breath.

I was raised in an era when governments and public servants were trusted people in our society.

You can only imagine my immense disappointment when I found it to be so different.

I expected both the CAA/CASA and BASI to search for the TRUTH as to why 'EDC would not continue to fly on one engine. Not only did they not want the truth known by myself and the public, but to me they appeared to have gone out of their way to 'pervert the course of justice', to deflect criticism of their own regulatory deficiencies by embellishing assumptions concerning my management of the ditching. I found CAA/CASA not only to be completely overbearing, but also intimidating and harassing. It continued to make one mistake after another with its insulting speculation and I dispute its findings.

BASI had two years to investigate this accident. I had a mere 46 seconds in which to assess the situation, evaluate available options, make a decision, select a site and carry out the ditching. I vehemently deny I was in any way responsible for the accident, and I maintain I did the very best I could in the circumstances. With the benefit of twenty-five years of hindsight, I would change none of my actions. Because I survived an aircraft accident, and have read the BASI report following my accident, it now puts a whole new perspective on other accident reports where the Pilot is not alive to defend himself or herself.

Indeed, I still derive immense satisfaction from the fact that, due to my actions, I was able to carry out a successful ditching in which everyone survived. At no stage was I willing to accept a different outcome. The CAA/CASA response has turned a straight-forward piece of professional aviating

Rod's Final Thoughts and Expectations

into a murky, convoluted and embarrassing mess which has reached up to despoil the great value of my actions. If I had been aware of the conditions that brought about this accident, I would not have flown the aeroplane on that flight or any other day. Clearly, the then CAA was extremely negligent in its surveillance of this whole operation, particularly in allowing that DC-3 to continue flying when they knew the left engine was suffering mechanical distress and with both engines on overhaul extensions.

The actions of two government authorities caused the destruction of my aviation career, which obviously incorporates loss of earnings for at least the past two decades, which has had an incredible impact on my personal life. It is an impossibility for me to ever regain the ground they took away from me. A lot of people say life is not fair. There is a lot of difference between fair and unjust.

* * *

It would be fair to say that I've suffered from Post Traumatic Stress Disorder (PTSD) but not in relation to the ditching. I would carry that out again under the same circumstances at a moment's notice. It's been the last twenty-five years of callous treatment by the authorities that has caused me endless grief. My desire to right a wrong has been my overwhelming priority for 25 years to the point where not a day goes by without my thoughts turning to how to resolve the issue.

How do you quantify compensation after decades of fighting for vindication, which includes loss of income as a professional Pilot, for destroying a person's life and having such a huge impact on the people close to you? A public apology would be a good start and recognition of the fact that 25 people survived because I made the correct flying decision and most importantly, retractions of false statements made against me, and the BASI report to be rewritten truthfully, factually and independently.

I ponder as to where the people are today who adversely affected my professional aviation and personal life all those years ago. I wonder if their own conduct eats away at them, although I doubt it, or if they even care about the damage they did to my career. At least I know I can sleep very well at night with a clear conscience.

Tony Hannam stated:

> 'To even consider that ditching is the best decision, is totally foreign to a Pilot and the commitment to believe that you have sufficient

skill and expertise would most likely scare off any further thoughts of going down that path! The mind-set of an average Pilot just does not contemplate such a course of action and they would revert to proven behavioural patterns of dealing with a mechanical problem using the normal tools to do the job, checklists, using known procedures and applying them to controls and switches that normally should work for them. In the meantime, it is very easy to either lose concentration or get distracted by talking on the radio and answering (perceived) trivial questions, setting new transponder codes and scanning instruments to turn onto required headings, apart from operating feathering pumps and reading more checklists, thereby not maintain the critical minimum airspeed for flight in a demanding configuration and hence losing control of the aeroplane at a height from which recovery is not possible. Rod Lovell rapidly understood the inevitability and gravity of the situation and chose to sacrifice the aeroplane in order to save the lives of the passengers and crew.'

* * *

One thing in particular concerns me regarding modern day airlines. No in-depth training of ditching occurs considering the vast amount of long haul, over water flights. I consider ditching a large aeroplane to be a high risk, very demanding manoeuvre which requires extensive training and therefore considerable cost. Is this the reason the airlines and aviation authorities ignore what should be undertaken? I would have thought it would be imperative to have at least an understanding of the complexities of a ditching and practise the elements in their simulator exercises. I can think of a few fatal accidents where if I had been the Captain, I would have seriously considered ditching the aircraft as an option. Pilots, through company operations manuals, should be given this option. Having been trained in the airline system, where Operations Manuals are the Bible, I am saddened, but understand, when some airline crews dare not think outside the square if an unusual situation arises. It's ironic that airlines and the regulators pay very little attention to the possibility of a ditching, yet all airlines carry life rafts and life jackets. At the beginning of each flight, passengers are required to pay attention whilst the flight attendant carries out the emergency procedures which include landing on the water. What is the point if the pilots are never trained to carry out a successful ditching? In 2009 the UK Civil Aviation Authority stated pilots

Rod's Final Thoughts and Expectations

are required to be informed about ditching technique and considerations, and ditching procedures must exist in their aircraft manuals and checklists. The only pilots trained for landing on water are military specialists. Airline pilots are not required to train, even in simulators, for landing an aircraft on water, confirms the CAA. But the pilots, along with the cabin crew, are required to carry out physical training practice for the post-ditching situation.

This is the excuse the Authorities use—simulators are made to behave and perform just like the real airplane. Well, they don't test ditching airplanes, so there's really no experience for most aircraft types on exactly what the airplane will do when it touches the water, and therefore, it's impossible to program a flight simulator for it. I think if we had data to program the simulators, we might do well to practice ditching and practice multiple engine failures more often. This is a cop-out. They do not realise the training is for the approach to the water. Once the plane has contacted the water the Pilot has no control over it.

Recently, I asked an online professional and airline pilots forum, 'Do airline and aircraft manufacturers teach ditching?' Apart from the overwhelming answer of 'no', comments posted said it would never happen, scoffed at the idea, but alarmingly the comment most reflected was 'it's the same as conducting a forced landing'. Sorry, fellow aviators, but it is nothing like that at all. It is flown entirely differently to ensure its success. I encourage pilots to research what I have said and practice it in a simulator—it is not easy. In my opinion, after listening to numerous accident reports, this ditching option is never even considered by the pilots. The 21st century is seeing the phasing out of four-engined aircraft which are being replaced with the more economical two-engined aircraft. The downside of this is the reduction of options in critical emergencies.

* * *

Possibly the most common question professional pilots get asked is, how long did it take you to learn to fly? I never know quite how to answer that question. We are always learning. Sure, we learnt the basic flying skills in just a few months, but the art and profession of flying and aviation requires constant renewing of skills and life-long updating, whether it be via examinations for new aircraft or new procedures. You add to your knowledge and skill base each time you read an aviation magazine, every time you go flying and every time you talk to a fellow aviator. It is called Continual Professional

Development (CPD). If a Pilot was to tell me that flying is easy, and that you can learn to fly in no time, they would be the last Pilot I would even consider boarding a plane with, let alone letting them Pilot it. We, as professional pilots, are not granted any equivalent tertiary education qualifications after possibly decades studying and working. This becomes very relevant when completing any forms that ask for your education status. The most we can put down is that we achieved L12 at high school which has no connection to flying at all. Interestingly, it is in recent years that policies have changed. A Bachelor in Aviation can now be awarded to an individual that passes some of the exams that we experienced pilots passed forty years ago and can attain the flying and simulator experience which consists of intense training for emergencies considered too risky to carry out in the air. We may not have degrees, but it should be comforting to the average passenger to know that an RAAF trained Pilot flying in General Aviation and airline operations with over 10,000 hours experience in the air commanding complex multi-engined aircraft, would be a pretty safe bet to be a candidate for a Master of Aviation.

* * *

Most of the media have been extremely supportive, the only exceptions were two of the media personnel who were both passengers on the flight when we ditched. I don't know what their problems were, but they were totally unsympathetic to my cause, even after I saved their lives. These people did not get the big picture of what actually happened on that day and how close they came to dying. It seemed paramount to embellish the story for the advancement of their careers without taking into consideration the consequences for others involved.

In a newspaper editorial from one of the journalists on board, he stated that, unlike Hollywood movies, DC-3s don't skip along the surface but they hit the water and just about everything rips off underneath and they keep going on towards the bottom. He also claimed the aircraft completely submerged, hitting the sand on the bottom, before slowly lifting itself back to the surface

Obviously, he considered himself on a Disneyland Fantasyland ride. His foolishness to even suggest an aircraft can dive 6 m under the sea striking the nose on the sand, and then lift itself back up to the surface and remain intact is absolutely beyond fantasy. He should be ashamed of himself for attaching his name to that article. We only had contact with the surface of the water, which caused a bow wave to go over the cabin and down the sides. I contacted this journalist and berated him for such irresponsible journalism. He apologised to me over the phone, in regard to this over-glorified story, but no retraction was ever printed. From time to time we all criticise the media and these are the very people that create the problems.

In the same editorial, the newspaper photographer also jumped on the bandwagon. He was proud of the fact that he ensured he was first off the aircraft to start taking photos by jumping into a life raft. He also bragged that he wasn't going to miss an opportunity to miss the biggest photo of his career. What an absolute hero! No consideration was given at all for the emergency evacuation of all those teenagers and women still on board. Thankfully the responsible crew members carried out their diligent duties to make sure everyone else got off safely.

The series of photos of the ditching taken by him earned him the prestigious Nikon Kodak Press Photographer of the Year Award for 1994-95. He is to be congratulated for this achievement, but I guess he's not in line for a bravery award.

* * *

Public support: The greatest and most common comment made after the accident was that, 'if my family and kids were on an aircraft, I would want you to be the Captain'. This is probably the best compliment that could be bestowed on any Pilot.

The obvious question is, what do I think caused the accident?

The CAA is the short answer! Had they regulated the maintenance of VH-EDC, it would have been grounded until made serviceable and airworthy by changing the engines and maintaining the faulty propeller as required at overhaul schedules. Instead they issued extensions for it to continue flying with both engines on overrun at the same time 'despite the indications that the (left) engine was suffering mechanical distress' as stated on page 18 of the BASI report. It then chooses to accuse Co-pilot Leach of mis-handling and lack of skill of the handling Pilot without ever defining how that was determined.

I was there; they weren't.

I don't tolerate mis-handling or lack of skill on any machinery whatsoever, particularly on an aircraft in my charge whether it be on an instructional flight, training flight or with fare paying passengers—I simply take control if deemed necessary, then there is no question of mis-handling arising! Please remember that I was a proven and authorised CAA Check and Training Captain on the DC-3, and previously a Training Captain on DC-9s, so it was my everyday job to recognise any such event and immediately take remedial action, therefore mis-handling by the Co-pilot was not the culminating factor that led to this incident as claimed on page 1 of the BASI report.

If you want my factual opinion (which hasn't changed since 1994) why the aeroplane failed to obtain climb performance after an engine failure after take-off, then factors, in no particular order, which accounted for the loss of performance, included:

- Left engine failure
- Left propeller failing to feather
- Right engine not producing rated power (never even considered in the BASI investigation even though it was operating beyond 1000 hours and overdue for an overhaul)
- Significant parasitic drag
- Incredible number of spark plugs unserviceable in both engines (this information came to light to me on 24th April 1997 but no mention of it was made in the BASI Report of March 1996!).

In reviewing the above it is obvious that these five dot points could be considered directly to have affected the ability to fly the aircraft, which as it turned out, was un-flyable without descending towards the sea.

Many of these points are thoroughly examined and expanded upon on the website (www.FromHeroToZero.com.au)—'Administrative Appeals Tribunal' which should be read in conjunction with this summary to fully comprehend the deficiency of the maintenance and regulatory surveillance thereof.

In my submission to the AAT my Queen's Council (QC) stated the following in support of my flying expertise, considering the increase in drag caused by this non-feathering propeller.

'20. No aircraft is ever flown with the propeller at 68 degrees or in the range 60 to 68 degrees. There are no test flights of any kind done in this configuration and Captain Lovell may be the first man in the world ever to have flown a DC-3 in this configuration.'

This is of huge significance in understanding the inadequate and deficient investigative analysis in the subsequent BASI report.

Conversely, the AAIB (Air Accidents Investigation Branch—investigating the Netherlands accident), considered propeller drag a major issue in the accident involving PH-DDA as they requested Hamilton Standard to produce the negative thrust (drag) figures for a propeller that was rotating and stationary. Yet the BASI report has the audacity to make the statement 'there would be a negligible drag increase above that of a fully feathered propeller.' It is mind-boggling to see such a stupid statement written into an aircraft accident investigation report that makes absolutely no mention of human factors whatsoever! Disgraceful, shameful and utterly un-professional!

The engine failed about 30 seconds after lift-off and we as the pilots, had to identify the malfunctioning engine and then instigate a specific procedure to ensure the wrong engine was not shut down by mistake! How many seconds are left now until splashdown—only 46 seconds after the engine failed? This was a 76 second flight from lift-off to ditching into the sea! Think about that for a few of your own seconds and now try to imagine how busy we were. Firstly we were reacting to the engine failure, applying hand and foot operated flight controls to avoid losing control of the aeroplane, scanning instruments, identifying which engine had malfunctioned and trying to understand why. On top of this we were co-ordinating checklist procedures then shutting it down, finding then that the aeroplane wouldn't maintain height on the only remaining engine. It was clear that our only safe option was to fly down towards the water to maintain sufficient speed and therefore sufficient airflow over the wings to keep it aloft. We had to plan a new course of action to turn it into a safe water landing by selecting a site clear of pleasure vessels and avoiding fishing boats, then setting it up with flaps selected down and at the correct speed to fly it onto the sea wings level, to avoid breaking up on impact!!

Thank goodness I was not overwhelmed by perhaps one of the most extreme and stressful situations a Pilot can face—an un-flyable aeroplane that is now going to have to be deliberately ditched into the sea. I knew what had to be done and was thoroughly competent in my ability to carry this out.

Simply put, the accident had nothing much to do with Co-pilot mishandling of the flight controls or even weight issues. These were just used to deflect attention from the true cause of the inability of the aeroplane to fly.

* * *

On reflection, I don't know why I, or others in the aviation industry, bother wasting all of our time and effort because nothing ever changes. Obviously, our expertise is not worth taking note of.

On the day of the ditching, there was no-one more appropriate than me to relate the facts, causes, circumstances and consequences. I was there, and yet the regulatory authorities chose to ignore my factual information. I consider myself an experienced and qualified multi-engined Check and Training Captain. I'm absolutely astounded and bewildered how so-called experts, sitting in an air-conditioned office with endless time on their hands, could wrongly speculate on my actions. The highly respected ex-DCA examiner of airmen, Macarthur Job, along with experienced DC-3 Captains, such as Captain Terry Blyth, Captain Paul Phelan, Captain Geoff Jones, Captain David Foulkes, Captain Jim McGowan and numerous others attested to my actions on that day.

Left engine precautionary shutdown after take-off from Port Vila 21st May 1993 (Author's Collection)

I firmly believe that the CAA/BASI investigative process incorrectly reviewed my actions and erroneously assessed the Pilot's response on that day culminating in the unwarranted Pilot Licence suspension and deeply flawed Investigation Report 9401043.

Both government authorities paid no attention to two previous engine shutdowns on 'EDC as well as my numerous qualifications and experience. On 21st May 1993, I shut down the left engine on a flight out of Port Vila, culminating in a safe return and landing. On 10th December 1993, I did a precautionary left engine shutdown on a flight out of Sydney with a safe return and landing. A bit of a pattern forming here with two shutdowns of the left engine and then some four months later a major failure of the left engine and the aeroplane was ditched. The pilots were the last to touch the aeroplane, so the finger gets pointed at them, but this is the last link in the chain. The responsibility of the regulatory authority and supervision of maintenance and management of the aeroplane ultimately dictates the quality of the

Rod's Final Thoughts and Expectations

Left engine undergoing maintenance after successful single-engine landing in Port Vila (Author's Collection)

equipment which they have to operate.

* * *

I mention the following two incidents to illustrate how flights do not always go according to plan, hence the crucial need for a Captain who can make instantaneous and sound decisions based on the facts presented to him at the time.

On 16th May 1995, Nimrod R1P, Serial No. XW666 ditched off RAF Kinloss[1] (no casualties) following a major engine fire during a test flight after a major overhaul. The Pilot, Flight Lieutenant Art Stacey, was exceptionally skilful in his handling of this very unpleasant emergency and succeeded in ditching the aeroplane thus allowing the crew to escape. The crew of seven were saved due to quick thinking. After hearing an explosion and receiving visual reports of fire consuming the wing, the Captain feared for the structural integrity of the aeroplane and decided to ditch before he lost control authority, even though the runway was only five miles ahead, and in full sight. He was awarded the AFC (Air Force Cross) for his actions. The investigating engineer's assessment was that they were less than 90 seconds from structural failure. Recently, after contacting Art, Chairman of the Goldfish Club (dedicated to the mutual experience of members surviving 'coming down in the drink'), I have become a member of this unique club.

On 18th June 2013, my youngest son, Kris, was a passenger on a Virgin Australia Boeing 737 (VH-YIR) bound for Adelaide after departing from

---
1 https://skybrary.aero/bookshelf/books/3309.pdf

From Hero to Zero

Brisbane, when, due to fog, the aeroplane had to divert. The crew were not advised of fog at Mildura when they diverted. Upon arrival at Mildura, fog had already formed below the landing minima. As the diversion to Mildura had not been planned, due to incorrect weather forecasting, thankfully, the wise and knowledgeable Captain acknowledged that he only had enough fuel for one approach and landing. A missed approach was not an option. He continued his approach to below legal minimum as stated by the ATSB report to put the aeroplane safely on the ground. If he had not done this and carried out a missed approach as is the normal and legal requirements under these meteorological conditions, the aeroplane could have crashed after running out of fuel on the missed approach. I told Kris to thank that Captain every day of his life.

APPENDIX 1
TESTIMONIALS

Flying Officer Lovell is a maritime Captain of a twelve-man P-3B Orion crew. He has 2,500 hours of Pilot flying time. He is highly skilled, talented and a thoroughly professional Pilot who demonstrates a high degree of maturity and aeronautical expertise in the handling of his aircraft. His airmanship is smooth and his judgement sound. He demonstrates an in-depth knowledge of the complex P-3B weapon system and of airways and DOT (Department of Transport) procedures, and his highly proficient in instrument flying.
A C Konczey, Lieutenant Commander, United States Navy
11th November 1976

Mr Lovell is a skilled Pilot and has discharged his duties conscientiously throughout the term of his employment with this company.
Captain KA Beattie, DFC, Chief Check and Training Captain,
IPEC Aviation
30th November 1979

I have known Rodney Lovell for a period of three years and was privileged to have employed him as Chief Pilot for our organisation.
David Chapman, General Manager, Airtex Aviation
20th September 1989

Captain Lovell's expertise as a Pilot goes without question and his demeanour and courtesy at all times has been exceptional.
Paul F Petersen, Executive chairman, Girvan Group
18th September 1989

It was my privilege and pleasure, recently, to have instructed Mr Rod Lovell during an endorsement for Boeing 747. Rod is a Pilot with great ability, who always prepares himself well for the task with the result that his operation of the aircraft is outstanding in all areas. His management of the cockpit and crew are of the highest standard and his overall manner is pleasant and well balanced.
Captain Geoffrey J Jones, QANTAS Airways Limited
1990

I confirm that you completed the ground school training required for an endorsement on the Boeing 747-200/300. It is further confirmed that you completed a flight simulator training course suitable for the issue of a first-class endorsement on the Boeing 747-200/300 aircraft. May I take this opportunity to thank you for your hard work and enthusiasm with which you approached your duties in QANTAS and at my personal regrets, that the economic climate necessitated the cessation of your employment.
Captain Dick Wilkinson, Manager Base Training, QANTAS Airways
26th February 1990

I received incredible support from Boyd Munro. Munro formed Software Design Inc (known as SDI) and began selling first in Australia, then Britain, and shortly thereafter the United States, through SDI Inc, a California corporation. Boyd continues to fight for the rights of aircraft owners and pilots here in OZ which by now must involve a considerable investment in both time and money after having to deal with 'our' inept bureaucracy that is entrenched in the government aviation division.

Boyd Munro is a businessman and a Pilot. He holds a British Air Transport Pilot Airline Transport Pilot Licence, an FAA Airline Transport Pilot Certificate fixed and rotary, and an Australian CPL fixed and rotary. He has been flying since 1966. Boyd has never flown for hire or reward and obtained professional licenses solely to demonstrate that he meets professional standards.

I received the two letters from Boyd, one following my ditching. Quotes from these letters as follows:
I have always felt utterly confident in you flying my family around, and I will miss the way you look after the aircraft so well.
Boyd Munro, CEO, SDI, UK
3rd November 1990

Appendix 1—Testimonials

My confidence in your piloting skill is as high as it was. My confidence in your judgement is even higher.
Boyd Munro, CEO, SDI, UK
27th April 1994

Every now and then, an event occurs on the world aviation scene, which makes you feel proud of your fellow aviator—one who has brought favourable comment on the industry by exhibiting a feat of exemplary flying skill. The results make good business for the world's media, but thankfully not for the world's hospitals and undertakers. There is no tragedy, so narrowly averted, because of the efforts of a human being who has used all the experience of his or her career to stop that terrible headline appearing. He is one of the very few 'natural' pilots I have come across in my twenty-five year, 12,000 hour plus career, most of that spent in a check and training capacity. Too often in aviation circles the verdict is concluded long before the trial begins and then without taking everything into consideration. Those who apportion blame do so in committee with many days or months to consider decisions taken in a mere split second by the aviator concerned. In Captain Lovell's case there are facts that speak for themselves. Firstly, he is thorough, conscientious and flies according to the rules. He is a highly principled individual. Secondly, the DC-3 failed to maintain altitude on one engine, rather unexpectedly. Thirdly, he very sensibly didn't turn back but took a painfully difficult decision to ditch, not what a Pilot wants to do to an aeroplane. Fourthly, he pulled it off! Exceptionally well! That is piloting skill under intense pressure. Why the aeroplane failed to fly is obviously at the root of the investigation, but I can guarantee one thing, it was not through lack of ability or understanding of the situation.
Rod Lovell knows how to fly twin radial engine tail-draggers, on two engines or one! I don't have any doubts about that. Captain Lovell is a professional aviator who operates to the rules. He would not jeopardise anyone's safety at any time. His thorough preparation for the flight testifies to that. I would hope that the investigation would not only exonerate Captain Lovell from any blame, but in fact praise him for his excellent handling of a nightmare situation. I hope we have moved out of the dark ages of aviation when 'pilot error' was the easiest and most

expedient way of kicking the problem under the rug. It saves the investigators a lot of trouble but nothing else.

Captain Tony Hannam, Training Captain, Boeing 747-200/300 Cathay Pacific Airways
29th June 1994

I am pleased to have this opportunity to be able to certify that, in my opinion, Captain Rod Lovell is a professional and very competent Pilot, especially so, as Captain on DC-3 aircraft. I have a total of over 14,000 hours, 8,000 hours of these being command experience on DC-3s. We experienced an engine shutdown (port engine) on departure Vila and his handling of the aircraft and systems was without blemish. We had further engine problems between Medang and Moresby and his decision to divert to Nadzab, carry out an instrument approach with one engine running rough, was competent and entirely correct. I think that in the case of the controlled ditching into Botany Bay, anyone criticising Rod's handling of this situation has either never flown with the professional Pilot or has a personal vendetta to satisfy! The latter, I think, being the case in this instance.

Captain Jim McGowan, Experience DC-3 Check and Training Captain
15th July 1994

During 40 years of active transport flying in aviation, I recall only a few people who impress me as having outstanding qualities as pilots. Rod Lovell is one of those people. I have on many occasions had the opportunity of observing Rod's professional aptitude to his flying on DC-3, Argosy, and DC-9 type aircraft. As said above, I have crewed DC-3 type aircraft with Rod on many occasions and I would argue to the end with anyone's idea of his inability to operate such aircraft. Some 12,000 flying hours of the 20,000 I have logged were accrued on DC-3 aircraft so I feel justly qualified to state the above.

Captain Terry Blyth, Check and Training Captain, IPEC Aviation (ex TAA Captain)
7th July 1994

I also flew with Captain Lovell on DC-9 aircraft throughout 1983 to 1986 when he was employed as a DC-9 Captain and later on as a DC-9 Training

Captain. I had the benefit of observing his flying standards during normal line flying and also in the line checking, simulator checking, and aircraft base checking environment during all of the above periods whilst carrying out my duties as a DC-9 Check and Training Captain. On all of those occasions I was always impressed with Captain Lovell's high professional standards, cockpit management was excellent and he showed leadership at all times. He has that rare ability to demand the highest standard in all areas and yet maintain a relaxed manner. With regard to the DC-3 ditching incident in Botany Bay, obviously I am not in a position to know the full circumstances. However, what I can say with the fullest confidence is that if Captain Rod Lovell was commanding the aircraft, then the situation would have been handled in a highly professional manner during the pre-fight, in flight and post-flight periods. Leadership would have been excellent, the decision making would have been correct for the information available at that moment and the aircraft would have been flown accurately and efficiently.

Captain David Foulkes, QANTAS Airways
1st July 1994

We at Jeppersen recently heard of the extremely skilful and professional manner in which you piloted a DC-3 with an engine out, thereby saving the lives of 25 people, with remarkably little injury. All of us wonder if we would be as clear thinking if we found ourselves in such a situation. Congratulations on an exceptional job.

Kevin Collins, Director Training Division and Aviation Marketing, Jeppersen Sanderson
9th April 1994

No doubt you have received many messages since your short trip to Botany Bay, but from the reports that I have seen it was a wonderful effort to get through the episode with everyone intact. It is easy for the critics to denigrate the work of proper training of aircrew, but as I heard one Pilot remark, he never had a problem with critics when he was at 30,000 ft (9,150 m). You demonstrated that the real skill is down around 300 ft (91 m), (and maybe minor a few feet) and congratulations to you on having the skill, presence of mind and character to cope with what could have easily been a major disaster.

Ian McNab, Partner, McNab, McNab and Starke
9th May 1994

From Hero to Zero

I saw in this morning's *Herald* that the CAA have grounded you without trial. This is absolutely in just. I have always admired true professionalism in any man, and your skill and coolness saved all your passengers from death or injury. My four young daughters and |I wish you the best of luck in your appeal and would like you to accept a small contribution towards your legal expenses.

The Mathers Family (a concerned member of the public), Belmore, NSW
5th August 1994

Our son, Scott, was a passenger in the now infamous DC-3. We would like to convey our sincere appreciation to you for your skill in 'ditching' the plane, in such a manner that injuries were minimal and lives were not lost. We were in Sydney at the time and, fortunately, first heard about the incident from our son himself, in a phone call from the hospital. We were therefore spared much emotional trauma. We trust that you are recovering well from your injuries and again extend our heartfelt thanks for your superbly executed 'landing'. We hope to be able to reiterate our gratitude in person at the BBQ Sergeant Saunders has organised for this Friday.
Leigh and Ian Howle, Parents
27th April 1994

I have not met you, but I am writing this letter to try and express my gratitude to you for bringing my son, Cameron, to safety last Sunday in Botany Bay. It is impossible to put into words how I felt about it, but I am sure that your skill and presence of mind are the main reasons why we have Cameron today. We were incredibly lucky that you were in charge and I will never forget the feeling of relief and gratitude. I thank you most sincerely. On behalf of all my family.
Roslyn Mackintosh, Parent
29th April 1994

I am one of the many who don't often put pen to paper in order to praise or congratulate someone for simply 'doing their job' but your handling of an incident (stemming from outside factors, beyond your own control) was exceptional to say the least, showing (1) skill; (2) excellent judgement; (3) superb appraisal of a most difficult situation; (4) professionalism in every

Appendix 1—Testimonials

respect and (5) utmost regard for passengers and crew. I'm sure I speak for the 'TRUE' aviation community in my admiration. If such an incident occurred in the USA you would be weighted down with medals, citations and be on the 'Roll of Honour'.

John Walton, Aero Associates Quality Aviation Products
(Son of Nancy Bird Walton AO, OBE—took flying lessons from Sir Charles Kingsford Smith at 18 years of age and was later awarded a commercial Pilot's Licence at 19 years.)
17th November 1994

I have known Captain Rod Lovell for a number of years and I wish to relate a situation which involved a great deal of skill, experience and remarkable action on his part. In August, 1992, I casually employed a part-time Pilot who sought work experience in general aviation. This Pilot was a full-time Career Officer with the RAAF, was an experienced First Officer on C-47s (DC-3s) and was about to undergo conversion as a Command Captain with the RAAF on C-47s. In order that he could work with this company as a First Officer, it was necessary for him to be endorsed or checked into our company on DC-3s by Rod Lovell, who was our Check and Training Officer. During this training, on approach to an airstrip, the RAAF officer encountered wind-shear near touchdown and lost complete control of the aircraft. Another Pilot observer and myself, who were on board, braced ourselves for the inevitable crash. We were amazed at the extremely quick reflex and action on the part of Captain Rod Lovell who took over and rescued the aircraft and occupants from a near-impossible split-second crash. This incident has highlighted to me the skill that Captain Lovell has in his knowledge and handling of DC-3s

Dick Lang, Desert Air Safaris
7th July 1994

APPENDIX 2
ROD LOVELL'S QUALIFICATIONS

A summary of the qualification that I hold or have held:
- Commercial Pilot Licence
- Senior Commercial Pilot Licence
- Student Pilot (Helicopter) Licence
- First Class Air Transport Pilot Licence (Australia)
- FAA Commercial Pilot Certificate (USA)
- Private Pilot Licence (Australia)
- FAA Airline Transport Pilot Certificate (USA)
- NZ Airline Transport Pilot Licence (New Zealand)
- Formation Endorsement (Civilian)
- Aerobatic Endorsement (Civilian)
- FAA High Altitude Training
- RVSM/TCAS/RNP
- Cat II Qualified
- RAAF High Alt Pressure Chamber Training
- RAAF Ejection Seat Training

I am endorsed as Captain on:
- P-3B Orion
- Boeing 747
- DC-9
- DC-3
- AW650
- Learjet 35
- Cessna Citation Jets
- Beechcraft Super King Air

and approximately 35 other aircraft.

Appendix 2—Rod Lovell's Qualifications

I have been trained and checked as a Captain by:
- The Royal Australian Air Force
- QANTAS Airways Ltd
- Trans Australia Airlines
- IPEC
- Norfolk Island Airlines
- Federal Aviation Administration
- FlightSafety International
- The Department of Civil Aviation/CAA/CASA

and, again, numerous others

Instrument Rating issue and renewal check flights total 37 to that date. All but a few are multi-engined command ratings.

29th August 1977	Right Hand Seat Captain Approval P-3Bs Chief Pilot Approval - Bi-Air
30th June 1980	Line Training Captain Approval LR35
11th February 1985	Line Training Captain Approval DC-9
18th July 1986	Chief Pilot Approval - Antique Airways
15th April 1987	Chief Pilot Approval - Aero Professional
12th June 1987	Endorsement Training and Testing DH82a and B18
8th April 1988	Chief Pilot Approval - Avtex
28th September 1989	Training and Checking Approval - Instrument Rating Renewals
13th January 1993	CAA agreed to my appointment as DC-3 Flight Captain
15th May 1993	Check Pilot Approval - Groupair Chief Pilot Approval - Antique Airways
21st July 1993	Check Pilot Approval - Desert-Air Safaris
30th August 1993	Check Pilot Approval - Antique Airways

Total flight time, at time of writing, is in excess of 10,000 hours. In addition to this, I have in excess of 500 hours logged in flight simulators. Flight simulators provide more in-depth training, particularly in the practise of emergency and abnormal operations, than can be accomplished in aircraft. We often say that in the flight simulator, if you are sitting there fat, dumb and happy there is a good chance you have missed something. Flight simulator training is normally periods of high intensity, non-normal operations.

APPENDIX 3
GLOSSARY OF TERMS

AAT	Administrative Appeals Tribunal
AD	Airworthiness Directive
Altitude	Height above mean sea level in feet
AOC	Air Operators Certificate
ATC	Air Traffic Controller
ATO	Approved Testing Officer
ATP	Air Transport Pilot
ATPL	Airline Transport Pilot Licence
ATSB	Air Transportation Safety Board (formerly called the Bureau of Air Safety Investigation (BASI)
AWI	Airworthiness Inspector
BASI	Bureau of Air Safety Investigation (now called the Air Transportation Safety Board ATSB)
CAA	Civil Aviation Authority (now called Civil Aviation Safety Authority CASA)
CASA	Civil Aviation Safety Authority (as of 6th July 1995—formerly Civil Aviation Authority CAA)
CAAP	Civil Aviation Advisory Publication
CAO	Civil Aviation Orders
CAR	Civil Aviation Regulation
Control Column	Controls the elevators
Control Wheel	Controls the ailerons
CRM	Crew Resource Management
DCA	Department of Civil Aviation
DOT	Department of Transport
EFATO	Engine Failure After Take-Off
ELT	Emergency Locator Transmitter
EM	Electronic Memo
EROPS	Extended Range Operations (sometimes called, engines run or passengers swim)
FAA	Federal Aviation Administration (USA)
FOI	Flight Operations Inspector

Appendix 3—Glossary of Terms

Height	Vertical distance in feet above a fixed point
IAS	Indicated Airspeed
ICAO	International Civil Aviation Organisation
IFR	Instrument Flight Rules
IMC	Instrument Meteorological Conditions
MAP	Manifold Absolute Pressure
MP	Manifold Pressure
METO	Maximum Except Take-Off power: 1,050 bhp (take-off power 1,200 bhp) per engine
MTOW	Maximum Take-Off Weight. The Maximum permissible Take-Off Weight of an aircraft as specified in its Certificate of Airworthiness
PF	Pilot Flying
PNF	Pilot Not Flying
PNG	Papua New Guinea
RAAF	Royal Australian Air Force
RFDS	Royal Flying Doctor Service
SOAP	Spectrometric Oil Analysis Program
SPA	South Pacific Airmotive Pty Ltd
TAA	Trans-Australia Airlines
TBO	Time Between Overhauls
V_1	Decision speed. The airspeed indicator reading defining the decision point on take-off at which, should one engine fail, the Pilot can elect to abandon the take-off or continue. In effect it is the last point at which a Pilot can safely decide to abandon a take-off in an emergency.
V_2	Take-Off Safety Speed. The speed at which the aircraft may safely be climbed with one engine inoperative.

APPENDIX 4
CHRONOLOGY

14th November 1938
Department of Civil Aviation (DCA) formed

During 1950s
Air Safety Investigation Branch (ASIB) formed

30th November 1973
DCA merged with Department of Shipping and Transport and became Department of Transport, Air Transport Group

7th May 1982
Department of Transport, Air Transport Group reformed into Department of Aviation (DoA)

1982
ASIB became Bureau of Air Safety Investigation (BASI) an operationally independent unit of DoA

24th July 1987
DoA absorbed by Department of Transport and Communications

1st July 1988
Civil Aviation Authority (CAA) formed to control aviation safety regulation and provide air traffic services

6th July 1995
CAA split into two separate government organisations: Airservices Australia and Civil Aviation Safety Authority (CASA)

1st July 1999
Air Transportation Safety Board (ATSB) formed from amalgamation of BASI and Marine Incident Investigation Unit (MIIU)

www.ingramcontent.com/pod-product-compliance
Lightning Source LLC
Chambersburg PA
CBHW020353170426
43200CB00005B/157